RETURN TO

Albion

Americans in England
1760–1940

NATIONAL PORTRAIT GALLERY

SMITHSONIAN INSTITUTION

HOLT, RINEHART

AND WINSTON

New York

RETURN TO

Americans in England

1760–1940

—

RICHARD KENIN

INTRODUCTION
BY
ALISTAIR
COOKE

Copyright © 1979 by National Portrait Gallery, Smithsonian Institution
Introduction copyright © 1979 by Alistair Cooke
Published by Holt, Rinehart and Winston, 383 Madison Avenue, New York, New York, 10017.

Published simultaneously in Canada by Holt, Rinehart and Winston of Canada, Limited.

Library of Congress Cataloging in Publication Data

Kenin, Richard.
   Return to Albion.

   1. England—Biography.   2. Americans in England.
I. Title.
CT775.K46   920'.042   78-1033
ISBN Hardbound: 0-03-042861-0
ISBN Paperback: 0-03-042856-4

First Edition

Designer: Robert Reed

Printed in the United States of America

10 9 8 7 6 5 4 3 2 1

A passage from T. S. Eliot's "Lines for Cuscuscaraway and
Mirza Murad Ali Beg," published in *Collected Poems
1909–1962,* is quoted on page 275 by permission of
Harcourt Brace Jovanovich, Inc. From the *Cantos*
(copyright 1934) and *Personae* (copyright 1926) by Ezra
Pound, material is reprinted on pages 106, 194, and 277 by
permission of the New Directions Publishing Corporation.

Men run away to other countries
because they are not good in their
own, and run back to their own
because they pass for nothing in the
new places.

    —Ralph Waldo Emerson

My choice is the Old World,
my choice, my need, my life.

    —Henry James

FOR JAMES PARTON

Contents

Acknowledgments

A great many individuals gave of both their time and energy so that this book might be written. To all of them I express a profound gratitude, in particular to the following: the Marquess of Anglesey, Lord Astor of Hever, David Astor, Sanborn C. Brown, Joseph T. Butler, Paul Channon, M.P., Winston Churchill, M.P., Lord Clark, the Earl of Drogheda, Leon Edel, Mrs. T. S. Eliot, Sir John and Lady Eliott, Sir Rupert Hart-Davis, Anita Leslie, Margaret MacDonald, the late Andrew MacLaren-Young, Raymond Mander and Joe Mitchenson, the Duke of Marlborough, Lady Alexandra Metcalfe, Sir Oliver Millar, the late J. A. P. Millet, Henry Morgan, Junius S. Morgan, José de Navarro, Nigel Nicolson, Richard Ormond, Wyman W. Parker, Michael Parkin, Jules D. Prown, Princess Mary de Rachlewiltz, Edgar P. Richardson, Jane Rittenhouse, Sir John Rothenstein, John Russell, Mr. and Mrs. John Schaffner, Lincoln Seligman, Charles Coleman Sellers, Helmut von Erffa, and the late Cecil Woodham-Smith.

To Ellen Miles and Ken Yellis, who read the manuscript and offered incisive criticism, I am most grateful. Without Katharine Ratzenberger it would have been impossible to find much of the material used in the preparation of the book. Eloise P. Harvey typed the manuscript more times than either she or I would like to count. Frances Stevenson Wein undangled my participles whenever they appeared and provided brilliant editing. Beverly Cox was instrumental in securing the illustrations which accompany the text. Douglas Evelyn administered the publishing of the manuscript with tact and grace, and without Marc Pachter's and Charles Blitzer's advice and critical support it is likely that the book would never have been completed.

Finally, a very special thank you to Marvin Sadik, the Director of the National Portrait Gallery. It was he who first commissioned *Return to Albion*; and what began as an impassioned idea was, through his guidance, translated into the reality of this volume.

RICHARD KENIN
Washington, D.C.

Introduction

I know how men in exile feed on dreams of hope.
—*Agamemnon*

At first glance, this is a straightforward historical account of the Americans, of the first generation and the latest, who responded to the pull of their ancestral roots and went back to England. They are seen to have done it from a variety of motives. To absorb traditions they feared they had lost. To acquire an expertise that had failed to make the Atlantic crossing. To counter the English charges of American "barbarism" with a crash course in Old World airs and graces. To prove to themselves, at least, that they were not simply transplanted and diluted Englishmen but were what Crèvecoeur saw and acclaimed: "The American, this new man."

But the story is more complex and fascinating than that, if only because human motives do not come singly but in clusters of contradictory impulses. This book, then, is a series of case records on a theme as old as Aeschylus and as new as Henry James, if not Erica Jong: the expatriate's adventure seen as a dilemma. It almost always begins as a rousing act of the will, a romantic plunge, and ends as often as not as a choice between alternatives—to stay, to go back—that are both unsatisfying. (We should not be put off by the lamentation of Copley that he never returned to America, or by Audubon's vow "to return no more to Europe." Elegant protestation was an eighteenth-century form of wish-fulfillment.)

Whether or not the expatriate claims to be satisfied with his voluntary exile, the reviewers of his memoirs always see him as the victim of a conflict of loyalties and habits. This may be no more than a highly sophisticated brand of sour grapes patented by writers who, having chosen to stick in their native mud, cannot bear to believe that distant pastures are as green as people say. Naïve tycoons who retire to London or Buckinghamshire may go on protesting that they have exchanged a brawling world for a serene one. But the testimony of businessmen, except in the fictional world of Dickens, Sinclair Lewis, and Louis Auchincloss, is not taken seriously. The more intellectual the reviewer, the more he may be depended on to uncover heartache in the expatriate's experience, whether it is W. H. Auden declaring his affection for Greenwich Village but going back to Oxford, or S. J. Perelman shaking the horrors of New York for civilized London and then beating it back to Gramercy Park after finding the English "too couth."

Of course, the general experience of leaving the native land for another has an enormous literature. But, in this record, the most psychologically interesting to us is the case of the Colonial expatriate. He does not exchange one culture for another, but for an amendment or parody of an original, which constantly reminds him of the forsaken roots and sets up, in people of character, an unending battle between a way of life that is taken for granted and another way of life that is built either on adapting the old traditions to a new climate or on reacting against the fatherland. I imagine that the diaries of Roman proconsuls would make fascinating source material of this sort, as do the letters of English soldiers of the early 1920s who stayed on the Rhine with German wives once the occupation was over, and as E. M. Forster and Paul Scott have provided in their novels about the last generations of Englishmen who were running India. One thinks, too, of Lord Kitchener, surely the archetypical English patriot, itching for the embassy at Constantinople or Cairo and balking at an appointment to the Committee of Imperial Defence in London on the grounds that he had not spent a winter in England in thirty-six years and had "no intention of spoiling my health by remaining at home." I presume, also, that the literatures of Portugal and Brazil are full of such tugs-of-war between the homeland and "the Brazilian, this new man."

Naturally, to Englishmen and Americans, the most familiar and most tantalizing of all such tribal experiences is that of the Briton who settles in America (Auden, Robert Owen, C. Aubrey Smith, Cooke[?]) and of the American who settles in England (Benjamin West, Henry James, Gordon Selfridge, T. S. Eliot). And until now they have been discussed strenuously as individuals or superficially as types of Americaphile or Anglophile.

What this book does is to show, in a parade of returning Americans, from before the Revolution to the Second World War, that Anglophilia is a very complicated affliction and by no means the downright inferiority complex implied by the Emerson quotation on the epigraph page, or the simple case of snobbery that popular magazines and newspaper interviewers take it to be. To me, the most revealing surprises come in the story of that group of early American painters who, hoping to emulate the success of Benjamin West, took off for London just before, or during, the Revolutionary War. The popular picture of the revolution is always woefully melodramatized in the clash of two groups of antagonists: in England, stupid ministers legislating for a chauvinist parliament to the cheers of the populace, while brave Franklin seizes the lion's tail; in America, an aroused people seething with righteous indignation against the hated monarch, while suspect Loyalists cower before the coming storm. But here we have Copley, Stuart, and Trumbull sailing blithely, as if on the regular Cunard run, and seeing in London not the enemy's bosom but "a receptive marketplace." The British were battering Long Island and White Plains, while Copley is being made a member of the Royal Academy. Throughout the war, Benjamin West is secure in the favor and friendship of the

King. True, Trumbull, as the son of a notorious rebel leader, was imprisoned within a few weeks of his arrival. But he was soon transferred to a comfortable form of house arrest and visited by Charles James Fox, and later released on the intervention of Edmund Burke.

Not all the records of the painter-expatriates make brave reading. Trumbull, having confessed to Jefferson the sole, pious aim of wishing to commemorate "the great events of our country's revolution," sees a lucrative market in glorifying the British commander at the siege of Gibraltar. Patience Wright, the waxwork queen, sculpts the King, first-names him, and passes on useful intelligence to rebel leaders. After these performances of Mr. Facing-Both-Ways, there is something almost endearing about the no-nonsense double-agentry of the gifted scoundrel, Benjamin Thompson.

As the eighteenth century waned, and the new republic started to flex its muscle, the pull of England as the source of art and invention began to slacken. Yet, so quintessential an American as Robert (Steamboat) Fulton spent seven years there trying to become a fashionable painter. And it is a shock to see S. F. B. ("What hath God wrought!") Morse departing in his twentieth year for England as the dutiful pupil of Washington Allston, and going back to study "the old masters" without a passing thought of the telegraph. Well into the nineteenth century, the protestations of the first generation of independent Americans that the old country could teach them nothing were firmly contradicted by the fact of Audubon's thirteen-year retreat to Scotland and England, because they were the only places that could produce color plates worthy of his bird drawings.

For such pragmatic reasons, if for no others, there must have been a steady stream of Americans into England during the nineteenth century: knowledgeable fusspots who knew that Britain retained a nucleus of incomparable craftsmen-printers, clock-makers, silversmiths, cartographers, cabinetmakers—whose skills grew from an apprenticeship system which was doomed in America once Eli Whitney had standardized interchangeable parts that could be fitted by drones.

With the coming of the Gilded Age, and the ostentation of the robber barons, there arrived in Britain a new type of expatriate that appears even in our day: the most self-conscious of all voluntary expatriates, the affluent exile who departs on the pretext that America has become intolerably philistine, a reaction against the vulgarity of the first industrial giants that was made all the easier since it was from them that the horrified fugitives usually derived their income. Of these hothouse flowers, Logan Pearsall Smith was the most fastidious example, and Henry James the most profound.

Around the turn of the century, there was a quite new type possessing a confidence in some transatlantic skill that the last Colonials could only boast about. This is the bustling American eager to amaze the British with the latest American marvel—the telephone, the noncreaking elevator, the elegant workable bathroom, the expert management of a penny paper, the introduction of the department store. And of these, much the most appealing in the beginning and most poignant at the end is the Dreiserian figure of Gordon Selfridge, who within a year or two of his arrival in London was gaped at as a sort of Maecenas, and at the end was an unrecognized bankrupt mooching off to a bed-sitter.

In our own time, the Anglo-American odyssey retains one constant—the hypersensitiveness of the Americans and the British to criticisms of each other, a three-hundred-year-old neurosis that was spawned when the first father saw his son sail away knowing he would not stay, and then was miffed to find that he did stay and—what is worse—prospered.

But there is a new and disturbing element that threatens to change the returned American out of all recognition. This is the unpredicted ferocity of nationalism that has sprung from the dissolution of the old empires. The United Nations started with 50 member nations. Today it labors to contain 150 states—large and ludicrously small—that claim the pride and panoply of sovereignty, even when their barren economies can offer their people little more than an ambassador to the UN, a secretary, and a hotel suite in New York. In the United States, the domestic expression of this newfound pride is the increasing chauvinism of immigrant or "ethnic" peoples who once were proud to abandon what Theodore Roosevelt called "hyphenated Americanism." They now cherish their separateness, a trend that threatens the ideal—and the achievement—of "E Pluribus Unum." If the trend continues, the return to Albion will be only one variation of the American paying a passing tribute to his old roots or replanting them. The expatriate experience will then embrace the North Carolina black returning to Liberia, the Italian going home to Tuscany, the retired Polish-American considering the advantages of free concerts and free medicine in Warsaw.

This solemn possibility aside, it may well be that the whole experience of the returnees will be anachronized, since the jet charter has recruited a legion of knockabout travelers and made every other college boy and girl a part-time expatriate. Certainly, for every Copley who once chose to try his luck in London, there are today scores of thousands of the young who choose to spend an offhand year or two in England or Scotland or Spain or Italy, not to mention the hippies who can claim an easygoing acquaintance with Algiers, Amsterdam, Katmandu, and Bangkok. There is, too, a new generation of movie and rock stars who decamp for keeps to Spain, Switzerland, France, the Channel Islands, or wherever, as precaution against a tax bite. In Britain alone, three or four doctors in ten think of emigration to Canada, Australia, or the United States. And the multinational corporations now employ about a quarter of their American staffs in places remote from home.

They are all a far cry from Benjamin West off to challenge and conquer the British Establishment, or from T. S. Eliot resolved to be the troubadour of dying Europe and yet "not to talk about the Rocky Mountains, the bold unfettered West."

The ease of travel, the vast spread of world trade, the universality of the movies, the lingua franca of satellite television have robbed the returnee of much of his romanticism and all of his courage. In 1979, the return to Albion can be seen less and less as part of a continuing saga, of natives now as then dissatisfied with the homeland. It is a closed book, a finished record of the lonely, voluntary expatriate. As such, it will very likely become all the more precious as a historical document.

—Alistair Cooke

Benjamin West, 1738–1820, with his son Raphael.   Self-portrait. Oil on canvas, circa 1773. 26⅞'' × 26¼''. (Yale Center for British Art, Paul Mellon Collection)

At the Court of King George:

The Benjamin West Circle

The great western gates of St. Paul's Cathedral stood open and waiting. It was ten-thirty on the morning of March 29, 1820.

A mile from the cathedral in Somerset House, that massive palace built by Sir William Chambers on the north bank of the Thames, a funeral procession was assembling in the apartments allocated by the Crown to the Royal Academy of Arts.

In a room on the ground floor of the Academy, hung and carpeted with black cloth so heavy that all daylight was excluded, stood an open coffin surrounded by tall wax tapers which provided the only illumination in the chamber. There, in state, lay the mortal remains of Benjamin West, second President of the Royal Academy and Painter of History to His Late Majesty King George III.

Slowly the coffin was taken up and conveyed to an elaborate hearse drawn by a half-dozen horses heavily laden with "rich trappings, feathers and velvets." The hearse, leading a cortege of over one hundred carriages, moved out of the courtyard of Somerset House into Fleet Street, past the site of Temple Bar, and into the precincts of the City of London. Pages and mutes, the traditional professional mourners at solemn occasions, escorted the body. One hundred police marshals of the City of London attended the procession to ensure that proper decorum and respect were maintained. Along the line of march, all intersections were closed. Nothing would be allowed to disrupt the procession as it moved slowly toward the cathedral.

All the orders of the establishment were represented in significant numbers. Five lords spiritual, including the Archbishop of York, accompanied by the dignitaries of the cathedral—canons and subcanons, a prebendary, an almoner, and vicars choral. Numerous lords temporal led by three dukes, two marquesses, and nine earls; members of the *corps diplomatique* and high-ranking officers of the army and navy; the Lord Mayor of London and his entourage of sheriffs and aldermen. Finally, the academicians, distinctive in their mourning garb of long black cloaks, black silk scarves, and hatbands, followed by a great many students of the Royal Academy who, as a body, had always been closest to the heart of the late president.

After a service of some length, the remains of Benjamin West were interred in the cathedral crypt between the coffins of Sir Joshua Reynolds, the first President of the Academy, and West's intimate friend, Thomas Newton, the sometime Dean of St. Paul's and Lord Bishop of Bristol.

In many respects it was a remarkable ceremony, more a spectacle than an occasion of sadness; the sort of event that the English carry off with such studied grace. But how ironic that such Anglican pomp and majesty were lavished on the memory of an artist, an *American* artist, and a Quaker to boot!

Benjamin West died convinced that he was, in truth, "the American Raphael." And though his artistic reputation would go into rapid decline in the years following his demise, few lives, when recounted, emerge as such positive success stories.

West, whose grammar and diction were appalling, was truly remarkable in his ability to survive in the world of intrigue so manifest at the Court of St. James's. There he was—the American colonial of transparently bourgeois temperament who remained a confidant of the King throughout the War of Independence; the prolific creator of numerous works of art; the teacher, mentor, and counselor to three generations of American and English painters who, emerging from his studio, were thought to bear the indelible mark of excellence; the great artistic innovator of his generation whose romantic neoclassicism knew no peer; and, for almost three decades, the administrating officer of the most distinguished artistic institution in the realm.

Honored not only in England but also in imperial France, in papal Italy, and in republican America, little wonder, then, that Benjamin West was accorded such a remarkable final tribute, for society adores paying court to great success. Few Americans would achieve comparable acclaim in Britain during their own lifetimes. Yet West's experience demonstrated that it could be done. He opened the door and pointed the way to those of his countrymen who sought recognition in the land which had nurtured the roots of the American experience. In so doing, he marked out a path for a return to Albion, to the England of American dreams, which a great many of his compatriots eagerly followed.

The pietistic West, whose intellect quietly resisted all the challenges and disturbing questions of the Age of Reason, burst onto the London scene on August 25, 1763, as an exotic bird loosed from the forests of the New World. Was he not the first American who had gone to Rome to study painting according to the neoclassic theories of the supreme theoretician, Johann Winckelmann? Had he not sat at the feet of the leading practitioner of the Roman school, Anton Raphael Mengs? And, finally, had not the greatest of the art connoisseurs, the Cardinal Alessandro Albani, placed his hands on the head of the young painter and pronounced him a man of unique quality?

As he rode into London from Shooters Hill on top of the Canterbury coach, West saw stretching before him the capital city where his future would be determined. From the Tower to the outskirts of the still-rural villages of Chelsea and Battersea, London straddled the Thames with a loverlike embrace. The commercial life of the metropolis remained close to the water, and on the wharves and quays, as well as in the countinghouses and coffeehouses of the City, the smell of money strongly scented the air.

But money was for spending, and London was a city of seductive distractions in the eyes of the newly arrived Pennsylvanian. There, David Garrick revived Shakespeare, and Oliver Goldsmith punned his way into prominence. Doctor Johnson and his alter ego, James Boswell, delighted a coterie of intellects by making maliciousness respectable. In the arts William Hogarth vied for attention, dissecting the weaknesses of his fellows by pulling back the curtain on a gin-sodden, egregiously overdone society whose pleasures strayed into perversion and vice. Armed with the skill of the draughtsman and the eye of the humorist, Hogarth survived in the marketplace of the arts because he appealed to the realities of popular passion. However, his was an area of competition that Benjamin West studiously avoided.

The "up-market" of the painter's world was dominated by the great portraitists Joshua Reynolds, Thomas Gainsborough, and Allan Ramsay, the official court painter. From their studios, and those of many others, were churned out a steady supply of standardized poses, costumes, and draperies for those among the aristocracy, gentry, and professional classes who aspired to pictorial immortality.

Portraiture was not an area that appealed to West. True, a fortune could be made—Reynolds's affluence was ample testimony to that. But West, fresh from Rome, passionately believed that if, as Pope had written, "the proper study of mankind is Man," he must be depicted as a heroic figure set within the epics of his greatest achievements, namely, the classical ages of Greece and Rome. His teacher, Anton Mengs, summed up this credo by advocating artistic work which embodied nobility, simplicity, and grandeur. The young West, as a devout disciple, carried this dictum with him to England. But at the outset, in order to survive, he had to paint portraits, and in order to secure clients he had to have contacts.

It was not West's original intention to remain permanently in England. He thought merely of continuing his studies at the St. Martin's Lane Academy before

Pen and watercolor over pencil, 1786 19⅛″ × 29⅜″ (Museum of London)

Skaters on the Serpentine.   In London's royal parks, the young Benjamin West first attracted public attention through his prodigious skill on the ice. Thomas Rowlandson, 1756–1827.

returning to his native Pennsylvania. But the capriciousness of fate dealt the young painter a positive hand. An accomplished skater, he took to the ice, first in Hyde Park and later on the frozen basin of Kensington Gardens, giving performances of the complicated "Philadelphia salute." It was a convenient way to attract attention, and, soon after, he secured a commission to paint a full-length portrait of Gen. Robert Monckton, Wolfe's principal lieutenant at the battle of Quebec. It is quite possible that conversations with Monckton were instrumental in inspiring West subsequently to produce what proved to be his most popular work, *The Death of Wolfe.*

The Monckton portrait was a success, and, at the urging of Joshua Reynolds and the landscapist Richard Wilson, it was shown the following year, together with two of West's Italian works, at the Spring Gardens exhibition of the newly founded Society of Artists.

West's comparatively delicate style of painting sharply differed from the beefy robustness of Hogarth. But public taste was changing, and his work was both noticed and generally well received in the press: thus was launched an artistic career that was to last for the next sixty years.

An important patron appeared who long remained a close friend of the painter. His Grace, Robert Hay Drummond, Archbishop of York and Primate of All England, found it pleasant to entertain artists at his table. With West he discussed "the honor which the patronage of genius confers upon the rich." It was clear that West was about to become a protégé. The Archbishop read aloud from the *Annals* of Tacitus about the great Roman general, Germanicus, who, in the first century, defeated the barbarians on the Rhine but, in so doing, aroused the envy of the Emperor Tiberius, who sent him to Syria and there arranged for a convenient assassination. Agrippina, the wife of Germanicus, had her husband's body cremated and, with his ashes and their children, set sail for Italy. She was received by a multitude of her husband's officers at Brundisium, who wailed with grief when she set foot on shore, bearing the funeral urn, as a direct act of defiance to the tyrant emperor.

It is a story embodying great nobility and courage, set in the most venerable of historic times. The Archbishop commissioned West to paint the subject for him, and so pleasing were the results that he attempted to raise 3,000 guineas from his friends in order that West might be amply supported and set free to continue his work as a history painter.

However, Archbishop Drummond was not completely successful. Only 1,500 guineas, half the amount that he estimated was necessary, were raised. Disturbed that West might be forced to return to the comparatively barren wasteland of society portraits, Drummond approached the King, asking that he view *Agrippina* as an example of the young American's skill and devotion to the nobility of classical art.

The King agreed and was quite taken with what was brought before him. His attendants were dismissed and the Queen was summoned so that she, too, might

Oil on canvas, 1768
64½'' × 106½''
(Yale University Art
Gallery, Gift of Louis
M. Rabinowitz)

Agrippina Landing at Brundisium with the Ashes of Germanicus.   The painting which first brought West to the attention of King George III. Benjamin West, 1738–1820.

share in the experience. George III instantly took to West, whose unaffected piety and sense of moral rectitude were complementary to his own. A commission was discussed. The King, like his archbishop, intended to select a theme from antiquity. He chose the story from Livy's *History,* of Regulus and his departure from Rome with the Carthaginian ambassadors. George asked whether West considered this a suitable subject, and of course the painter agreed. "Then," the King cried with great animation, "you shall paint it for me"—and proceeded to read the tale personally to West.

It was the beginning of a friendship that spanned five decades, surviving not only the American Revolution, but also the King's struggle with porphyria which relentlessly drew him into insanity and eventual blindness. When George III died in 1820, a few weeks before West's own demise, the painter remarked that he had lost the best and truest of friends.

In 1772, after executing a number of commissions for the Crown, West was appointed Painter of History to the King. It was a new post, well fitted for his talents, and in that capacity he produced some seventy-five major paintings, encompassing not only historic scenes but also devotional works and the occasional portrait.

The probability of success was now far too great to consider a return to Pennsyl-

*Benjamin West's Picture Gallery at 14 Newman Street.
John Pasmore (the younger), active 1830–45.*

vania. However, though he resided in England for the next half-century, West continued to surround himself with things American. His bride, Elizabeth Shewell, arrived from Pennsylvania, escorted by the painter's father and Matthew Pratt, who was to be West's first student in London. Pratt, in turn, was succeeded by Abraham Delanoy, Jr., who remained only a short time and then returned to New York, advertising himself as an accomplished disciple of the new American master. Delanoy never attained prominence but did spread the gospel of West's achievement. And one by one they began to cross the Atlantic, men whose names, in later years, stood forth among the most important American painters of the late eighteenth and early nineteenth centuries: John Singleton Copley, Gilbert Stuart, John Trumbull, Ralph Earl, Mather Brown, Charles Willson Peale, Joseph Wright, Henry Benbridge, Edward Malbone, Washington Allston, Charles R. Leslie, Samuel F. B. Morse, Thomas Sully, Rembrandt Peale, Robert Fulton, William Dunlap, and John Vanderlyn. Not all could claim the legacy of having been students of Benjamin West, but each did acknowledge his hospitality, guidance, and patronage.

As his responsibilities grew, West found it necessary to secure suitable quarters for himself and his extended family. The Painter of History to the King had an annual retainer and the expectation of royal commissions. But support by the Crown was not sufficient to maintain West's establishment in Newman Street, where he constructed not only lofty galleries large enough to hold his "ten-acre" religious pictures, which were destined for the royal chapels at Windsor, but also extensive painting rooms and living quarters for those who attached themselves to his rising star. And so, with the aid of his students, West produced hundreds of portraits and small works, many of little note, in order to support his expensive life-style.

He transformed his home and galleries into a kind of sanctum sanctorum of the arts. There, vast paintings were theatrically presented on projecting stages against backdrops of draped fabric. Velvet rope barriers, supported by stanchions, kept the public at a respectable distance from the religious and historic visions on the walls, while the natty West who, in Gilbert Stuart's eyes, looked as if he had just stepped out of a bandbox, appeared to his young kinsman, Leigh Hunt, "so gentlemanly that, the moment he changed his gown for a coat, he seemed full dressed." Even in the little garden at the back of the house, a plethora of classical busts reminded the visitor that he was ensconced at the center of the artistic revival of the nation, where could be found "the mild and quiet artist at his work; happy, for he thought himself immortal." Overdone, perhaps, but the effect was telling.

From his citadel in Newman Street, West and his students commuted regularly to Windsor, where the King provided him with quarters. His early works were comparatively delicate, but inevitably a more monumental style was imposed as the Sovereign demanded works such as *Cyrus Receiving the King of Armenia* and *Hannibal Swearing Eternal Enmity to the Romans,* which were more expressive of the grandeur and achievement of royalty. But, by the 1770s, West was ready for a major transformation of artistic style. He did not reject the subjects his patron demanded; they continued to be produced until the relationship cooled with the King's descent into insanity. But the time was ripe for an independent course more expressive of the painter's changing outlook.

In 1759, on the Plains of Abraham at Quebec, James Wolfe, the hero of the

Pen and ink,
circa 1785–88
7¼″ × 9⅛″
(The Toledo Museum
of Art, Toledo, Ohio;
Gift of Edward
Drummond Libbey)

Mr. West's Family in the Garden of Their Residence in Newman Street.   The artist is seated at the right. Benjamin West, 1738–1820.

British Empire, was slain. But Wolfe's armies were successful in terminating the French presence in Canada forever. Twelve years later West began a painting, commemorating the death of Wolfe, which from the outset was a subject of controversy. In all respects it was a conventional work, with one major exception. Rather than cast his figures in classical garb, West portrayed actual military uniforms of the day. Joshua Reynolds found the painting unsettling and urged West "earnestly to adopt the classic costume of antiquity as much more becoming the inherent greatness of the subject than the modern garb of war." He was joined by Archbishop Drummond, who feared that the painter's career would be irreparably damaged if the work, once presented, were to be rejected as being an act of defiance against established tastes.

West, however, was confident of a popular reception and urged his critics to withhold judgment until the painting was finished. He argued strenuously in favor of presenting his commemoration as a contemporary piece, for the death of Wolfe was, in his words, "a topic that history will proudly record, and the same truth that guides the pen of the historian should govern the pencil of the artist."

Both Reynolds and Drummond were skeptical, but they did agree to prorogue judgment until the work was finished. Weeks later, at a second viewing, Reynolds sat quietly before the canvas for about thirty minutes studying it carefully. It was not the first history painting to cast figures in contemporary dress, but it was by far the largest and most ambitious of such works. Finally, the great portraitist rose and, according to West's first biographer, John Galt, exclaimed, "Mr. West has conquered! I foresee that this picture will not only become one of the most popular, but will occasion a revolution in art."

Such extraordinary praise from the curmudgeonly Joshua Reynolds sounds somewhat apocryphal, for a year later, when the painting was publicly exhibited, he attacked West in one of his most famous discourses, charging that the painter had failed to appreciate the noble exigencies of historic perspective in casting his characters in the pedestrian vulgarity of the present day. Reynolds argued that paintings "which are built upon general nature live forever while those which depend for their existence on particular customs and habits, a partial view of nature, or the fluctuation of fashion can only be coeval with that which first raised them from obscurity. Present time and future may be considered as rivals, and he who solicits the one must expect to be discountenanced by the other."

West was unperturbed by the attack, for however apocryphal Reynolds's earlier prediction, it did come to pass. When the painting was publicly shown, the crowds thronged to see the latest novelty from the palette of "the American Raphael." Eventually it was sold to great advantage, and the King commissioned a copy for the Royal Collection. William Woollett, the master engraver on copperplate, was engaged to produce a print for the popular market. So great was the demand across

Oil on canvas, 1780
65⅛″ × 96¼″
(Royal Ontario
Museum, Toronto)

The Death of General Wolfe. The first of West's great paintings of contemporary history, and the most popular. Benjamin West, 1738–1820.

England and the Continent that West's name became universally known for the first time. And £15,000 was his share of profit from the engraving's sale.

Thus, as a classicist, West won popular acclaim in England twenty years before David achieved similar recognition in France with his *Oath of the Tennis Court.* West set history painting on the contemporary stage and not only received official approbation but great financial success as well. He carved out an area of expertise and enjoyed a proprietary monopoly over it, for there were no English painters prepared to compete with him in what was a very expensive and time-consuming genre.

The second half of the eighteenth century in England was financially a relatively good period for artists. It was a time of rising expectations. Affluence was becoming widespread as the Industrial Revolution wrenched the kingdom into the modern age. And as wealth grew, the number of men able to indulge in the polite pastime of patronage increased manifoldly. Large country houses required ample numbers of paintings for decoration. Men of substance, increasingly well traveled and cosmopolitan in outlook, felt the urge to collect in order to satisfy private passions and to give ample testament of their superior taste and sophistication.

A genuine marketplace for the contemporary arts was in the making. But as yet there were no proper art galleries where the public could easily go, and private collections and artists' studios were often inaccessible. The profession of art dealing had not yet become a public affair—only a few print dealers, whose clientele emanated principally from a much less exalted financial plane, were readily in evidence. But the time was ripe, and William Hogarth was the first of the great English painters to sense what was happening. He saw that a venue was required in London where modern paintings could be publicly seen by those who could afford to buy.

In 1740 Hogarth began to donate new works to the Foundling Hospital of Capt. Thomas Corum. It was a curious gathering place for society's fashionables, but gather they did, and soon many practicing artists were giving paintings to the institution. Not only was a distinguished modern art collection assembled in a relatively short time, but the artistic community arrogated to themselves a proprietary interest in the running of the charity and soon dominated the hospital's board of governors.

Here was a major step in the institutionalization of the art world in England. In 1759 the governors decided to stage a two-week public exhibition of the best of English modern painting at the newly formed Society of Arts near the Strand. Over one thousand people a day paid admission to see the latest works by the greatest artists of the age, and it rapidly became clear that a handsome profit could be turned at such events.

The creation of the Incorporated Society of Artists was a direct outgrowth of this exhibition, and it was at their premises in Spring Gardens that West exhibited his early works. But the ideal of an elite brotherhood, or guild, of artists, established to promote the general welfare of the profession and to celebrate standards of excellence in the manner of the ancient livery companies of the City, proved chimerical. The competitive sensitivities of eccentric temperaments made for constant dissension, and, in 1768, the Society of Artists almost destroyed itself when the board of directors was virtually purged of its most distinguished members.

Two hostile camps of artists now faced one another, with those possessing the greatest talent now, ironically, on the outside. Benjamin West, who benignantly attempted to get along with everyone, was the only director of standing left after the purge. But it was an impossible situation. And eventually, in conjunction with the architect Sir William Chambers, the painter Francis Cotes, and the medalist George Michael Moser, West, who had the ear of the King, drew up plans for a royal academy of arts modeled upon continental precedent, which would enjoy the subsidy of the Crown along with free apartments in Somerset House. It was an ample testament of West's popularity at court that he not only secured the King's support for such an academy, but also succeeded in convincing George III that, if the institution was truly to be a jewel in the crown of royal bounty, it must have, as its first president, Joshua Reynolds, whom the Sovereign disliked and consistently refused to patronize. With Reynolds ensconced in the presidential chair, the professional legitimacy of the Royal Academy was assured. And although the Incorporated Society of Artists did not disappear altogether, it did sink into a kind of limbo, only occasionally rising to the surface of public attention when an artist of merit, at odds with the Academy, chose to exhibit there as an act of defiance.

But, for all practical purposes, the Royal Academy, with its annual exhibitions, became *the* place in London for the artist of ambition and talent. To be allowed the dignity of adding *R.A.* after one's name was a sign that an artist had arrived, and under Reynolds's presidency the Academy became the unquestioned home for the artistic establishment of the kingdom.

Increasing prosperity signaled a boom in the English art market in the 1770s. From all over Europe, artists flocked to London to promote themselves and their wares, as the English capital became cosmopolitan and even chic. The walls of the Royal Academy were filled with the work of foreigners eager to provide the plutocracy with every artistic item, from engravings to frescoed ceilings. The word was out internationally that, for the artist, London had become a boon.

The Prince of Wales Being Welcomed at the Royal Academy by the Academicians. Johann Heinrich Ramberg, 1763–1840. Pen and gray wash, 1787. 6½'' × 20½''. (The British Museum)

Even in distant America this turn of events did not go unnoticed. As the thirteen colonies and their mother country drifted irrevocably apart, many artists were increasingly tempted to come to England and try their luck. They generally came, not as high tories or devout radicals, but as creative entrepreneurs moving into a receptive marketplace. America, bordering on revolution, might be a good locale in which to sell guns and ammunition, but works of art were another matter. "Painters cannot live on art alone, though I could hardly live without it," wrote an embittered John Singleton Copley. Resenting the comparatively low social status accorded to his profession in the colonies, he was one who craved the opportunity to study great works available only in Europe.

Cool, private, and aloof in his relations with others, Copley, a born elitist, had corresponded with West since the early sixties about the possibility of a successful career in England. Summoning up his courage, Copley submitted several paintings to the Society of Artists' exhibitions at Spring Gardens and was assured by both Reynolds and West that a bright future would be his if only he would come to Europe before his talent suffocated in the barren environs of Massachusetts. "You have got," wrote West, "to that length in the art that nothing is wanted to perfect you now but a sight of what has been done by the great masters, and if only you

John Singleton Copley, 1737–1815.
Self-portrait. Oil on canvas, 1780–84. 18½" diameter.
(National Portrait Gallery; Gift of the Morris and Gwendolyn Cafritz Foundation
and matching funds from the Smithsonian Institution)

*Pen and watercolor
over pencil, 1785–90
13¼″ × 18½″
(Victoria & Albert
Museum, London)*

*Spring Gardens. Within the galleries here, the paintings of Copley were first
viewed by London's connoisseurs. Thomas Rowlandson, 1756–1827.*

would make a visit to Europe for this purpose for three or four years, you would find
yourself in possession of what will be highly valuable."

West assured Copley that "you may depend upon my friendship in any way that's
in my power to serve"—an offer he was to make to a great many American artists.
But still Copley tarried. "My ambition," he confided to a friend, "whispers me to run
this risk, and I think the time draws nigh that must determine my future fortune."
But some years passed before Copley was finally ready to make the break, and it was
not until the spring of 1774 that this most prudent of painters threw caution to the
winds and set sail for Europe.

When Copley reached London in July, he found the British metropolis "an astonishing city." West took him everywhere and introduced him to everyone. From
Joshua Reynolds's studio to the life class at the academy—"where the Students had a
naked model from which they were drawing"—to the palace of the Queen, London
with its affluence and excitement washed over Copley's senses. And when he saw
West's *Death of Wolfe*, "which is sufficient of itself to immortalize the Author of it,"
the potentialities of history painting began to stir in his mind.

West saw Copley off on an eighteen-month tour of Italy, advising him to study
"*Raphael, Michal Angelo, Corragio,* and *Titan,* as the so[u]rce from wh[e]nce true
tast[e] in the arts have flow'd." It was a good time to be out of America for someone
of Copley's temperament, and of this fact he was all too aware. To Henry Pelham,
his half brother, he wrote, "Could anything be more fortunate than the time of my
leaving Boston? Poor America! I hope the best but I fear the worst. Yet certain I am

she will finally emerge from her present calamity and become a mighty Empire. And it is a pleasing reflection that I shall stand the first of the artists that shall have led that country to the knowledge and cultivation of the fine arts, happy in the pleasing reflection that they will one day shine with a lustre not inferior to what they have done in Greece or Rome in my native country."

This was a rather remarkable statement from one who was far from sure that he ever wanted to return to America again. Copley accurately foresaw that his countrymen would suffer "the miserys of War, Sword, famin and perhaps pestalence," but, in spite of this, "the Americans have it in their power to baffle all that England can do against them . . . so that Ocians of blood will be shed to humble a people which they never will subdue." It was an evocative and rather quixotic prognostication from a man who, when he returned to London in the autumn of 1775, initially· consorted almost exclusively with American expatriate Loyalists.

At the age of thirty-seven, Copley, now reunited with his family in the English capital, was ready for his attack on London's portrait market. History painting, much as he admired it, would have to await the appearance of a patron willing to provide a substantial commission. Copley, at the outset, would not take such risks.

Early in 1776 the Copleys took a fashionable residence at 12 Leicester Square, a convenient address far less remote than Newman Street where Benjamin West held court. Many others in Copley's profession had also recognized the square's attractions. In earlier years both Hogarth and Sir James Thornhill had maintained residences close to the Copleys' new home. And now Sir Joshua Reynolds, President of the Royal Academy, lived opposite. Number 12 was a well-lit house with ample studio space, and, for the next seven-and-a-half years, Copley used it as his central base in London.

While the Copleys began a new life in Leicester Square, there were other painters still in America who were drawn inexorably to London by the attractions of patron-

Oil on canvas, 1771
39¾" × 58"
(Her Majesty Queen
Elizabeth II)

The Academicians of the Royal Academy.   West (seen center left)
took Copley to the Academy's life class, where the Boston painter first
saw a nude model in pose. Johann Zoffany, 1733–1810.

Oil on canvas, 1778
16¾'' × 12¾''
(Redwood Library and
Athenaeum)

Gilbert Stuart, 1755–1828.   Self-portrait.

age and fame. Gilbert Stuart, who had been exposed to Copley's work in Boston, was no stranger to Britain. As a child of seventeen, he had accompanied the itinerant painter, Cosmo Alexander, to Edinburgh, only to be abandoned when Alexander died in August 1772. Forced onto his own resources, Stuart worked his passage back to America, but, by September 1775, the lure of Britain again preyed upon his mind. The battle of Bunker Hill had recently been fought and, though Stuart was not particularly political, such an altercation must have been a powerful incentive to leave while it was still possible to move freely.

But, once again in England, Stuart discovered that London was not an easy place in which to succeed without connections. It was simply not possible to obtain wealthy patrons without the benefit of salubrious quarters where they could be received, particularly if they were expected to sit for portraits over long periods of time. Thus it was really not surprising that the raw and largely untrained Stuart was soon reduced to penury. Having reached the end of his tether and the expiration of his pride, he turned desperately to Benjamin West in December 1776, begging for help:

> Sir, The Benevolence of your Disposition encourageth me, while my necessity urgeth me to write you on so disagreeable a subject I hope I have not offended by takeing this liberty my poverty & ignorance are my only excuse Lett me beg that I may not forfeit your good will which to me is so desireable. Pitty me Good Sir I've just arriv'd att the age of 21 an age when most young men have done something worthy of notice & find myself Ignorant withoutt business or Friends, without the necessarys of life so that for some time I have been reduced to one miserable meal a day & frequently not even that, destitute of means of acquiring knowledge, my hopes from hom Blasted & incapable of returning thither, pitching headlong into misery I have this only without being a Burthen, Should Mr. West in his abundant kindness think of ought for me I shall esteem it an obligation which shall bind me forever with grattitude with the greatest Humility.

Stuart subsequently called at West's home and was received with great kindness. His gifts as a portraitist were unquestioned, and West who, in Stuart's words, "never could paint a portrait," gave him work finishing commissions from the Crown. Stuart became a familiar fixture at Newman Street and, under West's guidance, his talent ripened and matured. In 1782 he achieved his first signal success at the Royal Academy by exhibiting a full-length portrait of William Grant of Congalton in the novel pose of a skater on the Serpentine. *The Skater,* as the painting was cryptically titled, received much critical acclaim in the press for its dewy freshness of color and unique treatment of pose. Stuart was sufficiently encouraged to set up an establishment of his own, as commissions for half- and three-quarter-length portraits increased in number. Years later he recalled with feeling how the portentous academician Sir Nathaniel Dance-Holland had advised him, "You are strong enough to stand alone—take rooms—those who would be unwilling to sit to Mr. West's pupil, will be glad to sit to Mr. Stuart."

West could not object to Stuart's declared independence, for the young man had arrived professionally, and there were others to take his place as assistants. One was John Trumbull who, armed with letters of introduction from Benjamin Franklin in Paris, had begun his apprenticeship two years earlier, in 1780.

For John Trumbull, a son of one of the leaders of the movement for independence, the decision to go to England four years after Stuart's departure was extremely difficult. Tied to the New World by family obligations, Trumbull nevertheless had scant respect for those who comprised the self-styled committees of safety, made up as they were of "the middling and lower classes" whom he considered political illiterates. It was far better to have the new America led by those born to

Oil on canvas, 1782
96⅝'' × 58⅛''
(National Gallery of
Art, Washington;
Andrew W. Mellon
Collection, 1950)

The Skater.   Stuart's portrait of William Grant of Congal-
ton which scored an immediate success at the Royal Academy.
Gilbert Stuart, 1755–1828.

rule, namely, gentlemen educated in the courtly traditions of courtesy, prudence, and justice.

Trumbull was an advocate of the virtues of simple Christian piety. The siren of modern materialism rarely whispered into his ear, and it was this quality of simplicity that particularly endeared him to Benjamin West. A Connecticut Brahmin of Puritan aspect, Trumbull nevertheless found it necessary to journey to England, not to pursue mammon but rather to court an artistic muse which was silent in his own land.

Trumbull did not appreciate the delights of London. With the rectitude of a Puritan, he was repelled by "the cabals, the palpable corruption, and the meanness of intrigue" so apparent in the corridors of power. And what pleasures he might have approved scarcely had a chance to grow on him, for, a few weeks after his arrival, he was summarily arrested as a treasonous rebel and committed, "among the common felons," to a new prison at Clerkenwell.

It really was remarkable that Trumbull, the son of a prominent leader of the American Revolution, thought that he could happily move about London as an apolitical painter. No doubt the rats of Clerkenwell were a rude reminder that this was not the case. The most he could do to mitigate his circumstances was to assert his gentlemanly station in life and demand transfer to better quarters. This was granted, possibly because Clerkenwell was jammed with felons from the riots of the

Oil on canvas, 1801
30″ × 24¾″
(Wadsworth
Atheneum, Hartford;
Bequest of Daniel
Wadsworth)

John Trumbull, 1756–1843. Self-portrait.

previous year. But in any case, it was at Tothill Fields Prison near Bridewell that Trumbull was made as comfortable as possible.

It truly was a most elegant imprisonment. Trumbull lodged in the house of the prison-keeper who, for one guinea a week, provided him with an acceptable room complete with "a handsome bureau bed." Twice a day his meals were ordered from a nearby public house, and, when the weather was clement, he strolled in the prison yard, conversing with his jailer who, as a former butler to the Duke of Northumberland, possessed "the manners of a gentleman."

Trumbull's incarceration, however mitigated by personal comfort, posed a significant threat to all Americans in London, who feared their own loyalty might be called into question. This was particularly the case now that the arch-Loyalist Benjamin Thompson, the future Count Rumford, had taken charge of internal security regarding Americans at the Foreign Office.

When Benjamin West rushed to the palace to plead for his young protégé's life, he was also immensely concerned that his own position in the eyes of the King had not been compromised. George III assured West that Trumbull was not destined for the gibbet, but refused to intervene in order to secure his release. After all, the rebels had only recently executed Maj. John André for espionage, and Trumbull's family name was far too infamous to allow him even the unofficial freedom of the city.

Thus Trumbull remained a prisoner for almost seven months. West sent him paintings to copy, and Stuart, who could find humor in almost any situation, visited his friend whom he dubbed "Bridewell Jack."

While few in London were aware of John Trumbull the painter, as a political prisoner he was definitely news. Charles James Fox, leader of the not so "loyal opposition," called to express sympathy. In May 1781 the great Edmund Burke himself visited the prison and agreed to negotiate with the government on Trumbull's behalf. This resulted in an Order-in-Council granting bail of £400, on condition that the would-be painter depart from the kingdom within thirty days and not return until peace was reestablished. Trumbull was able to raise half the required sum, while Copley and West each pledged £100 as sureties to make up the difference. Once released, Trumbull departed from England as swiftly as possible, and on July 6, 1781, he arrived in Amsterdam, where John Adams was unsuccessfully attempting to secure loans for the all but bankrupt United States.

While Stuart and Trumbull remained acolytes to Benjamin West, John Singleton Copley, possessed of far greater experience, opened a public practice as soon as his house was in order. Copley's skill was certainly not unnoticed, and a question arose as to which artistic society, the Royal Academy or the Incorporated Society of Artists, he would choose to send his pictures for exhibition. It would have been a feather in the collective cap of the Incorporated Society if Copley could be drawn within their fold, for there were precariously few artists of the first rank who had not chosen the Academy as their public showplace. Consequently, in order to convince the newly arrived master, John Greenwood, a compatriot and old friend, was delegated to wait on Copley in order to present the Society's compliments.

Greenwood, a director and fellow of the Society, had not been in America for over twenty-three years. Born in 1727, he left Boston for Surinam in 1752, and from there migrated to Amsterdam, where he painted portraits and mastered the art of the mezzotint. He arrived in London the same year as Benjamin West and thereafter was a continuous exhibitor at the Society of Artists until his death at Margate in 1792.

However, Greenwood was never particularly successful as a practicing artist, though he did manage to obtain regular work providing engraved illustrations for books produced by the great publishers of the day, including John Boydell. As a painter in America, Greenwood was originally known as a ruthless delineator of the human face. But the years in England softened and mellowed his style, and his subject matter changed from the coarseness of *Sea Captains Carousing in Surinam* to the poetic harmonies of *Palaemon and Livinia* and *A Gypsy Fortune Teller,* so soft in their delicacy as to be considered effeminate.

Yet it was as an auctioneer and art dealer that Greenwood was most widely known. A man of natural business instincts, he predictably was drawn to London as

Mezzotint, after 1792
6⅝" × 5"
(Museum of Fine Arts,
Boston; George R.
Nutter Fund)

John Greenwood, 1729–92.   William Pether, 1731–95?

*Oil on canvas,
date unknown
34'' × 48''
(National Art Gallery
of New Zealand)*

The Seven Sisters of Tottenham.   A view of Greenwood's country home near London, reputed to be his last painting. John Greenwood, 1729–92.

the art market expanded. As a major competitor of James Christie, Greenwood maintained "Great Rooms" both in the Haymarket and near Copley's house in Leicester Square. And it was there that Titian's *Death of Actaeon* passed under his hammer, for £20, into the collection of Benjamin West.

From his home at Tottenham, Greenwood conducted a profitable private art business, arranging purchases on the Continent on behalf of collectors who recognized his talent for skillful and discreet negotiation. A multilinguist of great affability, the "friendly Mr. Greenwood," as a posthumous portrait engraving called him, was a dealer of significant volume. In 1770 he claimed to have imported over 1,500 paintings into Britain for purposes of sale. And four years later he traveled to Germany to purchase, en bloc, the extensive collections of both Count von Schulenbourg and Baron Steinberg. When William Hogarth died, it was Greenwood who disposed of all his prints and paintings, as he subsequently did of extensive portions of Joshua Reynolds's collection of continental prints.

Yet, however successful an art dealer Greenwood was, his powers of persuasion were not sufficient to lure Copley into the Incorporated Society of Artists. The Royal Academy was clearly the place to establish contact with the great patrons of the arts, and after exhibiting a conversation piece in the spring of 1776, Copley was rewarded, the following November, with an academic associateship.

Copley was now a master approaching middle age, yet was still eminently adaptable to new influences. By 1780 his portraits had abandoned the closely observed detail so notable in his American works, in favor of the more fashionable style of the "grand manner" practiced by Reynolds and Gainsborough.

Oil on canvas,
1779–81
90'' × 121''
(The Tate Gallery,
London)

The Death of the Earl of Chatham. With this giant group portrait, Copley established himself as Benjamin West's chief competitor. John Singleton Copley, 1737–1815.

Copley hoped that his new style, so eminently harmonious with established tastes, would sell, so that, with increasing financial security, he would be able to devote more attention to the highly speculative but more venerable arena of history painting. It was in the illustration of great contemporary historic events that American painters made their most prescient contribution to English art. Painting on a monumental scale, they produced commemorative and documentary works redolent of the secular spirit of the Enlightenment, emphasizing the virtues of heroic individualism and civic authority. And with their freedom from allegorical imagery and their penchant for realism, these works of historic reportage, which by no means represented the entire *oeuvre* of the painters involved, marked these Americans out as the new men of the day.

Certainly, when treated as painters of history, West, Copley, and Trumbull were in advance of their time, both in England and on the Continent. They were the modern artists whose native sense of commercial showmanship awakened and conditioned a new level of public consciousness and appreciation of the arts.

Such paintings, enormous in size, were what the public wanted, or so the artists hoped. They were to be a new form of entertainment, appealing to popular sentiment anxious to celebrate the glorious fallen leaders of recent memory.

West's *Death of Wolfe* had struck a responsive financial chord, not only for the painter, but for the publisher of its derivative print. Copley hoped to match this when, in 1779, he began to recreate on canvas the scene in the House of Lords on April 7, 1778, when the terminally ill William Pitt, Earl of Chatham, wrapped in his crimson flannels and supported by crutches, rose to debate the question of American rights only to collapse in a fit and die a month thereafter. The collapse of "the great commoner" was an event of national importance, personally witnessed by the most important peers of the realm. Copley labored for more than two years on the work, freed from competition when Benjamin West generously abandoned his own plans for such a picture in order to aid his friend. When it was completed, *The Death of the Earl of Chatham* was seven-and-a-half feet high and ten feet across. A magnificent example of group portraiture laid in a historic setting.

Such a picture was bound to be the centerpiece of the Academy's 1781 exhibition, ensuring a great financial success for the organization which had recently moved into its reconstructed quarters at Somerset House. But Copley had too well developed a business sense to want to hang his masterpiece, the product of so much labor, in a general academic exhibition. Instead, he went into direct competition with the Academy by renting a private gallery with the intention of charging the public a fee to view his great work.

The academicians were furious that one of their most junior members should so flagrantly violate the spirit of the organization. After significant pressure, Copley's

Oil on canvas, 1782–84 97'' × 144'' (The Tate Gallery, London)

The Death of Major Peirson. John Singleton Copley, 1737–1815.

picture was forced from its original venue in Pall Mall. But the canny Bostonian, unperturbed by the storm he was raising, engaged a second site at Spring Gardens, where over 20,000 people flocked to see his novel creation, paying a total in excess of £5,000 into the painter's coffer, while revenues at the Academy's exhibition fell almost 33 percent from the previous year's takings. Sir William Chambers, a leading academician, reflected the dismay and hostility of many of his colleagues when he wrote to Copley, "No one wishes Mr. Copley greater success, or is more sensible of his merit, than his humble servant, who, if he may be allowed to give his opinion, thinks no place so proper as the Royal Exhibition to promote either the sale of prints or the raffle for the picture, which he understands are Mr. Copley's motives. Or if that be objected to, he thinks no place so proper as Mr. Copley's own house where the idea of a raree-show will not be quite so striking as in any other place, and when his own presence will not fail to be of service to his views."

But a raree-show it was to be. Copley's subscription list for 2,500 large engravings of *The Death of the Earl of Chatham* was quickly sold, though the prints were long overdue in production. And many merchant princes of the City who were admirers of the dead Earl now conferred their patronage on the man who had immortalized him.

Determined to extract as much money as possible for the painting, Copley refused to accept less than 2,000 guineas. However, there were no takers at such an exalted figure, and a quarter-century was to pass before Copley finally raffled off the painting to twenty subscribers who each committed 100 guineas. A hard man over money, John Singleton Copley eventually got his price. Years later, Anthony Pasquin satirically jabbed at the Bostonian's financial instincts when he wrote, to the tune of "Yankee Doodle,"

> *From Massachusetts rebel state,*
> *When loyalty was crying,*
> *I ran on shipboard here to paint*
> *Lord Chatham who was dying.*
> *Then I hung up the House of Peers*
> *(Though some were quite unwilling)*
> *And gave the groupe to public view,*
> *And showed them for a shilling!*
>
> *Let* David *paint for hungry fame;*
> *And* Wilkie *subjects funny;*
> *Let* Turner *sit and study Storms*
> *But we will paint for money!*

After such a success, Copley moved to a gracious new house on George Street, near Hanover Square, and it was there, in 1784, that he completed his next historic tour de force, *The Death of Major Peirson,* which placed him at the zenith of his career.

When Copley failed to capture a portion of the royal patronage market with his group portrait of Their Royal Highnesses the Princesses Mary, Sophia, and Amelia, he returned to safer ground with portraits of City aldermen and merchants who, through the Corporation of London, commissioned *The Defeat of the Floating Batteries at Gibraltar*. Visitors to his studio reported that the battle had almost literally been fought indoors by the painter, who erected models of fortifications, ships, guns, and even the rock itself. But when, after six years of labor, the vast canvas, covering five hundred square feet, was finished, no private gallery was large enough to hang such a work. Yet Copley was determined not to send it to the Academy which would do little to augment his own income. An enormous oriental tent, eighty-four feet long, was therefore erected in Green Park, and Copley hired his fellow academician, Francesco Bartolozzi, to engrave an elaborate admission ticket which itself became a collector's item. But the crowds that flocked to see the picture so disturbed the nearby residents of Arlington Street that Copley was forced to move his tent three times, finally settling near Buckingham Palace after an assurance from the King that "my wife won't complain." According to Copley, sixty thousand people paid admission to see *Gibraltar* which, as before, competed directly with the Royal Academy's exhibition, costing that body a severe decline in revenue—though some said that the Academy building was structurally unsound which, if true, would frighten many would-be visitors away.

Oil on canvas, 1782
58⅝″ × 47⅝″
(The Art Museum,
Princeton University)

Elkanah Watson.   In the background of this portrait of a prosperous American merchant is an American flag— the first, according to the sitter, ever hoisted in England. John Singleton Copley, 1737–1815.

Americans in London, like everyone else, knew that the Revolution was drawing inexorably to a close. And, after the defeat of Cornwallis at Yorktown, it was clear what the end result would be. On December 5, 1782, John Singleton Copley, accompanied by his friend Elkanah Watson, went to the House of Lords to hear King George hesitantly announce the Crown's acknowledgment of American inde-

Oil on canvas, circa 1781–83 60'' × 40'' (Anonymous loan to the Boston Athenaeum)

Patience Wright, 1725–86. The redoubtable Mrs. Wright proclaimed herself the greatest Yankee patriot in London. Attributed to John Hoppner, 1758–1810.

pendence. Benjamin West was also there, trying to look as stoic as possible so as not to give offense. Copley, however, was so excited that, when he returned to his studio, he seized his almost-completed portrait of Watson, in the background of which he had inserted a ship bound for the New World, and, in the words of the sitter, "With a bold hand, a master's touch and I believe an American heart, he attached to the Ship the stars and stripes. This, I imagine, was the first American flag hoisted in England." There was still a bit of the Yankee left in John Singleton Copley.

When John Adams arrived, as the first American minister to the Court of St. James's, it was in Copley's studio that he sat for a full-length portrait. Abigail Adams was pleased with her husband's likeness and admired Copley's establishment. But for diversion, the Adamses went on to the greatest colonial raree-show in London, which was held daily at the Cockspur Street premises of Patience Wright, America's first sculptor and the greatest Yankee patriot in town. There they encountered a reception far in excess of anything Abigail Adams could have anticipated.

Upon my entrance (my name being sent up) she ran to the door and caught me by the hand. "Why, is it really and in truth Mrs. Adams, and is that your daughter? Why you dear soul how young you look. Well I am glad to see you. All of you Americans? Well I must kiss you all." Having passed the ceremony upon me and Abby she runs to the gentlemen. "I make no distinction," says she, and gave them each a hearty kiss from which we would all rather have been excused for her appearance is quite the slattern. "I love everything that comes from America," says she, "here," running to her desk, "is a card I had from Mr. Adams. He came to me and gave me a noble present. Dear creature, I design to have his head." "There," says she, pointing to an old man and woman who were sitting in a corner of the room, "are my old father and mother. Don't be ashamed of them because they look so. They were good folks (these were their figures in wax work), they turned Quakers and would never let their children eat meat and that is the reason we're all so ingenious. You had heard of the ingenious Mrs. Wright in America I suppose?" In this manner she ran on for half an hour. . . . There was an old clergyman sitting reading a paper in the middle of the room, and though I went prepared to see strong representations of real life I was effectually deceived by this figure for ten minutes and was finally told it was only wax.

Patience Wright had arrived in London in 1772, two years before Copley, accompanied by her three children. The redoubtable Quaker lady caused a sensation when she opened her waxworks in Pall Mall. It was not only the lifelike quality of her sculpture that aroused attention. Mrs. Wright herself was an incandescent showpiece whose opinions were pronounced with all the flair of a marching band.

It was not long before *tout* London was seen at the Wright establishment, which became the newest of fashionable lounging places. With a lump of wax on her lap, Patience Wright regaled her visitors with a torrent of radical unorthodox views. A unique creation, she was so great a curiosity that word of her crept even into the confines of the Court. The King and Queen paid calls to Pall Mall, both to be sculpted and with hopes of entertainment. They were rewarded with a character whose "sharp glance was appalling; it had almost the wildness of a maniac's," or so thought Elkanah Watson. King George and Queen Charlotte may have been shocked at being addressed by their Christian names by Mrs. Wright, but it was only good Quaker custom—not one, however, that Benjamin West would ever have dared indulge. The King apparently did not mind such familiarity, for his presence at Mrs. Wright's was noted on more than one occasion. But when the artist turned her wrath on the Sovereign and publicly berated him for his treatment of her American brethren, the bounds of good taste were finally transgressed, and royals came to the Wrights no more.

The pro-Americans, however, did continue to come. The historian Catharine Macaulay sat for a bust, as did both John Wilkes and the great Pitt whose wax effigy still stands, in his peer's robes, in the undercroft of Westminster Abbey. They and others were prime sources of political information which the voluble Mrs. Wright systematically passed on to Benjamin Franklin and other leaders of the independence movement. No one took her rantings seriously, and this in itself was heady protection once the Revolution began in earnest.

Mrs. Wright became celebrated both for her skill in modeling the human visage in wax as well as for her "strong masculine understanding." Horace Walpole was immensely amused when he reported that Lady Aylesbury literally spoke to a wax figure of a housemaid, failing to recognize it as a work of artifice. *The London Magazine* of December 1775 reported, "Mrs. Wright . . . has been reserved by the hand of nature to produce a new style of picturing superior to statuary and peculiar to herself and the honour of America, for her compositions, in likeness to the originals, surpass paint or any other method of delineation; they live with such a perfect animation, that we are more surprised than charmed for we see art perfect as nature."

Benjamin West was one of those seen on occasion at Mrs. Wright's salon. It was a good place to meet David Garrick, Benjamin Franklin, or Silas Deane. West was fond of the Wrights. He took Patience's son Joseph into his studio as a pupil for a brief period, and her daughter Phoebe, who married the painter John Hoppner, stood as a model for some of West's domestic canvases.

The Wrights were an intensely political family, who occasionally lacked the discretion so necessary for Americans to survive in London. In 1780 Joseph Wright exhibited a portrait of his mother at the Royal Academy, showing her modeling a head of the "blessed" Charles I with King George and Queen Charlotte looking on. Appearing at a time when the monarchy was held in extreme disrepute, with talk rife of revolution and a potential flight to Hanover, the painting bore unpleasant allusions to the monarch and his unfortunate ancestor who had lost his head. Some, like Walpole, thought the Wrights were making an avowed political gesture, a view supported in the contemporary epigram:

Wright in her lap sustains a trunkless head
And looks a wish—the King was in its stead.

Not altogether surprisingly, Joseph Wright did not stay long in England, though his mother, after a few halfhearted attempts to return to the United States, did remain until her death in 1786. Her financial success, in spite of hostility to things American, appears to have been sufficient to discourage any serious attempt at repatriation. Sadly few of Patience Wright's works survive today as testimony to her genius. Such are the attendant risks when working in a medium of extreme fragility.

Benjamin West, with an ever-watchful eye, saw immediate financial potential in the end of the War of Independence. He conceived a plan for a series of history paintings, on a monumental scale, depicting the great events of the Revolution. West anticipated that the market for prints alone in America would more than justify his effort, and subsequently wrote to a former pupil, Charles Willson Peale, asking for military uniforms and portraits of the most important leaders of the movement.

But it was a risky business producing visual paeans to the defeat of the King's armies, and, after consideration, West turned the project over to John Trumbull, who had returned to England in 1784, having discovered that, for the painter, Connecticut was not Athens.

West turned his attention instead to George III's massive commission, to produce thirty-five, mural-size paintings on the subject of "Revealed Religion" for the chapels royal at Windsor. It was a controversial project which, in the end, was rejected by the King's successor, but did mark a turning point in the style of West's painting. By the time of his death in 1820, West had exhibited almost one hundred religious canvases at the Royal Academy, almost all painted in a romantic style, seminally important for British art, and far removed from the neoclassicism of his early works.

For the young and inexperienced John Trumbull, West's project was the most golden of opportunities. Not only was there money to be made, but fame to be earned, as the patriot painter of the Revolution. Trumbull was perfectly suited for the task. He had actually served as an officer on Washington's staff and personally knew a great many heroes of the day. After making a copy of West's *Battle of La Hogue,* Trumbull began his series in 1785–86 by producing *The Death of General Warren at the Battle of Bunker's Hill, June 17, 1775,* modeled closely on Copley's *Death of Major Peirson.* And, the following June, Trumbull finished *The Death of General Montgomery in the Attack on Quebec December 31, 1775,* which employed West's *Death of Wolfe* as an obvious prototype. These would be followed by other paintings, including the *Surrender at Yorktown,* the *Battle of Trenton,* and the *Signing*

Oil on canvas, 1832–34 replica after the original completed in London in 1786 72'' × 108'' (Wadsworth Atheneum, Hartford, Museum Purchase)

The Death of General Warren at the Battle of Bunker's Hill, 17 June 1775. John Trumbull, 1756–1843.

of the Declaration of Independence. For Trumbull, so like Copley in spirit, so like West in philosophic outlook, this was the most exciting of times, as he moved to create art as historic documentation. Three years after completing his *Death of Montgomery,* Trumbull wrote to Thomas Jefferson, in Paris,

> The greatest motive I had or have for engaging in, or for continuing my pursuit of painting, has been the wish of commemorating the great events of our country's revolution. I am fully sensible that the profession, as it is generally practised, is frivolous, little useful to society, and unworthy of a man who has talents for more serious pursuits. But to preserve and diffuse the memory of the noblest series of actions which have ever presented themselves in the history of man; to give to the present and the future sons of oppression and misfortune, such glorious lessons of their rights & of the spirit with which they should assert and support them, and even to transmit to their descendents, the personal resemblance of these who have been the great actors in these illustrious scenes, were objects which give a dignity to the profession, peculiar to my situation.

West explained to Trumbull the intricacies, both legal and practical, of publishing derivative engravings. He had been extremely successful, while Copley, on the other hand, had had occasionally to resort to the courts for financial redress from his

Oil on canvas, 1832–34 replica of the original completed in London in 1786 72″ × 108″ (Wadsworth Atheneum, Hartford, Museum Purchase)

The death of General Montgomery in the Attack on Quebec, 31 December 1775. John Trumbull, 1756–1843.

engravers. West recommended that Trumbull contract with Antonio di Poggi, an Italian artist turned publisher, to produce engravings of the deaths of Warren and Montgomery. Poggi would handle all the details and, in return, he would take a hefty share of the profit.

As a business relationship, the affair proved disastrous. Three years would elapse before the first of Trumbull's engravings appeared, and almost ten years passed before the second copperplate was ready. The work produced by continental engravers was more than competent, but so long was the time lapse that any hope of enormous profits, based on public enthusiasm for the events depicted, faded with the years.

Trumbull, meanwhile, in an attempt to capture a British market for his art, produced, in 1787, a painting depicting the end of the historic three-year siege of Gibraltar, when the victorious Gen. George Elliot (later Lord Heathfield) finally expelled the Spaniards from the rock on the night of November 26–27, 1781. It was an eminently successful picture, perhaps Trumbull's best. His composition, again based directly on West's *Death of Wolfe,* was reproduced at least five times by the painter between 1787 and the year of his death.

The one incident in the painting that most interested the artist was the heroic death of the Spanish commander, Don José Barboza. For his third and largest version, painted in 1789, Trumbull secured as his model the then nineteen-year-old

Thomas Lawrence, who would one day sit in Benjamin West's presidential chair at the Royal Academy.

The painting was generally well received. Horace Walpole declared that he "regarded it as the finest picture he had ever seen, painted on the northern side of the Alps." William Sharpe produced an elegant engraving after the picture, which sold extremely well, and so euphoric was Trumbull that he declined an offer of 1,200 guineas for it, expecting that he stood to make much more if he followed the example of John Singleton Copley. Unfortunately, his hopes were disappointed, and years later when the painting was sold for a third of the original price offered, he had to admit that he had made a serious blunder.

John Trumbull never achieved the prominence of West or Copley as a painter of history. His subject matter offended the English, and his own compatriots lacked the enthusiasm of active patrons. By the time he left Britain after the War of 1812, Trumbull had spent almost a quarter-century away from his native land, though his expatriation was not an uninterrupted one. He was no longer a full-time painter, having acted, first, as one of the American commissioners appointed to negotiate the Jay Treaty with Great Britain, and, second, having dealt in commodities as diverse as casks of brandy and old master paintings purchased from the ruined noblesse of France. None of his commercial ventures were particularly successful, and the end result was disappointment for expectations unrealized.

Many American painters who came to England to find Elysium vowed that they would never return to the United States until their success as artists was unques-

Oil on canvas, 1788
20'' × 30''
(Cincinnati Art Museum, John J. Emery Endowment)

The Sortie of the British Garrison from Gibraltar, 26 November 1781.
John Trumbull, 1756–1843.

tioned. For John Trumbull, the choice was not so prescient. Possessed by the passion of the patriot, he could, after many years abroad, still write:

> My future movements depend entirely upon my reception in America, and as that shall be cordial or cold, I am to decide whether to abandon my country or my profession. I think I shall determine without much hesitation . . . if I will follow the general example of my profession by flattering the pride or apologizing for the vices of men, yet the ease, perhaps even elegance, which would be the fruit of such conduct, would compensate but poorly for the contempt which I feel for myself, and for the necessity which it would impose upon me of submitting to a voluntary sentence of perpetual exile. I hope for better things.

The choice that faced Trumbull was less pressing to Gilbert Stuart, who had precious little interest in the majesty of historic, mythical, religious, neoclassic, and romantic fantasies. Stuart, with good humor, occasionally mocked Benjamin West, asserting that "no one would paint history who could do a portrait." To re-create the human visage was something Stuart could do with consummate skill, excelling not so much in the creation of portraits as of faces—faces virtually alive in the luminosity of their flesh tones. Everything he produced was geared to the quality of flesh; it was for Stuart a sensuous object worth endless praise, "Like no other substance under heaven. It has all the gaiety of a silk-mercer's shop without its gaudiness and gloss, and all the soberness of old mahogany without its sadness."

Critics would object to his "milk and rosewater" images, many looking unfinished, devoid of costume, drapery, or background. But, at its best, the liquid, dewy freshness of Stuart's brilliant flesh tones ranked him, in public esteem, with the very greatest of his peers—George Romney and, later, Thomas Lawrence.

In 1783, independent of West with his own painting rooms, Gilbert Stuart, now of New Burlington Street, cut an elegant swath across London. He apologized to no one for his choice of subject: "I will not follow any master. I will find out what nature is and see her with my own eyes. Rembrandt saw with different eyes from Raphael. Yet they are both excellent and for different reasons. They had little in common but each followed nature."

He was, like Gainsborough, the master of exact resemblance, "the Van Dyck of the time," who saw the personality behind the mask, brought it out into the open, and laid it bare to the eyes of the beholder. But Stuart was also a maverick. His close friend, Benjamin Waterhouse, remembered that, with him, "It was either hightide or lowtide. In London he would sometimes lay abed for weeks waiting for the tide to lead him on to fortune, while Copley and West had the industry of ants before they attained the treasure of bees."

As Stuart's reputation increased, he came to the attention of Alderman John Boydell, the greatest of the art entrepreneurs of the age, who had done much to

Pen and ink, 1783
7″ × 5″
(The British
Museum)

Mr. Stuart Painting Mr. West's Portrait.
Benjamin West, 1738–1820.

create the boom in English art. Boydell made a small fortune as the publisher of West's *Death of Wolfe.* He purchased Copley's *Death of Major Peirson* and hung it in his print shop, where the works of many artists, including John Greenwood, were on view.

Stuart was commissioned by Boydell to paint a portrait of Copley which was hung above *Major Peirson.* This was followed by orders for fourteen other portraits of artists and engravers actively employed by the publisher. A veritable Gilbert Stuart exhibition could thus be seen at the Pall Mall premises of the great Boydell, who was soon to present London with the first of its large, public picture galleries, where the themes of Shakespeare were illustrated by West and eighteen other leading artists.

London was full of art critics, amateur and professional, who lodged frequent notices in the daily and weekly press. Gilbert Stuart was one of the favored, for reviews of his work were almost always positive. Even Patience Wright's son-in-law, the acerbic John Hoppner, found it possible to say kind things about the young American.

But tragically it all came to a crashing end. After 1785 Stuart ceased to exhibit at the Royal Academy, thus forfeiting any chance of gaining the academician's laurels that surely would have been his due. Living in great splendor, "the gayest of the gay"

Stuart spent with a profligacy which apparently far outdistanced his respectable income, and soon he was forced into rather unorthodox measures. How surprised Benjamin West must have been, when he called at Boydell's gallery one afternoon, to find his own portrait by Stuart hanging among the alderman's collection. Stuart, who had given the highly praised picture to West, had borrowed it briefly to make certain "alterations," which included selling it. West was able to reclaim his property, but Boydell was out of pocket.

Late in the summer of 1787, Stuart, hounded by his creditors, and no doubt in fear of debtors' prison, fled London and surfaced in Dublin the following October. He hoped to paint the aged Lord Lieutenant of Ireland, the Duke of Rutland, who was one of the few serious patrons of the arts in the kingdom. But the Duke unfortunately expired just as Stuart was reaching the Irish capital. Nevertheless, there were far worse places for the painter than Dublin. He was, after all, a portraitist of some reputation, and there was virtually no competition for the patronage of the Protestant ascendancy and the hierarchy of the Catholic Church.

In the briefest of times, Stuart was engaged to paint numerous high panjandrums of Irish society; members of the Privy Council; the Lord Chancellor and the Speaker of the Irish House of Commons; elegant prelates of the church including Euseby Cleaver, the sometime Bishop of Cork and future Archbishop of Dublin, as well as the Bishop of Ossory who presented the painter with a fine monogrammed snuffbox. It was the perfect gift for the son of a snuff grinder, known throughout his career as an enormous user of the stuff which stained his shirts and, surprisingly, did not become mixed on his palette.

Stuart remained in Ireland for five years, residing first in Dublin, and later in the suburban village of Stillorgan where he continued to lead a life of "extreme conviviality." There he produced enough work to finance his return to America in 1792 at the age of thirty-seven. His daughter Jane would have us believe that the exile's return was a passionate pilgrimage to the feet of the beatific George Washington. More likely it was a case of moving on before Irish creditors closed in, as had the tradesmen of London.

When Stuart died, eulogies of his character appeared in the American press, stating that he had given up the brightest prospects in England out of patriotic fervor for the New World. In London this news was received with more than mild surprise. Charles R. Leslie, an American expatriate much younger than Stuart, recalled an exchange on the subject between Sir Thomas Lawrence and Lord Holland.

Lawrence opined that he knew Stuart well, "And I believe the real cause of his leaving England was his having become tired of the inside of some of our prisons."

To which Lord Holland quipped, "Well then, after all, it was his love of freedom that took him to America."

In 1792, while Gilbert Stuart was slipping out of Ireland, Benjamin West was settling into the presidential chair of the Royal Academy. His election was no more than a ceremonial confirmation. During the previous year West, as Deputy President, had taken effective control of Academy business as Joshua Reynolds slid quietly toward death in February 1792.

As he rose to address the general council of the Academy for the first time as President, the fifty-four-year-old West is reported by his first biographer to have said, "Therefore, gentlemen, not on account of any personal merits on my part, but to do honour to the office to which you have so kindly elected me, I shall presume in future to wear my hat in this assembly." Three years later, Henry Singleton commemorated the custom when he painted *The Royal Academicians in General Assembly,* showing West, in true Quaker fashion, sitting among his colleagues, a black hat firmly placed on the presidential brow. (Perhaps this was a gesture to his Quaker heritage, but more likely it was in emulation of the presiding officers of Parliament who always covered their heads at official occasions.) At the side of the council stood John Singleton Copley with his familiar wandlike staff in hand. Copley was not pleased, for the presidency was a post he too coveted. What had begun, over a quarter-century before, as a warm personal relationship between himself and West had cooled into a rivalry of intense bitterness.

West and Copley were competing in the same marketplace. While Copley succeeded in underbidding for the commission to paint the *Siege of Gibraltar,* he was convinced that West was using John Trumbull as a pawn to undercut him by en-

Oil on canvas, 1795
78'' × 102''
(Royal Academy of
Arts, London)

The Royal Academicians in General Assembly.   Copley stands at the right, a staff in his hand, and West sits in the presidential chair. Henry Singleton, 1766–1839.

couraging Trumbull to paint his own version of the famous event. In truth, Copley may not have been wrong, for, as the famous diarist, Mrs. Papendiek, noted in her *Court and Private Life in the Time of Queen Charlotte,* the "saintly" West was "the friend of no one who might possibly interfere with his success."

Copley was losing his touch as a painter. In vain attempts to recapture the popular acclaim engendered by the *Death of Chatham* and his other history paintings, he continued to grind out large works on similar subjects, but the results were pathetically disappointing. The nadir of Copley's career was reached in 1803 when he exhibited a huge group portrait of Sir Edward Knatchbull and his family, both living and dead, which was received in the Academy with hoots of derision. Copley was mortified, but he was bound to suffer further indignities when Knatchbull, outraged that the picture had been shown at all, demanded successfully that it be withdrawn.

For West, this was a brief moment of satisfaction. Since his election to the presidency, Copley had seized every opportunity to provoke divisiveness within the Academy. No more so than in this very exhibition, when Copley succeeded in having one of West's own reworked paintings expelled on the grounds that it had been shown before, albeit in a somewhat altered state.

West was not invulnerable to such attacks. In the Court it was whispered that the King's Painter of History was a rank jacobin and democrat whose loyalty was far from unquestioned.

West committed a classic blunder by taking advantage of the Peace of Amiens to visit Paris to exhibit his most romantic works, which were avant-garde by any standard. He returned to England voicing loud and jubilant praise for the Emperor Napoleon, Britain's inveterate enemy, which was too much for the ailing King George who all but withdrew his patronage from West. Copley would have enjoyed such a situation, were it not for the fact that the King hated him as well. At one point the Sovereign exploded to the painter William Beechey, "West is an American,— and Copley is an American,—and you are an Englishman, and if the devil had you all, I would not enquire after you."

Such internecine fighting was destroying the utility of the Royal Academy. The painter Joseph Farington confided to his diary, "Copley has done more injury to the arts and the character of artists than any man of his time." And it was to Farington on November 29, 1805, that West confided his decision to resign the presidency rather than continue to battle against Copley and his cabal in the absence of support from the Crown.

But it was a Pyrrhic victory for West's enemies. The architect James Wyatt was elected President, and West retired to Newman Street to paint his *Death of Nelson,* the last of his large history pieces. It was a work he had promised himself for over a year, since several evenings before Trafalgar, when he and the great admiral sat at dinner discussing the *Death of Wolfe.* West had promised, half in jest, that if Nelson's intrepidity furnished him with a similar subject, he would be happy to paint it.

It was now Benjamin West's turn to exhibit his painting in competition with the Academy, as Copley had done on so many previous occasions. Over 20,000 people flocked to see the *Nelson,* which came as a great financial relief to one whose fortunes were sadly depleted due to the withdrawal of royal support.

One short year passed, and West returned to his seat as President of the Academy. The Wyatt party had proved itself incapable of governing effectively, and almost everyone was glad for a return to the comparatively quiet days of the old President's suzerainty.

Copley was a beaten man. His wife confided to his daughter in Boston, "Your father often regrets that he did not return [to America] many years since, but these retrospects are vain." On September 17, 1811, the young Samuel F. B. Morse wrote from London, "I visited Mr. Copley a few days since. He is very old and infirm. I think his age is upward of seventy, nearly the age of Mr. West. His powers of mind have almost entirely left him; his late paintings are miserable. It is really a lamentable thing that a man should outlive his faculties."

A little over three months after Morse penned his letter, Copley attended his last meeting of the council of the Royal Academy. With an "absent bewildered manner," he lingered on, attempting to produce a valedictory work of merit, but it was not to be. On August 11, 1815, Copley suffered a stroke and died twenty-eight days later.

West, on the other hand, seemed indestructible. Farington noted that his face had become thin and long as early as 1805, but, while Copley was struggling merely to get to the Academy in 1811, the seventy-two-year-old West was hard at work producing the "ten-acre" *Christ Healing The Sick,* which was sold to the British Institution for 3,000 guineas—the largest sum of money ever paid in Britain for a work of modern art. This, in turn, was followed by *Christ Rejected,* for which the painter refused an offer of 8,000 guineas.

During the last decade of his life, Benjamin West retained his title as the grand old man of the British school. At the libidinous court of the Regent, his piety was clearly out of place and his radical politics genuinely suspect. Lord Byron's famous jape,

> Meanwhile the flattering feeble dotard West.
> Europe's worst dauber, and poor England's best,
> With palsied hand shall turn each model o'er
> And own himself an infant of fourscore

was an accurate representation of his standing at Carlton House. But among the public, he was still a much-revered figure who had escaped the opprobrium attached to old age much longer than any of his contemporaries.

When he died in 1820, shortly after the King whom he had served for over a half-century, West, together with George Dance, was *the* surviving member appointed at the foundation of the Royal Academy. He left many students who freely acknowledged his influence on their careers, but few followers who imitated his technique or subject matter, for West was much more concerned with implanting in the minds of those who came to him an appreciation of the great moral responsibilities attending the production of high art.

Charles R. Leslie was one of those students, who recalled vividly the afternoon of West's death, when a caller at the master's home was received by an old retainer who asked, "Sir, where will they all go now?" It was a question that went unanswered.

2

The Rewards of Invention:
Count Rumford, Robert Fulton,
and John James Audubon

It was the middle of September 1783. At Dover a packet was ready for the crossing to France. Edward Gibbon, the historian, was revisiting the Continent for the first time since the restoration of peace between the great powers. It was filthy weather and the crossing was extremely rough, but, in a letter to Lord Sheffield, Gibbon remarked that the journey had been made interesting by the company of two distinguished Americans. The first was Henry Laurens, a former President of the Continental Congress, who had been imprisoned in the Tower during the Revolution and who, after recuperation at Bath, was on his way to France to join Benjamin Franklin. The second was described by Gibbon as "Mr. Secretary, Colonel, Admiral, Philosopher Thompson," the future Count Rumford.

Benjamin Thompson was truly a *Wunderkind* of his era, and even those, like Gibbon, who did not like him had to admit that he was possessed of extraordinary abilities. Thompson had no use for kings or congresses except as they suited his purposes. Thirty-seven of his sixty-one years were spent abroad; he was an exile who never found a *patria*.

Thompson was a comely individual with a shock of red hair and bright blue eyes, who knew how to exploit his good looks to maximum advantage. At the age of nineteen he was courted by, and married, one of the richest widows in New Hampshire, a woman many years his senior. And, with her money and connections, he naturally gravitated into the circle of John Wentworth, the Royal Governor of New Hampshire, through whose patronage he obtained a major's commission in one of the provincial regiments of the colony.

Thompson was a natural elitist, absolutely convinced of his own superior abilities. But, as these were times of political turmoil, his posturing only succeeded in raising suspicions that he was "unfriendly" to the cause of colonial liberty, and this was a dangerous position to hold after the evacuation of Boston in 1776. They were not just suspicions, however, for as early as 1774 Thompson had been active in the pursuit and capture of British deserters from General Gage's command, an occupation hardly likely to win him popularity among his fellows.

As a Loyalist refugee, he abandoned his wife and fled Massachusetts with the British garrison between March and April of 1776 and made his way to England with, in his own words, "Public Dispatches and a Letter of Recommendation from Governor Wentworth to Lord George Germaine, the Secretary of State" for the American Colonies. The report was, in fact, a highly detailed account, penned by Thompson, on the state of the American army, its ability to recruit, arm, and supply itself, and the strategic position it occupied at the time of Thompson's departure.

Germaine was immensely impressed with the articulate young officer who stood before him. Thompson played his cards very well and, within days, was appointed to the sinecure of Secretary of the Province of Georgia, at a nominal salary of £100 per annum. Some whispered that it was not his political skills that mattered but rather those that he exercised in the boudoirs of Germaine's household.

Thompson virtually became a member of the family, and it was at Stoneland Lodge, Germaine's country house, that he began the first of his noted scientific

Oil on canvas, 1812
29'' × 24''
(American Academy of Arts and Sciences, Boston)

Sir Benjamin Thompson, Count Rumford, 1753–1814.
Rembrandt Peale, 1787–1860.

experiments with ordnance that was to earn him a fellowship in the Royal Society in 1779, at the age of twenty-six. There was always some remnant of the schoolmaster in Thompson; he loved to give demonstrations of the practical applications of his ideas, and under Germaine's protective wing he commanded the attention of the British capital.

In the years following his election to the Royal Society, Thompson received an important promotion to Undersecretary of State in the American Department. He was now Germaine's right-hand man, both in and out of the office, and they were seen everywhere together, almost as father and son, eating, drinking, and discussing state business.

As Undersecretary of State, Thompson was able to fully indulge his penchant for things military, and as an eminently practical man, he devoted considerable time to the development of new designs for "horse furniture and accoutrements" and light dragoon uniforms. Thompson was also directly in charge of considering the claims of his fellow Loyalist refugees, and it was said, not too quietly, that he was making a great deal of money at this time through gratuities for the services of this office. Certainly his quarters in Pall Mall provided no evidence of an ascetic life-style.

Even the King became aware of Thompson's existence. He had a natural gift for attracting notice and somehow came into possession of the revolutionary correspondence between Benjamin Franklin and Dr. Cooper, which he had bound in red morocco, tooled in gold, for presentation to the Sovereign. The letters were regarded as a great curiosity, and Thompson's name was not forgotten.

But his position was by no means inviolable. In 1781, as prosecution of the war went from bad to worse, murmurs of discontent with the Germaine administration grew more vocal. As Germaine's familiar, Thompson was also vulnerable, and a young man who had risen so far so fast was bound to have enemies. Imputations were made, and sincerely believed by men of distinction, that Thompson was engaged in treasonous activity with the convicted spy, Francis Henry La Motte, who was sentenced "to be hanged by the neck, but not until dead; then to be cut down,

Count Rumford's drawing instruments
(Massachusetts Historical Society)

and his bowels taken out and burnt before his face, his head to be taken off, his body cut into four quarters, and to be at His Majesty's disposal."

It was the Earl of Sandwich, First Lord of the Admiralty, who wanted to prosecute Thompson, but he dared not. For his own maladministration was the subject of a parliamentary enquiry, and Germaine made it clear that he would crucify Sandwich if Thompson were threatened. How lucky the young Undersecretary was for such a protector. George Hammond who, ten years later, would go to America as the first British Minister to the United States, could only explain it in terms of the "scandalous intimacy" that existed between Germaine and his deputy.

But despite Germaine's protection, Thompson sensed it was unwise to tarry in London much longer. As Undersecretary he still had position but, should Germaine fall from power, he would be completely helpless. Better to secure a new station now rather than wait for the walls to cave in.

Thompson asked Germaine for an effective command of that regiment of dragoons in America of which he was already titular colonel. Once it was granted, Thompson was off to the New World to win his spurs in a great military adventure, or so he thought. He landed at Charleston with the intention of proceeding on to New York to take charge of his troops, but, due to misadventure, found himself trapped there with no option but to offer his services to the local commandant. After involvement in a number of skirmishes on the Santee River, in February 1782, Thompson finally made his way to New York four months after Cornwallis had surrendered at Yorktown. While the peace negotiations dragged on, he was relegated to fighting a little war of his own against American whaleboats on Long Island Sound—a discordant image in the remarkable career of Colonel Thompson, who professed only to be interested in the dash and fire of a cavalry charge.

With the conclusion of hostilities, Thompson returned to England to press claims on the government for recognition of himself as a regular army officer entitled to the retirement benefit of half-pay. Having read numerous petitions as Undersecretary, Colonel Thompson was expert in drafting and pressing his own, and within a short time he secured the support of a number of important members of the government, including Lord North who represented his case successfully to the King. But what is the fate of an unemployed military man retired on half-pay at the age of thirty? Does he remain in England where the army is still licking its wounds? On the Continent the Russians and Turks appeared to be on the brink of combat, and the Austrians might be drawn in. Good military minds were always in demand, and, as far as this American soldier of fortune was concerned, "On one side or another I am determined to have a hand in it."

And so, by the middle of September 1783, Thompson was at Dover to catch the packet to France. On his way to Vienna, where he hoped to obtain a commission, Thompson stopped at Strasbourg to witness a review by the garrison. Always conscious of making a strong impression, he rode to the edge of the parade ground dressed in the scarlet uniform of a full colonel of the British army, a sight that had not been seen in France for years. His appearance naturally attracted much attention, especially in the eyes of one particular officer serving for pleasure in the French army. This was the Prince Maxmilian of Zweibrücken, who would one day sit on the throne of Bavaria.

Naturally, the Prince asked to meet the British officer whose appearance was so calculatingly impressive. They took to one another immediately and spent some time discussing the battles of the Revolution where many of the Prince's men had fought. Naturally, Thompson had maps and plans at hand, detailing his own important role in the course of events.

The Prince invited Thompson to visit Munich to meet his uncle, Charles Theodore, the Elector of Bavaria, and provided him with enthusiastic letters of introduction. Thompson hardly needed further encouragement, particularly after his visit to Vienna failed to produce an attractive position.

Perhaps it was time to abandon martial pursuits. The wife of a German general "opened his eyes to other kinds of glory," and, when he was offered a place at the Court of the Elector, there were a great many ladies of leisure from whose beds he climbed close to the seat of power.

Charles Theodore, impressed with the letters Thompson carried from his nephew, appointed him colonel and aide-de-camp with duties that included tutoring his bastard son, the Count von Bretzenheim. It must have been a trying experience for both pupil and master, as Thompson knew no German and precious little French.

However, before confirming his position, the Elector insisted that Thompson, as a serving British officer, return to England to obtain King George's permission for his secondment. Not only was this forthcoming, but at Lord North's suggestion the King dubbed Thompson a Knight Bachelor of the British Empire, and a parchment diploma was ordered from the College of Arms confirming his rank and status.

So there he was at the age of thirty-two, Sir Benjamin Thompson, a Yankee soldier of the Loyalist persuasion who was about to become, for the next thirteen years, a social reformer or an enlightened despot (historians have disagreed as to the exact extent of his power) in a South German principality in the late eighteenth century.

Charles Theodore gave Sir Benjamin a cavalry regiment to command, made him a major general and a privy councilor, and provided him with a vast residence in the heart of Munich. In 1785 he was elevated to the position of Court Chamberlain to the Elector and, the following year, at the request of his master, was knighted by the King of Poland with the Order of St. Stanislaus. The Elector of Bavaria was one of the vicars of the Holy Roman Empire, and in 1791, during the interregnum between the Emperors Joseph II and Leopold II, he ennobled Thompson as a count of the Holy Roman Empire and secured for him Poland's highest order of chivalry, the Order of the White Eagle. Thompson took the name Count Rumford, after the ancient name of Concord, New Hampshire, where he had first achieved success.

All these honors were in recognition of Rumford's many services to Bavaria. In the name of the Enlightenment and of practical ingenuity, he had, with the Elector's consent, completely reorganized the army so as to improve the living conditions of the common soldier; established schools in every regimental headquarters to raise the literacy rate; introduced the steam engine into Bavaria through his contacts with James Watt in Birmingham; developed new techniques of horse and cattle breeding; laid out the famous English garden in Munich where new agricultural techniques could be demonstrated; and opened soup kitchens and workhouses for the poor which eliminated the persistent problem of beggars in the streets. This last innovation was emulated all over Europe. In Geneva, Rumford's portrait was actually printed on tickets which admitted the indigent to that city's soup kitchens. The Count himself produced a series of recipes guaranteed to provide nourishing meals for hundreds at a time for only pennies per serving. The amateur scientist who had experimented with cannons now experimented with human beings, confident that, if the poor could be made happy, virtue would surely follow.

His achievements were manifold. Rumford even saved Munich from occupation by the French army and was rewarded with the post of Commissioner of Police in Bavaria. This was a position of enormous importance in South German states, for it placed the holder in complete charge of state security.

But, if he was an absolutist in forcing his programs on the people, Rumford was a much-beloved figure. When he lay ill, the populace of Munich marched in solemn procession to the cathedral to pray for his recovery—a tribute, he noted with pride, to "a private person! a stranger! a Protestant."

Yet such sweeping changes were bound to have repercussions. Rumford was liberating the peasantry from their feudal shackles, and in so doing was earning the implacable enmity of the aristocracy and landed gentry. By 1798 he began to sense that his master was growing tired of him. And again, rather than wait for a fall which seemed inevitable, he requested appointment as Minister Plenipotentiary to the Court of St. James's, which was readily granted. And so Rumford departed from Bavaria, as

> *Round him the labourers throng, the nobles wait*
> *Friend of the poor and guardian of the state.*

But how bizarre that he should return to London as a German diplomat. The British, seeing an obvious conflict of interest, would simply have none of it. After all, Rumford was still a colonel on half-pay in the King's army. He had served in a confidential capacity as Undersecretary of State, and from the Sovereign's own hand had received the honor of knighthood. Rumford took the rebuff well and retired from the Bavarian service, "a free, independent citizen of the world," with ample pensions now from the two heads of state. But he was not about to return to Germany. There was far too much potential for social reform in England.

He began to publish essays on social questions which earned him a reputation as the greatest living authority on philanthropy in the kingdom. Out of one essay grew the Society for Bettering the Condition of the Poor; and out of another developed the Royal Institution, dedicated to the popularization of new inventions for the improvement of the commonweal. It remains today perhaps the greatest monument to Rumford's genius.

The Royal Institution was set up as a technological institute under the Count's direct supervision and management. He succeeded in enlisting the support of Sir Joseph Banks, the President of the Royal Society, which held a virtual monopoly over scientific activity in the country. And, at the organizing meeting of the Institution in Banks's home, it was decided to ask the King for the grant of a charter so that Rumford's creation could be known as a "Royal" body. Nine prominent philanthropists were brought together to act as managers of the Institution, and a blue-ribbon standing committee of scientists, including Henry Cavendish, Nevil Maskelyne, and Sir Charles Blagden, was formed to ensure the maintenance of high standards. In April 1799, a house in Mayfair's Albemarle Street was purchased for the Institution's quarters. Within a year, refurbishment was all but finished, at least one prominent scientific lecturer engaged, and a syllabus drawn. Rumford then proceeded to publish his famous prospectus, inviting the support and patronage of the moneyed classes for the betterment of society as a whole. The response was overwhelming, so great was public interest in the novelty of scientific inventions.

Rumford, with his new coffeepots, reflecting lamps, chimney flues, fireplaces, and roasters, together with his systems of central heating and advocacy of regular bathing, was the great drawing card and stimulus of the Royal Institution, who thought he could bridge the gap between the scientist in his laboratory and the industrialist in his factory. But, to the manufacturer, Rumford's scheme was anathema, the plaything of a dilettante who did not have to live off the income of his inventions. It was fine for Rumford to refuse patents on his many creations, but others could not be so magnanimous. Thus, a primary goal of the Royal Institution was thwarted at the outset, when the elite of the manufacturing world absolutely refused to divulge publicly any of their precious trade secrets.

Instead, the Royal Institution became a kind of scientific club for the upper classes; a new source of diversion for the intelligent rich. It was a far cry from Rumford's dream, and gradually he disassociated himself from its daily operations, devoting more and more time, in and out of England, to the betterment of living conditions for the poor.

Yet the Royal Institution did survive, and under the leadership, first, of Sir Humphry Davy and, later, Michael Faraday, it was transformed, phoenixlike, into one of the most famous laboratories of pure science in the world. It was a transformation which Rumford, who, as a pure scientist, is remembered chiefly for his experiments on the nature of heat, would have eminently approved.

A thought had crossed the Count's mind. Why not return to the United States? In

The Comforts of a Rumford Stove. So pleased was Rumford with this caricature that he purchased several copies of it to present to friends. James Gillray, 1757–1815. Engraving, published June 12, 1800, by H. Humphrey. 9¾″ × 7⅝″. (Library of Congress)

1798 he had been elected a member of the Massachusetts Historical Society, surely a sign of rehabilitation in the eyes of his countrymen, in response to which he wrote, "I have ever loved my native country with the fondest affection; and the liberality I have experienced from my countrymen—their moderation in success, and their consummate prudence in their use of Independence have attached me to them by all the ties of Gratitude, Esteem and Admiration."

Rumford might have returned to America if they had let him come "in the character of a German Count." Indeed, James McHenry, the Secretary of War, did go so far in 1799 as tentatively to offer Rumford the Inspector-Generalship of the Artillery of the United States, together with the first superintendency of the military academy to be established at West Point. A remarkable offer to one who, only sixteen years earlier, had been branded an apostate for leading troops against his own countrymen.

But, in truth, America was far too liberal a place for Rumford to reside in comfortably. The smell of democracy there was far too strong for his delicate palate. Indeed, even in London he felt ill at ease being exposed personally "to the lowest class of people," the very people whom he hoped to aid, albeit at a respectable distance.

And so, in the autumn of 1801, Rumford, the eternal Ishmaelite, moved on again, this time to imperial France where, like Benjamin West, he was immensely impressed with the figure of the grand Bonaparte. He found the word *citoyen* completely out of fashion, and *liberté* "hopelessly obsolete." Paris had become just his sort of place, and it did not take long for Rumford, who was being lampooned increasingly in the British press, to decide to give up England altogether.

In 1804 he married the widow of the great French scientist, Lavoisier, who directed one of the most glittering salons in the capital. The marriage was hopelessly

Aquatint, in Microcosm of London, May 1, 1809 7¹³/₁₆'' × 10³/₁₆'' (Greater London Council Print Collection)

The Library of the Royal Institution, Albemarle Street. Founded by Rumford, this institution survives today as the greatest monument to his genius. Joseph Stadler, 1780–1812, after Thomas Rowlandson, 1756–1827, and Augustus Pugin, 1762–1832.

inappropriate, and, two years after the wedding, Rumford wrote, "We are, besides, both too independent, both in our sentiments and habits of life, to live peaceably together—she having been mistress all her days of her actions and I, with no less liberty, leading for the most part the life of a bachelor."

In 1809 they separated, and Rumford retired to Auteuil in the Paris suburbs to continue his experiments with heat and to father an illegitimate child as a final indiscretion to his last mistress. The Count died in 1814, in the midst of the ruins of Napoleon's empire. He was, with Franklin, America's first great scientist and inventor. Never an expatriate but always an exile, still Rumford cannot be labeled as a malcontent. Even more than Franklin, he was *the* great cosmopolitan of his era, the man for whom very little was beyond reach or imagination.

Robert Fulton and his steamboat are quintessential native images in the consciousness of America. But it is often forgotten that he spent over twenty years abroad, first as a painter and subsequently as an inventor and promoter of lethal instruments of destruction, who bartered with the governments of emperors and kings to secure the highest price for his precious secrets.

Having given up his apprenticeship to a Philadelphia jeweler, Fulton arrived in London in 1787, at the age of twenty-two, with forty guineas in his pocket and a letter of introduction from Benjamin Franklin to Benjamin West, the painter whom Fulton considered "an Ornament to Society and Stimulus to young men."

It is not clear just how dependent Fulton was on West. Certainly he never occupied an acolyte's position, in the studio of the master, comparable to that of

Gilbert Stuart or John Trumbull. For Fulton was an independent creature who felt "happily beloved by all who knew me." He exhibited portraits in the Academy in 1791 and 1793, and also sent genre pictures to the Incorporated Society of Artists, a few of which were reproduced by the great mezzotinter, James Ward. By January 1792, Fulton was sufficiently confident to write to his mother that he was just now beginning to get a little money and hoped within six months to clear all his debts "and then start fair to make all I can."

Oil on canvas, circa 1807 29¾" × 24½" (Nelson Gallery-Atkins Museum; Nelson Fund)

Robert Fulton, 1765–1815.   Self-portrait.

But twelve months later he was, after seven years' practice, still only a promising young man in a marketplace of incredibly keen competition. And so, in what was to prove a momentous decision, Fulton all but abandoned painting and turned his practical mind to questions of invention with hopes of "making all he could."

Fulton inaugurated what was to be a thirteen-year correspondence with Charles, third Earl Stanhope, one of the better-known practitioners in the physical sciences, outlining plans ranging from canals dug on inclined planes to a steamship whose paddle imitated the spring in the tail of a salmon. Stanhope was not overwhelmed with Fulton at the outset, but saw in his drawings that most precious of gifts: a union of creative imagination and engineering flair. Consequently, he offered encouragement and constructive criticism to his young correspondent, for canals were eminently a moneymaking operation. Since 1767, when the Duke of Bridgewater began to plow up the countryside with artificial waterways, the mania for canal construction remained unabated. So great, in fact, was the demand for improved transportation arterials that, between 1790 and 1794, no fewer than eighty-one canal and navigation acts were obtained from Parliament authorizing capital expenditure in excess of £5.3 million.

Hoping to ride this crest of enthusiasm, Fulton, in 1794, was all over the countryside looking at waterways and dreaming of ways to improve them. Having conceived of a machine that would excavate new canals and dredge old ones in a manner heretofore unknown, Fulton, while lodging in Manchester's Brasenose Street, struck up a friendship with the young Robert Owen who was, at that point in his life, managing two cotton mills in the vicinity.

Fulton was a natural salesman. He had a gift of gab and succeeded in convincing Owen that a partnership between the two of them, utilizing his genius and Owen's money, would realize a fortune. "Robert Fulton, Engineer," as he now styled himself, took Owen's money but was only able to repay a portion of it after some time. The problem was that, while his canal-digging equipment was ingenious in conception, it was an unqualified failure as a piece of engineering.

Fulton, however, was enraptured with the possibilities of new kinds of small canals, aqueducts, and bridges. In his *Report on the Proposed Canal Between the Rivers Heyl and Helford* and his better-known *Treatise on the Improvement of Canal Navigation,* published in 1796, his infectious enthusiasm was everywhere evident, even if his engineering know-how was subsequently challenged by professionals in the field.

Fulton sent copies of his *Treatise* to everyone he thought could do him some good, including George Washington who was grateful for the gift but did not have "leisure yet to give it the perusal which the importance of such a work would merit." It seemed that neither England nor America was yet ready for Robert Fulton and his patented systems of canals. Thus, in the autumn of 1797, he sailed for France to pursue new schemes while residing in the Paris home of his friend Joel Barlow.

France under Napoleon did not require canals, however new their design. What she did need were effective weapons of war. This fact dawned on Fulton, and, shortly after his arrival in Paris, by utilizing a scheme of that most ingenious of all Yankee inventors, David Bushnell, he created a design for an undersea ship, or "submarine," which he dubbed the *Nautilus,* that would be capable of wreaking havoc on the British navy.

Wrapped in the mantle of a rabid Anglophobe, he wrote to Napoleon, "It is the naval force of England that is the source of all the incalculable horrors that are committed daily. It is the English navy which supports the English Government, and it is that Government which by its intrigues has been the cause of two-thirds of the crimes that have marked the course of the revolution."

Fulton tempted Napoleon with visions of a fleet of Nautiluses blocking the Thames, choking the life out of the monarchy and thus precipitating a general rising that would end in the proclamation of a republic. The idea was too attractive to resist, and Fulton was given permission to construct a submarine at Rouen, which was launched on July 24, 1800; with Fulton on board, it made its first submersion five days later.

Fulton had designed torpedoes which could be fired underwater at conventional ships of the line, but his demonstrations at Le Havre were less than successful. The French lost interest, and Fulton, full of righteous indignation, now denounced Napoleon as "a man who has set himself above all law . . . a wild beast unrestrained by any rule." He let the English know, through his old correspondent, Lord Stanhope, that his submarine and its secrets were now for sale. The British security network in France was already well aware of the nature of Fulton's experiments, and it did not take much persuasion on the part of Lord Hawkesbury, a future prime

Ink and watercolor, circa 1793 8⅛″ × 13¹¹/₁₆″ (The New Jersey Historical Society; Gift of Solomon Alofsen, 1855)

Machinery for a Canal.   This drawing represents a mechanism, thought to be an alternative to the lock system, for powering an inclined plane that could transfer boats from one canal level to another. Robert Fulton, 1765–1815.

minister, to convince the inventor that he would get far better treatment in England.

On May 19, 1804, traveling under the assumed name of Robert Francis, Fulton arrived in London demanding £100,000 for his invention from Pitt's government. The legitimacy of his proposal was examined by a scientific commission, including Henry Cavendish, Sir Joseph Banks, and three others, who reported adversely on the project without interviewing its creator. But Pitt and Lord Melville thought there was potential in Fulton's submarine and torpedoes, and a contract of sorts was drawn, allowing the inventor £40,000 should the vessel prove acceptable. Again, tests were tried and, although more successful than those carried out in France (Fulton actually succeeded in destroying a target brig), no authorization was ever signed to put the *Nautilus* into production.

The fates had conspired to eliminate all sense of urgency concerning the submarine. Six days after Fulton's successful sinking on October 21, 1805, Nelson defeated the combined French and Spanish fleets at Trafalgar. British dominance of the seas was thus assured, and from then on it was an uphill battle for Fulton to secure enforcement of his contract.

Watercolor, 1804
19'' × 23''
(Manuscripts and Archives Division; The New York Public Library; Astor, Lenox and Tilden Foundations)

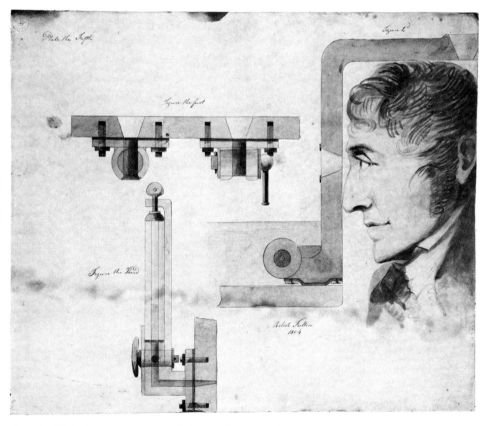

Plate the Fifth from a prospectus on Fulton's submarine, the Nautilus. *It includes a self-portrait of Fulton looking through a periscope. Robert Fulton, 1765–1815.*

Pitt died in January 1806, and Melville was impeached. The new government headed by Lord Grenville remained unmoved by Fulton's pleas. His letters went unanswered and, in frustration, Fulton became increasingly strident and threatening in his communications.

It was not until two years after his arrival in England that Fulton was finally told that his submarine had been rejected. Eventually, arbiters were appointed to adjudicate his claims for compensation, and, in the end, he was lucky enough to receive £15,000 as salary from the government he had once described as the single greatest threat to world peace.

Lord Grenville had hoped to buy Fulton's silence. He did not want the *Nautilus* sold to any other power but simply hoped to suppress it. Fulton was incensed. He assured Grenville that he had no particular desire to introduce these new weapons of war "unless my country should have need of them and which I hope will not be necessary as long as England and America understand the true interest of their commerce." It was an extraordinary argument from one whose patriotism had never shown before. Almost all of Fulton's active working life had been spent abroad, and it never occurred to him to offer his submarine first to the United States, where the financial rewards would be infinitely smaller, until it was clear neither Britain nor France would buy it.

But, in spite of the financial settlement, Fulton was bitterly disappointed. Twenty years in Europe had passed; he was forty-one years old and felt he had no solid achievement recorded to justify his existence. His submarine alone had occupied nine years of effort which now seemed pitifully ill-spent.

In October 1806 Fulton set sail for America, his dreams of a financial windfall in England hopelessly destroyed. On paper there was but one idea left—his steamboat, the *Clermont*.

> *Some men live for Warlike deeds,*
> *Some for women's words.*
> *John James Audubon*
> *Lived to look at birds. . . .*
>
> —Stephen Vincent Benét

The journey of John James Audubon to England, in 1826, was not a passionate pilgrimage. Rather, it was a matter of the utmost necessity. Of those who went to Britain, none loved America more profoundly and emotionally than this scion of a French admiral. But his dreams of creating an illustrated guide to the birds of North America, based on his own drawings, transcended American technology. For Audubon wanted engraved and hand-colored plates, not in octavo, quarto, or even folio size—he demanded nothing less than double elephant folio, life-size engravings—the largest printed book ever produced.

No one in America had the talent or the know-how to meet Audubon's exacting standards. And few possessed the financial wherewithal to purchase such a book after it was finished. And so, after years of running a shop, dealing in land, and managing a mill, Audubon, supported by funds saved by his eminently resourceful

Oil on canvas, 1826
38'' × 26''
(The White House)

John James Audubon, 1785–1851.   John Syme, 1795–1861.

English wife, sailed for England convinced he was "entering on a sacred object." He wrote, "As I approached the coast of England, and for the first time beheld her fertile shores, the despondence of my spirits became very great. I knew not an individual in the country; and although I was the bearer of letters from American friends and statesmen of great eminence, my situation appeared precarious in the extreme."

He was not a man to go unnoticed, this frontiersman with shoulder-length hair long enough to resemble Gray's "bard," and pantaloons so full in their cut that women's petticoats could easily have been fashioned from them. Audubon, in his wolfskin coat, with his giant portfolio of drawings hoisted on his shoulder in defiance of any porter's importunities, and his long rifle firmly grasped in one hand, cut a magnificent figure on the Liverpool docks.

One letter he carried was important above all others, for it was an introduction to William Rathbone, the great merchant prince of Merseyside, whose Gothic revival estate, Green Bank, was full of "a beautiful collection of the birds of England, well prepared and arranged." Audubon entered the house on July 25, 1826, "panting like a winged pheasant." He untied the fastenings on his portfolio as the Rathbones gathered round. And, as the drawings were produced, their praise was so munificent that Audubon once more breathed freely. He dubbed Mrs. William Rathbone, Sr., "the Queen Bee," and for her, two months later, he produced a remarkable self-portrait drawing with the inscription

AUDUBON AT GREEN BANK
Almost Happy!!

Audubon explained his dream for the *Birds of America* and was assured that, in England, not only was the talent available to carry out the project, but there was a sizable market of potential subscribers who, as collectors of finely illustrated color-plate books, could readily afford the high price that such an edition would command.

The Rathbones took up their new protégé and boomed him incessantly. Introductions were provided to prominent naturalists, scientific writers, and book dealers. An exhibition of Audubon's drawings was arranged at the Royal Institution at Liverpool, and the admission charges that were received provided much needed capital for the furtherance of the venture.

At the insistence of the "Queen Bee," Audubon produced a tiny drawing of the American wild turkey which was used by a local jeweler to make a seal. Across the top he placed his personal motto, America My Country.

The Rathbones toured Audubon throughout the district: to Matlock, and Buxton, and on to Manchester. And from there to Edinburgh, armed with introductory letters to the "multitude of learned." Again, his reception was most gratifying, and it

John James Audubon.   This was executed for his Liverpool patroness, Mrs. William Rathbone, Sr. Self-portrait.

was predicted that Audubon soon would be invited to join the university's select learned society, the Wernerians.

Audubon was taken to the home of Edinburgh's most famous engraver, William Home Lizars, whose color-plate books were famous throughout the kingdom. Lizars, a founder of the Royal Scottish Academy, was astonished at the quality of what was laid before him. "My God," he exclaimed, "I never saw anything like this before!" The following day, while the engraver's inspection of the drawings continued, Audubon held court in his shop to a crowd of aristocratic and scientific callers. Edinburgh was still a relatively small place, and the word had gone out that a great curiosity was to be seen at Lizars's.

Audubon's drawings of the "Mockingbird," the "Wild Turkey Hen and Young," and the "Whooping Crane" elicited murmurs of admiration. But when the magnificent "Great Footed Hawk" was produced, Lizars stood silently before it. He asked Audubon to lower it a little and then exclaimed, "I will engrave and publish this!"

Back at his lodgings that evening, the ecstatic artist penned excitedly in his journal, "Fame, expand thy universal pinions, and far, far, and high, high, soar away! Yet smoothly circle about me where ever I go. Call out with musical mellowness the name of this child of Nature, her humble but true admirer. Call out, call out, call out—and loud, loud, loud, 'AUDUBON!!!!' "

Visitors to Audubon's exhibition at the Scottish Royal Institution rarely saw the artist himself. Although not self-conscious about his appearance, Audubon disliked being pointed out as "The Great Unknown."

He waited expectantly for Lizars to finish his first plate, and when the beautifully engraved and colored aquatint was placed on his hands, Audubon knew that his time had arrived. He wrote to William Rathbone that he was off in search of "300 good substantial names of persons, or bodies or institutions" to subscribe to his massive publishing venture, which would take years to produce.

On March 17, 1827, Audubon began distribution of his prospectus, which solicited subscribers for the *Birds of America.* Shortly afterward he received a great boost to his ego when news of his election to the Royal Society was announced.

Nineteen days after publicly proclaiming his intentions to the world, Audubon left Scotland by stagecoach, heading south for England. He stopped at Newcastle, home of the great ornithologist-engraver, Thomas Bewick, who secured him eight subscriptions and membership in two learned societies. On to Leeds, York, Manchester, and back to Liverpool, adding names to the list at an appreciable rate.

Audubon's reputation as a great and talented curio preceded him from town to town. Everywhere he was fêted with enormous meals, rich beyond description. Yet all he yearned for was "roast ibis or sun perch . . . or jellied venison"—the foods he relished in Kentucky. Finally to London and the receptive arms of the Royal and Linnean societies, whose initials Audubon placed after his name for the rest of his life. His fame as a naturalist, though not without criticism, did nothing to compromise Audubon's eminence as an artist. Sir Thomas Lawrence considered the

Pencil,
October 14, 1826
7¾" × 12⅛"
(H. Bradley Martin)

View of Matlock from the Heights of Abraham. This was entered into the manuscript journal of Audubon's first journey through England. John J. Audubon, 1785–1851.

birds "very clever indeed" and was helpful in securing Audubon a number of much-needed commissions to paint rabbits, partridges, and other wildlife so popular on the walls of English libraries and dining rooms. Lawrence was also instrumental in providing an entrée for Audubon to Sir J. Walthen Waller, Bart., the King's oculist, who secured not only a most coveted royal subscription to the *Birds of America,* but also an imprimatur from the Sovereign, granting the book his especial "Patronage, Protection, and Approbation." This endorsement by the King was of great importance in adding further subscriptions, though Audubon never achieved more than two-thirds of the original three hundred names he desired.

Getting subscribers and holding their names on the list over a long period of time was only possible if the goods could be promptly and regularly delivered. Unfortunately, in Edinburgh, serious complications developed. The colorists employed by Lizars went on strike for higher pay, and all work on the *Birds* ceased. After a reasonable period, it became clear that the Scottish engraver would never be able to cope with the long-term demands of Audubon's project.

In desperation the painter naturalist approached the London publisher, Robert Havell, whose Newman Street studio, close to the old Benjamin West gallery, was well known for the excellence of its color-plate productions. Havell, at fifty-eight, found it impossible to consider a project of such immensity. He thought it would take at least fourteen years to produce the book according to the original plan. All

Engraved copperplate, 1830 26½'' × 39¾'' (Division of Graphic Arts, National Museum of History and Technology, Smithsonian Institution)

Virginian Partridge.   Robert Havell, Jr., after John James Audubon.

he could suggest was that Audubon approach Dominic Colnaghi, his chief competitor, who might be able to produce someone suitable.

Colnaghi had only one name in mind. Ironically, it was that of Robert Havell, Jr., the son of Audubon's contact, who years before had retired to Monmouthshire rather than follow the dictates of his father. The thirty-four-year-old Havell jumped at the chance and produced on copper a superlative "Prothonotary Warbler" whose quality was all the equal of that engraved by Lizars. Audubon danced for joy, shouting, in his French accent, "Ah, ze jeeg is up, ze jeeg is up!"

The young Havell returned to London to rejoin his father and, with a coloring staff that eventually numbered fifty men and women, began in earnest to produce the *Birds of America*.

During the next ten years, Audubon recrossed the Atlantic several times, collecting new subscriptions and adding additional drawings of birds not yet represented. On June 20, 1838, twelve years after the first proof of plate number 1 had been pulled, Havell produced an impression of two small dippers cavorting near the Columbia River. It was the final plate, number 435, of Audubon's dream. Soon the birds would be reproduced in a variety of media, testifying to their national popularity.

The project had run continuously but almost always in a beleaguered state. Money was terribly short, for subscribers kept dropping off the list. Audubon

Lancashire,
circa 1834
17½'' × 24½''
(Victoria & Albert
Museum, London)

"The American Robin" (Plate 131 in The Birds of America). *Reproduced on cloth by a Lancashire mill, this was printed in purple and red from engraved copper rollers, with pink and yellow added by surface rollers.*

produced numerous artistic potboilers to keep the project alive, but never knew if he would make a profit in the end, so expensive was the entire undertaking. Yet there was never any doubt in his mind that each completed set—and estimates range between 165 and 200 of these—would one day be of immense value. He was not at all wrong, and today his four-volume *Birds* is considered one of the most expensive of all printed books. The original subscriber's price was £182 14s in Europe and $1,000 in America. That figure today has increased several hundred times.

In September 1839, almost thirteen years from the day he first arrived in England, Audubon and his wife, who had joined him some time before, set sail for America on the *George Washington,* soon to be followed by Havell who had absorbed Audubon's infectious interest in the New World. They were going home for the last time, confirming a wish Audubon had expressed five years earlier: "After all I long to be in America again, nay if I can go home to return no more to Europe, it seems to me that I shall ever enjoy more peace of mind, & even physical comfort than I can meet with in any portion of the world beside."

For John James Audubon, as for Count Rumford and Robert Fulton, England never commanded emotional allegiance. On the contrary, it was a venue of the most rigorously pragmatic interests. But, for many of their compatriots who followed in years after, England communicated an evanescent intangible that could only be imparted to the spirit, rather than the intellect: a level of consciousness which, for want of a better word, we call romanticism.

3

The English Romance
of Washington Irving

The world had gone mad; or so a great many people thought. Reason, authority, science, tradition—all the pinions of Western civilization—were challenged in a sweeping revolt at the end of the eighteenth and the beginning of the nineteenth centuries. This reformation—social, political, and moral—was called romanticism. It is with us still today.

The neat paradigm of Enlightenment thought, so French, so neoclassic in outlook and content, came crashing down amid a wave of hostile anomalies. Napoleon and his wars of expansion were a prime catalyst, as romantic nationalism, a doctrine which exalted local cultural origins, swept the Continent. England, always antipathetic to the cultural hegemony of France, was midwife to the movement.

William Wordsworth and Samuel Taylor Coleridge published *Lyrical Ballads* in 1798. It was a collection of poems, commonplace in speaking motif yet often supernatural in subject, employing an extremely calculated diction. It was the literary manifesto of English romantics, proclaiming "the spontaneous overflow of powerful feeling." This, in turn, became the watchword of a movement whose restless experimental principles, so often in conflict with one another, propounded the doctrine of man's heroic struggle for self-expression in a world where obstacles were overwhelming.

The harmonious rationalism of the neoclassic ethic came under sharp fire. Man was now considered to be as irrational as his environment. The gateways of perception were thrown open with abandon, revealing the duality inherent in humankind—a lusting affirmation of life, existing on a tenuous balance with an ever-present death wish; a Janus-like face of good and evil; an omnium-gatherum of the senses.

In literature, music, and art, all bound inextricably, it was this striving for individuality against the hostile forces of Nature and Nature's God that corded the English romantics together. Yet, within the most general of theses, the range and intensity of emotion, together with the choice of subject matter, was as diffuse as it was diverse, allowing a great many designs refuge under the protective mantle of the romantic label. Here was a convenient tool for the codifying instincts of scholars anxious to provide cogent explanations for cultural chaos.

Newly independent America was not immune from this cultural revolution. The tides of European influences still washed omnipresently on her shores. Some felt the romantic call with an intense acuity, and for those, there was little choice but to go to Europe, particularly to England—as if on a passionate pilgrimage of discovery. It was an emotion that Americans, from Washington Allston through Henry James to Ezra Pound, would understand.

Washington Allston was "a painter born to renew the sixteenth century," wrote Coleridge. A romantic South Carolinian of independent means, Allston left Harvard Yard in 1801, bound for England. He was determined "to resolve matter and spirit into one vision and one truth" in an art that was impassioned and masculine, while at the same time evoking the emotive, subconscious impact of the "supernatural agents" of the psyche. He often chose biblical themes for his subjects, as allegories

Oil on canvas,
date unknown
25½″ × 17½″
(National Academy of
Design, New York)

Washington Allston, 1779–1843.   Charles Robert Leslie,
1794–1859.

encompassing both the most privately spiritual of ecstasies and the most public of emotions. It was not an easy task for one bred in the strictures of Puritan theology to leap headlong into the mysteries of the Coleridgean vision. Allston would endure periods of intense depression, bordering on despair, as he attempted to bridge in art the strange duality of his life experience.

He reached England in the middle of June 1801, "big with anticipation of every species of grandeur." And while the countryside was beautiful beyond his expectation—"every leaf seemed to embody a sentiment and every cottage a Venus"—London was an object arousing mixed emotion: "Indeed, the whole city appears to be composed of princes and beggars. I had no idea before of pride unaccompanied by some kind of merit. But here no one has pride without fortune."

Like so many before him, Allston and his companion, Edward Malbone, trod the well-worn path to Benjamin West's gallery in Newman Street, where they were received with customary kindness. And to Allston's great surprise he found himself ranking West, some of whose works were in direct anticipation of the romantic era, as the first among all English painters.

Through West's sponsorship, Allston entered the Royal Academy schools the following October, at the age of twenty-one. There he labored intermittently for the next three years before departing on his own sentimental journey through France and Italy.

It was in Rome in 1805–06 that Allston met two of the many men whom he would intellectually and emotionally captivate throughout the rest of his life. The first was the twenty-two-year-old Washington Irving, ever the detached observer of places if not people, who had been sent to Europe by his family after a bout with tuberculosis. Irving was instantly enamored of his new friend who "was of a light and graceful form, with large blue eyes, and black, silken hair waving and curling round a pale and expressive countenance." He recorded that a young man's intimacy took place between them which established a bond so strong that, years later, Irving would refer to Allston as "the man I would have liked to have always at my side—to have gone through life with."

Samuel Taylor Coleridge, archpriest of the romantic creed, experienced a similar reaction when meeting the charismatic Allston several months later. The visionary Coleridge, author of *The Ancient Mariner* and *Kubla Khan,* found a kindred spirit in the person of Washington Allston. They explored Rome together and retreated into the Sabine Hills near Vivegano for three weeks. But Napoleon was marching south, and Coleridge, fearing imprisonment if captured as a hostile alien, fled suddenly back to England. En route he wrote to Allston in a letter of great emotion, telling the young American of his attachment, "My dear Allston, somewhat from increasing age, but much more from calamity & intense pre-affections my heart is not open to more than kind good wishes in general. To you & you alone since I have left England, I have felt more, and had I not known the Wordsworths, should have loved and esteemed you *first* and *most,* and as it is, next to them I love & honor you."

Oil on canvas,
1811–13
156'' × 132''
(The Pennsylvania
Academy of the
Fine Arts)

The Dead Man Revived by Touching the Bones of the Prophet Elisha. *Among the most celebrated of*
the painter's English canvases. Washington Allston, 1779–1843.

*Oil on canvas, 1814
44" × 33½"
(National Portrait
Gallery, London)*

*Samuel Taylor Coleridge. This archpriest
of the romantic creed found in Allston a
kindred spirit. Washington Allston,
1779–1843.*

For Allston this feeling was mutual, though somewhat less emotional. He frequently recalled the times when he and Coleridge walked beneath the pines of the Villa Borghese, discussing Coleridge's golden rule to never judge any work of art by its defects. It was a dictum "as wise as benevolent" that spared Allston much pain in the years that followed, as his own works failed to measure up to his personal high standards.

Allston returned to America, to Boston, where he married and established himself as a painter of repute. But in 1811, at the age of thirty-two, he again set out for England, this time accompanied by his wife and the young Samuel F. B. Morse, his student and acolyte. The reasons for Allston's second journey are not clear. Perhaps he wished to avoid the entrapment drudgery of endless portraits. Perhaps he sensed that an entire generation of his peers was making cultural history across the Atlantic. In either case, by the autumn of 1811, the Allstons and Morse were ensconced in the London borough of Marylebone.

Allston's work was much admired. He sold at least two paintings to the prominent American art dealer, John Wilson, who had been active in London trade since 1789. It was at Wilson's European Museum that Londoners had one of their first opportunities to view Allston's pictures.

Through Coleridge he met the great connoisseur, Sir George Beaumont, who, in 1812, commissioned *The Angel Releasing St. Peter from Prison.* War was now raging between England and America, but this did not deter Allston from publishing his poems, the *Sylphs of the Seasons,* or from continuing to exhibit publicly. His painting, *The Dead Man Revived by Touching the Bones of the Prophet Elisha,* was shown at the British Institution, an organization patronized by the Prince Regent in competition with the Royal Academy. Benjamin West thought it a marvelous picture. He told Allston, "You have been studying in the highest school of art. There are eyes in this country that will be able to see so much excellence." West's pronouncement was confirmed when Allston was awarded a prize of 200 guineas for the work. This was a remarkable accolade to a citizen of a country at war with Great Britain, a testament either of the open-mindedness of the British public or of the total unimportance they attached to the American conflict, a mere sideshow to the life-and-death struggle then being fought with Napoleon's legions. In either case, when the war was finished, Thomas Sully and others energetically raised $3,500 to purchase the painting for the new Pennsylvania Academy of the Fine Arts in Philadelphia, where it has hung since 1816.

Allston was worshiped by young Samuel Morse. In a letter he told his parents that they should never describe him to others as a pupil of West, only of Allston. "They will not long ask who Mr. Allston is, he will very soon astonish the world." Twenty years later the emotion was just as strong when Morse exclaimed, "I go to Allston as a comet goes to the sun." Such was the painter's hold on those around him.

Morse had artistic pretensions equal to those of his master, but never approached Allston's level of intellectual abstraction. He took rooms at 4 Buckingham Place, just off Fitzroy Square. The Allstons were close by in London Street, as was Benjamin West in Newman Street. The American artist Charles Bird King, who was to give Morse some instruction, was not far away. Neither were Berners and Queen Anne streets where Coleridge and J. M. W. Turner would soon take up residence. It was here, in the artists' quarter of Marylebone, that much of the great work of the American romantics would be carried out.

In December 1811, a few months after Morse settled into Buckingham Place, there arrived in London a boy of seventeen who would soon be one of his most intimate peers. Charles Robert Leslie—"the good, the gentle, the beloved" as Thackeray called him—born in London of American parents, but taken by them at a young age to Philadelphia where he was raised, was the first student of art sent to London under the sponsorship of the Pennsylvania Academy. Leslie, whose diffident manners corresponded absolutely to the English ideal, who "always preferred to associate as much as I could with my superiors [in art]," was among the best-liked members of the English artistic fraternity.

Morse and Leslie, spurred by fears of solitude in a strange city, found they had much in common and so lived together in what were said to be Robert Fulton's old rooms in Great Titchfield Street. Although Leslie was three years his junior, Morse considered him his equal as a painter. Morse wrote, "He is enthusiastic and so am I, and we have not time, scarcely, to think of anything else, everything we do has a reference to art, and all our plans are for our mutual advancement in it."

Regularly at five in the morning, they rose and walked the mile and a half to Burlington House to copy for a few hours from the Elgin Marbles, returning home just as London was beginning to rise for the day. In the summers they painted together in the open fields before breakfast, sometimes just before sunrise, to study the effects of light on the landscape. Back in their rooms, they stood as models for one another. Morse painted Leslie as a Spaniard and, in turn, was painted as a Scot.

Oil on canvas, circa 1814 30'' × 25'' (Addison Gallery of American Art, Phillips Academy, Andover, Massachusetts)

Samuel Finley Breese Morse, 1791–1872. Self-portrait.

All around them London swarmed with life, pulsating at a tempo neither had previously experienced. The noise of street criers was constant outside their window from morning until midnight. Morse complained, "I don't know how many times I have run to the window expecting to see some poor creature in the agonies of death, but found, to my surprise, that it was only an old woman crying 'Fardin' apples, or something of the kind. Hogarth's picture of an enraged musician will give you an excellent idea of the noise I hear every day under my windows. . . ."

Oil on canvas, circa 1814–30 24½'' × 19½'' (Sleepy Hollow Restorations)

Charles Robert Leslie, 1794–1859. Self-portrait.

Pen and watercolor over pencil, 1784 19'' × 29½'' (Victoria & Albert Museum, London)

Vauxhall Gardens.   The first of London's great amusement parks, frequently visited by Morse, Leslie, and their circle of friends. Thomas Rowlandson, 1756–1827.

Crime was rife in the city. Only two doors from Leslie and Morse, someone was murdered one night. It was a frightening experience, and thereafter the two painters slept in the same room, armed with two pistols and a sword, with homemade burglar alarms attached to their door and windows.

But in spite of the danger, London offered numerous amusements to distract even those who had little to spend. Shortly before Leslie's arrival, Morse walked four miles out of town one afternoon to witness a great balloon ascension at the village of Hackney. He estimated the crowd at some 300,000, and however inaccurate his figures may have been, it was certainly the largest assemblage of humanity he had ever witnessed.

There was a visit to the annual St. Bartholomew's Fair in Smithfield Market, where Morse saw "an assemblage of everything in the world; theatres, wild beasts, *lusus naturae,* mountebanks, buffoons, dancers on the slack wire, fighting and swearing, pocket-picking and stealing, music and dancing, and hubbub and confusion in every confused shape."

There were frequent excursions to Vauxhall Gardens with its music and dancing, its fireworks and fountains. Morse was "struck blind" with the blaze of light from thousands of colored lamps. "Everyone is in motion," he wrote, "and care, that bane of human happiness, for a time seems to have lost her dominion over the human heart."

Leslie and Morse were passionate in their love of theater, an emotion evinced by most romantic painters. Their first year in London was the final season of the great Mrs. Siddons, and both Leslie and Morse practiced the strictest economy so that

Oil on canvas,
date unknown
30⅛'' × 25''
(Museum of Fine Arts,
Boston; Gift of George
Robert White and
Howard Payne)

John Howard Payne, 1791–1852, in the role of Hamlet.
Charles Robert Leslie, 1794–1859.

they might be able to afford the expense of seeing her often. They were witnessing the end of an era and were painfully aware of the fact.

As the weather became inclement, rendering outdoor amusements and painting from nature impossible, the Americans met in one another's rooms to drink Madeira, tea, or coffee; to read novels aloud; and to enjoy "music by Morse." A number of medical students from Boston enlarged the circle. Coleridge arrived to renew his friendship with Allston. And, as time progressed, the English painters, Benjamin Robert Haydon and James Lonsdale, became regular visitors. Finally there was the American actor, John Howard Payne, a successful child star fast losing his boyish charm.

Payne, the first American to play Hamlet, landed in England in February 1813. He was immediately imprisoned as a national of a belligerent power but, after fourteen days' confinement, was released and proceeded to London to launch his career as "Young Norval," in whose character he was painted by Leslie.

Child actors are so appealing that thespian flaws are often overlooked in favor of precocity. But once the bloom is off the rose, and age has transformed a soprano to a baritone, it is the rare theatergoer who remains indulgent if talent is not supremely evident. Payne, said to be the bastard of Tom Paine, never grew on his audiences in England. And, after 106 performances in 22 different roles, he abandoned the boards in favor of what he thought would be a more secure life as a playwright and theater manager.

But, regardless of failure, Payne was readily accepted into Allston's circle as their resident thespian and link with the fantastical world of the dramatic arts. Morse's parents were not at all pleased when they learned of his increasing intimacy with Payne, whose morals they called into question—indeed, any actor would have been suspect in their eyes. But such objections carried little weight in London, where Payne's connections with theatrical managers proved invaluable in procuring tickets to popular events.

The war between England and the United States, which had begun in June 1812, was a serious distraction for many Americans resident in London. But neither Charles Leslie nor Washington Allston was very political. For them, England was "the seat and nursery of the arts" they loved. And the only real question was whether, as enemy aliens, they might find it impossible to work. For young Samuel Morse, however, there was an intense feeling of involvement. Unlike his Federalist parents, who opposed the American-initiated conflict, Morse loudly applauded his country's cause. With the poet William Cowper he could say in one moment, "England, with all thy faults I love thee still," and with his very next breath argue that "the only way to please John Bull is to give him a good beating and such is the singularity of his character that, the more you beat him the greater is his respect for you, and the more he will esteem you."

Cast of preparatory sculpture for painting, 1812
20″ × 9″ × 22½″
(Yale University Art Gallery; Gift of the Rev. E. Goodrich Smith)

The Dying Hercules. Samuel Finley Breese Morse, 1791–1872.

If nothing else, the war had a profound effect on Morse's ambitions to succeed in what he termed the "intellectual branch of art." Like Benjamin West, he believed that "portraits have none of it; landscape has some of it, but history has it wholly." So aroused was Morse's indignation at the supposed ill-treatment of his countrymen in England that he yearned to become "the greatest painter *purely out of revenge*." But such high dudgeon did not really square with the facts. For while Allston was winning his 200-guinea prize at the British Institution, Morse himself was exhibiting his giant painting of the *Dying Hercules* at the Academy, to great critical acclaim. Even more significantly, in emulation of Allston's technique, Morse had made a clay model of Hercules as an aid in painting the picture, and this piece of sculpture, when shown at the Royal Society of Arts, was awarded a gold medal and a cash premium. How ironic that in England, the country Morse counted as the greatest enemy of his own, he could stand in front of a phalanx of ambassadors to receive an accolade from the hands of the Earl Marshal, the Duke of Norfolk. Perhaps the contradiction never crossed his mind for, as he wrote to friends in the spring of 1814, "I think I shall not be able to see my native country for some years yet to come; I must return *a painter*." Yet, just over a year later, Morse, out of funds, was on the high seas sailing for America with hope for the future and an encouraging letter from his master. If nothing else, his years in England had reinforced and strengthened his sense of national identity.

Charles Leslie, whose views regarding success echoed Morse's, was busy launching his own career. He was awarded two silver medals in the Royal Academy life class. And when his first large work, *Saul and the Witch of Endor,* modeled after paintings of West and Allston, was completed, it was sold, through West's patronage, to the great art connoisseur, Sir John Leicester, the first Lord de Tabley. Leslie always maintained close relations with the President of the Royal Academy. Emotionally they were so much alike, and it was occasionally mooted that Leslie

Monochrome watercolor, June 1823 10'' × 12'' (City of Bristol Museum and Art Gallery)

Merchant Tailors Hall, Bristol. Here Allston exhibited his work for the benefit of West Country connoisseurs. Henry O'Neill, 1798–1880.

would emerge as the spiritual heir of West in years to come.

When it became difficult to sell pictures in London, Allston removed to Bristol, where he held an unsuccessful exhibition at the Merchant Tailors Hall. Morse credited the lack of business to anti-American bias, but artists of all nationalities were suffering, for the art market had reached a new low, as public interest waned in the face of continuing war.

In the second year of Leslie's residence in London, Washington Allston's health tragically broke. He was never fully to recover. Allston and his wife decided to remove to the home of an uncle at Clifton near Bristol, hoping that a change of air would effect a cure. As always, Leslie and Morse accompanied them. But, by the time they reached the village of Salt Hill, Allston's condition had become so precarious that he was forced to stop for a number of days. Morse instantly returned to London to fetch Coleridge, whose mystical presence had always been a source of strength in times of trial.

The poet arrived posthaste and spent most evenings sitting up indulgently with Allston. The inn in which they lodged was completely full, so that Coleridge and Leslie were forced to share a double-bedded room. Leslie was flattered at being supposed capable of understanding the poet's metaphysics. "Indeed," he wrote, "men far advanced beyond myself in education might have felt as children in his presence."

Coleridge, always keen for new books, spied Leslie's copy of *A Knickerbocker's History of New York* and began to go through it. The young painter nodded off to sleep, and when he awoke the following morning, he found Coleridge still fully absorbed in reading. So entertained and delighted had he been with Washington Irving's prose that the passing of time had gone unnoticed. Coleridge had discovered an author whom all England would be celebrating.

Washington Irving arrived in Liverpool in 1815, as a little-known writer sent to rescue the tottering family business of his bachelor brother, Peter, who was as hopeless in love as he was in commerce. It was a Dickensian farce, for neither of the brothers Irving were capable of surviving in the world of commerce buffeted by insecurity in the aftermath of the Napoleonic wars. When the firm eventually did fail, Irving was forced upon his own resources and removed to London for support from Washington Allston, whose friendship he had never forgotten.

But Irving found his compatriot in a state close to desperation. After several months' convalescence in Bristol, Allston, with his wife, had returned to London, but within a few weeks it was Mrs. Allston who lay dead of causes that remain unclear. Four mourners only followed her coffin: her widower, Samuel Morse, Charles Leslie, and John Howard Payne.

In the days that followed, Allston passed from grief to despair, and it was feared that his life might be in danger. Morse and Leslie convinced him to move into the house they occupied, if for no other reason than the prospect of ever-present companionship. It was there that he slowly recovered his mental composure. Irving recalled many evenings at Buckingham Place where he, Leslie, and Allston "would sit up until cock crowing and it was hard to break away from the charms of his [Allston's] conversation. He was an admirable story teller; for a ghost story none could surpass him. He acted the story as well as told it."

There was only one who did not regret the death of Allston's wife, and that was Coleridge who, ever since the painter's return to England as a married man, had felt

Oil on canvas,
circa 1830
29'' × 24''
(John Murray)

Washington Irving, 1783–1859.   Gilbert Stuart Newton, 1794–1835.

himself locked apart from his "most kindred of spirits." It was not only Allston's wife but his penchant for exclusively American company that hurt and angered Coleridge. In a letter to a friend he complained:

> The same game in Bristol as in London—A. can visit *me*; but his own House and real feelings belong as exclusively Property to his "Countrymen," as he called one of the Beasts last Night: when to Wade's great delight I gave him a justly complimentary, but from that very cause a most severe Reproof. "Countrymen?" (said I) "Live the age of Methusalem, and you *may* have a right to say *that*, Allston.—At present, either the World is your Country, and England with all it's faults your home, inasmuch as it contains the largest number of those who are capable of feeling your *Fame* before the idle many. (the same in kind in all places but better (even these) in *degree here*, than in any other part of the world) have learnt to give you *Reputation*, or you are *morally* not worthy of your high Gifts, which as a Painter give you a praeternational Privilege, even beyond the greatest Poet, by the universality of *your* Language: and you prefer the accident of Place, naked *Place*, unenriched by any of the associations of Law, Religion, or intellectual Fountaincy, to the essential grandeur of God in Man.

After 1816 the friendship between the two men gradually became less profound, though in the following year, in his *Sibylline Leaves*, Coleridge did print Allston's poem "America to Great Britain," which expressed one American's gratitude for the cultural heritage of the English people.

In 1818 Allston returned to America for the last time, citing "a homesickness which (in spite of some of the best and kindest friends and every encouragement that I could wish for as an artist) I could not overcome." His major patrons, Sir George Beaumont and Lord Egremont, attempted to dissuade him, but to no avail. And shortly after his departure, he was elected an associate of the Royal Academy. Years later Charles Leslie opined that an academician's laurels would soon have been placed on Allston's brow had he elected to remain in England; such was the regard in which he was held by his fellow painters.

For his own part, Allston returned to America much more anglicized than Samuel Morse. In April 1819, he wrote to his friend, the English painter William Collins, "Should it be my lot never to revisit England, I still hope to preserve my claim as one of the British School, by occasionally sending my pictures to London for exhibition—a claim I should be most unwilling to forgo; my first studies and the greater part of my professional life passed in England, and among English artists."

Allston attempted nothing less than the establishment of an English school, or manner of painting, on American soil. As a painter, theorist, and poet, he was one of the major links between the English romantics and their American brethren. It was through Allston that Coleridge met William Ellery Channing, who, in turn, was a prime forerunner of the Transcendentalists. Four years before *Thanatopsis* appeared, Allston produced *The Sylphs of the Season*. In many of his greatest paintings, the mysterious power of God's empyrean was portrayed as an expression of the inner, the ultimate reality that lay at the heart of man's humanity—the essence of the human soul.

Though never a technical master of the first rank, Allston died in 1843 universally admired as a central figure of the romantic movement. One writer described him as an "expatriated Southerner and repatriated New Englander" who, in the prime of his career, discovered in England, in his own words, "that even the commonplaces of life must all in some degree partake of the mental, there can be but one rule by which to determine the proper rank of any pursuit, and that is by its nearer or more remote relationship to our inward nature." Such thoughts superficially seem light years away from the epistemology and metaphysics of Emerson, Thoreau, and those romantics who came after. But, if we look closer, we do find in Allston's philosophy a seminal font of New England thought; a source of the Transcendentalist ethic so venerated in American writing in the latter part of the nineteenth century.

With Allston gone from London, both Coleridge and Irving focused their attention on Charles Leslie. The former wrote, "Why, my dear *Leslie,* do you so wholly desert us at Highgate? Are we not always *delighted* to see you. Now, too, more than ever; since, in addition to yourself, you are all we have of Allston." But Leslie was not seen much at Highgate. One senses that, although his admiration for Coleridge was unbounded, he felt a certain uneasiness in the presence of so mercurial a personality. He was drawn instead to Washington Irving and to the Anglo-American painter, Gilbert Stuart Newton, whom Irving found captivating as well. Leslie wrote, "Nothing could be more agreeable than my daily intercourse at this period with Irving and Newton. We visited in the same families, chiefly Americans resident in London, and generally dined together at the York Chop House in Wardour Street .... Delightful were our excursions to Richmond or Greenwich, or to some suburban fair, on top of a coach. The Harmony that subsisted among us was uninterrupted. . . ."

It was an extremely sympathetic relationship for both Irving and Leslie: the one through words and the other through pictures described for the public a fantasized England that never really existed, an Albion to which romantically inclined Americans, seeking to establish identities within the complexity of Europe, yearned to return. England, as Irving saw it, "rich in the accumulated treasures of age," full of relics of the past, of experiences beyond the range of any parochial America, was picturesque and mysterious—richly endowed with literary and oral tradition that almost cried for visual representation. How remarkable the sheer denseness of a civilization, encumbered with layer upon layer of local customs tracing their origin into a murky past, all demanding loving, if occasionally irreverent, description from a writer who could romantically appreciate it in its entirety from the vantage point of unencumbered and even passive observance. Irving and Leslie saw what they wanted to see in England, just as Henry James was to do decades later. Theirs was an eclectic celebration of that which the English admired most in themselves, an elitist if not aristocratic view, which embraced eccentricity as quaint and endorsed privilege as a natural right.

With appropriate "indescribable emotions," Irving and his compatriot James Renwick toured the countryside from cathedral town to cathedral town. From the Cotswolds to the deepest recesses of the Welsh mountains, they visited ruins and country palaces, castles and rural inns. For Irving, these were salad days of "chivalry when we emulated the deeds and adventures of Don Quixote," with never a thought for the seamier side of British life, the side which apparently never intruded on Irving's consciousness.

The result was *The Sketch Book of Geoffrey Crayon,* first published as a serial in England and America in 1819 and subsequently reprinted as a book the following year. In its fifteen essays, Irving sought "to escape . . . from the commonplace realities of the present, and lose myself among the shadowy grandeurs of the past." And how successful he was. From *Rip Van Winkle* to *The Legend of Sleepy Hollow*; from the quiet nooks and corners of the Hudson River valley to the charming byways of the English countryside, Irving carried his readers into a mythical past where fantasy was the most elegant expression of artistic license; where romanticism could exist happily apart from the profound brooding introspection so evident in the

Stipple engraving, circa 1830–33 9'' × 5⅜'' (Sleepy Hollow Restorations)

Washington Irving.   The author of The Sketch Book of Geoffrey Crayon *at the height of his popularity in London.   William Keenan, active 1830–55.*

works of Coleridge and Wordsworth and so absent in the essays of Sir Walter Scott and Leigh Hunt.

The English critics waxed poetic in their praise of *The Sketch Book.* Francis Jeffrey, in *The Edinburgh Review* (August 1820), marveled at "the work of an American, entirely bred and trained in that country . . . written throughout with the greatest care and accuracy, and worked up to a great purity and beauty of diction, on the model of the most elegant and polished of our native writers." How ironic that *The Sketch Book* should appear precisely at the time of Sydney Smith's famous attack on American culture: "In the four quarters of the globe, who reads an American book? or goes to an American play? or looks at an American picture or statue?" It was the perfect rejoinder.

Irving was loved in England, not because his writings were refreshingly different, but because they were precisely what the English had come to expect from the masters of their own tongue. But he was an American, and this fact alone separated Irving from his fellows: "I was looked upon as something new and strange in literature; a kind of demi-savage, with a feather in his hand instead of on his head, and there was a curiosity to hear what such a being had to say about civilized society." His was a facile, mellifluous, polished prose just suited to the romantic temperament of the mass market. Irving himself, always sensitive to potential critics, had no doubts or regrets as to the sort of writer he was. In writing *The Sketch Book,* he frankly stated "I have attempted no lofty theme, nor sought to look wise and learned, which appears to be very much the fashion among our American writers, at present. I have preferred addressing myself to the feeling and fancy of the reader, more than to his judgement. My writings, therefore, may appear light and trifling in our country of philosophers and politicians; but if they possess merit in the class of literature to which they belong, it is all to which I aspire in the work." He sought "only to blow a flute accompaniment in the national concert" and left "others to play the fiddle and French horn."

Success in England assured acclaim in America for her first native son to earn a living exclusively by his pen. Even those whose strong patriotism caused them to question Irving's obvious Tory tastes welcomed his works, so far removed from political rancor, into their homes as exemplars of American achievement. And it was not long before Irving became a venerable living object of literary devotion among his countrymen.

In the eyes of Charles Leslie, Irving was certainly without peer. He told the writer, "I not only owe to you some of the happiest social hours of my life, but you opened to me a new range of observation in my own art, and a perception of the qualities and character of things which painters do not always imbibe from each other." Leslie found Irving's fantasized view of the world infectious. There was no longer a market for historic paintings, due to lack of patronage. One critic warned publicly that "it was unwise and unsafe for any young man of genius . . . to devote the prime years of his study, in that high department of art." Thus Leslie and Gilbert

Stuart Newton found it tempting to follow Irving's lead, visually, into the creation of genre scenes more acceptable to changing tastes.

Irving, Leslie, and Newton were a triumvirate, in the early 1820s, that was inseparable. There were seen everywhere together and spent endless evenings in one another's company. Irving indulged his penchant for wearing fancy jewelry. He requested Leslie and Newton to paint him in a romantic coat with a high fur collar, for "modern dresses are apt to give a painting a commonplace air." They thought the realities of life could be as fantastical as the books and paintings they created. Newton, known to his intimates as "the Childe" after Byron's hero, went so far as to paint himself in an imaginary Venetian costume reminiscent of a Shakespearian incantation.

Leslie, whose suggestion provided the inspiration for one of the tales of *Bracebridge Hall,* the sequel to *The Sketch Book,* contracted with John Murray to make illustrations for a new English edition of Irving's works. Newton executed a portrait of the author as a frontispiece, and even Washington Allston was co-opted into making a contribution. Irving was delighted that the work of his friends should be interwoven with his own, particularly in the case of Leslie to whom he had become especially close. While on a trip to Paris in October 1820, Irving wrote to his protégé, "My dear boy, it is a grievous thing to be separated from you and I feel it more and more. I wish to heaven this world were not so wide, and that we could manage to keep more together in it—this continual separating from those we like is one of the curses of an unsettled life: and with all my vagrant habits I cannot get accustomed to it." The relationship continued intensely on a plane of mutual affection until Leslie's marriage of 1825. As he had done with so many of his bachelor friends, Irving drifted away once Leslie had been called to the altar. Always affec-

Aston Hall, Birmingham. The site which inspired Irving's Bracebridge Hall. *(Photograph courtesy of Aston Hall Museum, Birmingham)*

tionate, Leslie credited Irving's distant attitude to his increasing success: the endless breakfasts at Samuel Rogers's celebrated home, overlooking Green Park; the afternoon literary soirees at John Murray's establishment in Albemarle Street; the gala evenings at Holland House with all the "nobility and mobility" of the capital. But for Irving there was emotional satisfaction only in an all-male environment. Perhaps this was why England, with its masculine bastions, was such a source of refuge for intense observers such as he.

Women had a place in Irving's life and literature, but always as foils of social repartee and intercourse. The capacity for greater intimacy was simply not in his makeup. When the mistress of horror, Mary Shelley, attempted to use John Howard Payne (himself a lifetime bachelor) as an intermediary in establishing a relationship with Irving, she encountered little but the most polite and civilized of silences.

Watercolor, 1811
7'' × 9½''
(Greater London
Council Print
Collection)

The Principal Entrance to the Fleet Prison.   Within the "Rules" of this prison, John Howard Payne was incarcerated for debt. George Shepherd, circa 1760–post 1831.

John Howard Payne's manuscript of "Sweet Home."   (Columbia University Libraries; John Howard Payne Collection)

England was not kind to Payne, whose tragicomic life provided Irving with a plot for his adventure, "Buckthorne and his Friends." After his failure as an actor, Payne took over the management of one of London's suburban theaters at Sadler's Wells, but with such disastrous financial results that he found himself committed to the Fleet Prison for debts in 1820. Fortunately, enough money was raised to enable Payne to live in the prison "Rules," an area just outside the walls reserved for prisoners of good character. In an alley called Naked Boy Court, Payne found a room and continued with the writing of what was eventually to be an *oeuvre* of fifty stage plays. He wrote in all styles, from tragedy through melodrama to comedy and even opera. Some of his works, such as *Brutus* and *Charles the Second,* were immensely popular, and, just as Irving was the first American writer of fiction to achieve success in England, so was Payne the first of his countrymen to introduce popular drama on the London stage. But financial success did not accompany notoriety. Payne made a mistake by selling most of his copyrights during the plays' first runs in order to obtain ready cash, and, consequently, he was not to enjoy the benefits of many of his dramatic successes.

In the 1820s Payne lived peripatetically in France and England, occasionally collaborating with Irving on adaptations of continental pieces as well as works of original design. Irving, who felt close to Payne, was anxious to give him work, but was always a little patronizing of his friend and never allowed his own name to appear in the capacity of coauthor.

It was while in France that Payne wrote his so-called opera *Clari or the Maid of Milan,* which was produced at Covent Garden on May 8, 1823, with music by Henry Bishop. It was not a great success and enjoyed only a few performances. But one song from the score, "Home Sweet Home," the quintessential expatriate lament, did attain great popularity. In the first year alone, it was reported that more than 100,000 copies of the song sheet were sold. (Some have estimated the figure at three times that number.) And though Payne received nothing in royalties for his effort—the copyright again having been sold—"Home Sweet Home" survived as the one link by which its author was remembered by posterity.

In the summer of 1832 Payne returned to America where he remained for the next ten years, a figure of popular celebration—an exile returned. It was in Cincinnati, in December 1834, that Payne jotted down on a single sheet of paper a Whitmanesque testament, expressing his elation at being a part of America once again.

> I've stood on shores where strangers stand
>   But there could never see
> Scenes half so sweet or wonderful
>   As fling their witchery
> Round thine my own, my native land
> Land of the brave and beautiful
>   Land of the Great and Free.
>
> I've heard the voices which command
>   The world's idolatry
> But voices of Heaven's health as full
>   Oft lift their melody
>   In thine my own, my native land
> Land of the brave and beautiful
>   Land of the Great and Free!
>
> I've look'd on eyes where glances bland
>   Thrill hearts with ecstasy
> Yet were their brightest glances dull
>   To some whose brilliancy
>   Lights thine my own, my native land

Land of the brave and beautiful
Land of the great & free!

And oft as from a foreign strand
I gazed where solemnly
The world of waves before me roll'd
I've sighed so far to be
From thine my own, my native land
Land of the brave and beautiful
Land of the Great & Free!

Yet, despite such sentiments, Payne was possessed of the wanderlust, and in 1842 he secured a consulship in Tunis from President Tyler. It was there, but for a hiatus of three years, that he remained; and it was there that he died in self-imposed exile in 1852.

Printed song sheet of "Home! Sweet Home!"
Philadelphia, circa 1823. (Library of Congress)

Allston, Morse, Payne, Irving, and Leslie: their life experiences were inextricably intertwined for over a decade in England. Allston and Morse, self-appointed heirs to the traditions of high art and noble purpose propounded by Benjamin West, reached for the stars but seldom discovered the magic of genius on the tips of their brushes. Payne, who dreamt of the achievements of Shakespeare and Garrick, had to content himself with a mantle of much less exalted hue, ultimately claiming immortality through the popularity of a music-hall ballad.

Washington Irving, whose imagination and fantasies shrouded a figure rushing headlong from loneliness and isolation to the comforting, if superficial, arms of critical and social acclaim, never overestimated the extent of his talents; never risked cozenage in his mind's eye. From the role of London's literary lion of 1820, through a career as historian and diplomat in Spain, to a second almost exclusively social existence in London as Secretary of Legation in 1829, Irving never consciously lost a sense of perspective about himself. With gold medals from the Royal Academy of History in Madrid and the Royal Society of Literature in London, and with an honorary doctorate in civil law from Oxford, Irving was entitled to a sense of self-worth and achievement. In 1832, when he returned to America after almost two decades of sophisticated expatriation, it was as an aristocrat bearing little enthusiasm for the jingoistic slogans of Manifest Destiny which sought to embrace him. Rather, he celebrated and molded his life-style around the civilized country pleasures that could be found in the Hudson River valley, about which he had so often fantasized. His home near Tarrytown became a shrine, an object of pilgrimage, where Irving, the oracle of Sunnyside, held court in the manner of an English country squire. He remained, until his death, a living icon to those of his countrymen whose romantic yearnings for the rural idyll of Nature under man's control found solace and satisfaction in all that he represented.

For Charles Leslie, content to remain within the limitations of his talent and skill, and supported by the domestic happiness of a wife and family, there was little temptation to leave England—"that most benighted of realms," as he called it. Leslie's sympathy was with the household literature of the English language; with Shakespeare and Sterne; with Goldsmith and Smollett and the popular translations of Cervantes. These provided all the inspiration he required to create quiet dreams and mythical scenes that found their way, not only into the collections of well-known patrons of modern art such as the Lords Egremont and Holland, but also into the homes of numerous industrialists and capitalists, who found in Leslie's work a pleasant and comprehensible diversion from the industrial realities of a countryside being ripped apart, by these selfsame individuals, in the name of economic progress.

Leslie, who honored Benjamin West above Raphael, who inherited the mantle of Hogarth and Wilkie, knew honor and success, as in all things in his life, in moderation. The pinnacle, perhaps, was reached when he received a royal bounty for his large group portrait of the new Queen Victoria taking the sacrament at her coronation. It was the most distinguished painting of contemporary history in Leslie's

Oil on canvas,
November 1857
24¼'' × 30''
(The Forbes Magazine
Collection, New York)

Sancho Panza in the Apartment of the Duchess.   Among the most famous of Leslie's literary genre
paintings, this was reproduced on canvas for a number of patrons and was eventually made into a
popular print. Charles Robert Leslie, 1794–1859.

Oil on canvas, 1837
38⅛'' × 73½''
(Her Majesty Queen
Elizabeth II)

Queen Victoria Receiving the Sacrament at her Coronation.   Charles Robert Leslie, 1794–1859.

generation. But, like all his works, it was a picture of refinement not extremes, for Leslie was a limner of manners as Irving was in language; a charmer of the mind whose excursion into comedy and pathos rested firmly on definite images rather than on the vague and haunting fancies of his romantic contemporaries.

Charles Leslie, the first biographer of John Constable, the much-beloved professor of painting at the Royal Academy, the creator of visual nostalgia which inspired whole generations of English painters, was the most anglicized American of his circle. Only once, in 1833, was he tempted to return to the New World as a teacher of drawing at West Point in Washington Irving's Hudson River valley. He soon found that it was impossible to stay, for both he and the America he knew had changed profoundly. For Leslie, there was no choice, no decision, but to return to England to his house in Pineapple Place, not as an exile but as one who claimed a new land as his own. There the circle came full, and Leslie died just two doors away from the house in which he had been born.

Coatee of the diplomatic suit worn by Washington Irving
when he served as Secretary of Legation in London.
(Sleepy Hollow Restorations)

4

The Lords of Change Alley:
George Peabody and "Co."

Morley's Hotel occupied the east side of Trafalgar Square, an imposing if somewhat overdone structure in the heart of London. It was a fashionable place. The food was particularly good and the rooms appealed to those county families who did not keep town houses in the capital.

Morley's was also a mecca for Americans, ever-present amid the swirling din of the hotel's crowded bar as well as behind the closed doors of its many private dining rooms. If one were an American in mid-nineteenth-century London, one eventually came to Morley's, and likely as not one would see Henry Stevens, "a hearty, fat, plump, jolly redfaced bachelor, weighing 163 pounds avoirdupois weight, healthy, happy and not destitute of friends." Stevens startlingly resembled his contemporary Karl Marx, although his outlook on business was rather different.

Henry Stevens of Vermont, king of the rare-book dealers, who, in true English fashion, liked to place the letters G.M.B. after his name (standing for "Green Mountain Boy"—though his younger brother often remarked that they really stood for "Grubber of Musty Books"!), was a fixture at Morley's, eating, drinking, exchanging gossip with his compatriots. But every day was also a business day for this entrepreneurial genius, who virtually created a market for rare Americana where none had existed before.

He arrived in London in July 1845, with only forty sovereigns in his pocket and an unyielding sense of confidence that here lay an undiscovered treasure-trove that deserved cultivation. His timing was absolutely perfect. As the enthusiasm of Manifest Destiny swept the United States in the 1840s, fanned both by the push of westward expansion and the jingoism of the Polk administration, the great American historians Bancroft, Prescott, Sparks, and Parkman were hard at work grinding out an ever-increasing number of volumes, each describing the glorious history of the New World and of the republican colossus that soon would straddle the continent.

Such popular scholarship awakened an interest in the sources of American history; in the scarce early imprints, pamphlets, broadsides, and manuscripts which appealed to the acquisitive instinct of wealthy collectors always on the watch for the rare and precious. And there was Henry Stevens, ready to service this private passion, he who bought and sold that others might shelve for posterity.

At the outset he had little competition. There were only two dealers of substance in London who dealt in rare Americana. The first was Obadiah Rich, a peripatetic compatriot of Stevens who, as American consul in Valencia and Madrid, ambulated between Spain and his retail premises in Holborn's Red Lion Square. It was Rich's famous Spanish library which was used by Washington Irving when he wrote his biography of Columbus. The second was George Palmer Putnam, who ran the American Literary Agency in Waterloo Place, but who is much better known to history as the founder of one of the most distinguished American publishing houses.

Of the two, Rich was by far the premier dealer. It was he who purchased the famous library of Americana assembled by the French traveler Henri Ternaux-Compans, whose *Biblothèque Américaine* was basic to any collector or dealer seeking to master the bibliography of the American past. Rich showed the Ternaux-Compans library with pride to Henry Stevens shortly after the latter's arrival, and was pleased when Stevens reserved £650 worth of books for his American clients. Rich had dealt transatlantically before, but his connections were never very good when handling Americana. He thought Stevens would provide a useful link and not only accorded him storage space for his books but agreed to wait for payment until Stevens had actually resold the books in America.

For Stevens it was a heaven-sent opportunity. He paid no business tax, having no premises like his competitors, and one by one the great American collectors Peter

Lithograph, 1852
11½'' × 16¼''
(Greater London
Council Print
Collection)

Morley's Hotel (center building), *Trafalgar Square, as seen during the funeral of the Duke of Wellington. The gathering spot for London's American financial community. Emily S. Drummond, dates unknown.*

Force, John Carter Brown, Samuel L. M. Barlow, and Henry C. Murphy fell completely within his orbit. He possessed an uncanny ability to locate and purchase the most highly coveted of items, and as his knowledge of bibliography increased he became more than just a dealer; he became an authoritative expert. Through his hands passed the famous Columbus letter of 1493; works by Peter Martyr; first editions of Hakluyt, Las Casas, Cortés, and Champlain. Vendors sought him out, for, according to Stevens, "As I pay *full prices* I secure almost a monopoly." Years later Stevens recalled that his first years in London "were indeed happy days, when on a July morning one might run down a hundred brace of rare books on America in London at as many shillings a volume as must now be paid in pounds. . . . They were scrambled for in Boston and New York like hot buck-wheat cakes at a College breakfast."

Oil on canvas, date unknown 50" × 36" (Yale University Art Gallery; Bequest of Henry Stevens)

Henry Stevens, 1819–86. William Page, 1811–85.

The greatest of Stevens's customers was the reclusive and fabulously wealthy James Lenox of New York, whose collection eventually served as one of the founding bases of the New York Public Library. For nearly twenty-five years, "all Europe was ransacked for bibliographical rarities for Mr. Lenox," who insisted on absolute secrecy regarding his collecting habits. Stevens and Lenox depended on one another, "he a buyer and I a seller, he collecting to shelve, I collecting to disperse—one's calling necessary to the other's. If there were any real differences of rank it is not likely either of us ever saw or thought of it."

It was to Lenox that Stevens supplied a copy, for £80, of the Bay Psalm Book of 1640, the first book ever printed in America. He sold him a Gutenberg Bible for the unbelievably low price of £500. And in 1855 Lenox received a collection of the first four folios and about forty of the quartos of Shakespeare for £600—such prices were never to be repeated or even dreamed of again.

But Stevens was not always so successful with Lenox. On one occasion, while attempting to turn his hand to picture-dealing, he offered his New York client a full-length portrait of George Washington which had been authenticated by Charles Leslie as having been painted by Gilbert Stuart. Bargains in books were one thing, but when Stevens asked only $1,000 for the painting, Lenox balked. When asked to explain his refusal, the quiet collector replied, "It is because it is *yours* and you cannot give its pedigree. You do not profess to be a connoisseur in portraits, and your price is too low for a genuine Stuart." Stevens eventually took the painting back to London and sold it for £150 to the American banker Russell Sturgis, whose family was intimate with Henry James.

Juggling the competitive interests of great private collectors was not the only occupation that claimed Henry Stevens's time. Shortly after his arrival he came into contact with Anthony Panizzi, who had skillfully extracted considerable sums of money from Parliament for the creation of a truly national library within the British Museum. Again it was a case of being in the right place at the right time. Stevens, using his knowledge of American bibliography, presented Panizzi with an extensive list of lacunae in the Museum's collection and offered his services to fill them. To his surprise Panizzi not only asked for everything on the list, but suggested that the twenty-six-year-old Vermonter now undertake to supply all American books to the British Museum. Such was the reward of a unique expertise, for, as Panizzi put it, "I want a few agents who are experts in their departments and can find out and supply such books as we ought to procure, and not a mere bookseller to receive and execute an order."

And so in 1847, just two years after he departed Boston with little save his ambition, Henry Stevens returned to America on the greatest shopping expedition imaginable—charged with buying a copy of every book printed in or related to the Americas not then in the British Museum. His presence did not go unnoticed, and vendors flocked to him in droves. In the spring of 1848, he scored a spectacular coup in purchasing a large section of the library of George Washington for $3,000.

Stevens thought a fortune could be made off this most celebrated of collections, but it was to prove a millstone round his neck. For when no major collector appeared ready to absorb the collection, he considered offering it to the British Museum and precipitated a public outcry against exporting the books. It was even suggested in some quarters that Stevens was placing profits above patriotism, and there were those in Congress who wondered whether exportation of the Washington library could be prohibited. Stevens eventually relented when advised, privately, that the British Museum would probably not purchase the library unless there were books of great intrinsic merit in it. He found himself forced to offer the collection at bargain rates to a syndicate of literary luminaries in Boston for housing in the Boston Athenaeum. Thirty years later Stevens impatiently recalled how little financial substance he found behind the patriotic utterances of Boston's Brahmins: "I sold the collection to a parcel of Bostonians for $5,000, but after passing that old Boston hat round for two or three months for $50 subscriptions, only $3,250 could be raised, and therefore, as I had used a few hundred dollars of the money advanced to me by the promoters and was in a tight place, I was compelled to subscribe the rest myself to make up the amount of the purchase."

Any American of importance in London could be sure of meeting Henry Stevens. He sought them out, some for the pleasure of their company and others for the pleasure of their custom. When the two were intertwined, Stevens was doubly blest.

One of those Stevens assiduously cultivated was Joshua Bates, at whose country home in the London suburb of East Sheen many select parties were held. Bates was one of the first American kingpins in the world of English finance. He was already in his sixties by the time Stevens knew him, and commanded a senior partnership in the venerable house of Baring Brothers which had acted as the official British agent for the United States government since the foundation of the republic.

Bates had come abroad early in the century as the agent for a prominent New England mercantile establishment. And, by capriciousness of fate, he established a friendship with Peter Labouchère whose distinguished family was allied by marriage to the Barings. Bates was an extremely adroit manipulator of men. In 1826, when Samuel Williams, a wealthy American banker and merchant, went bankrupt in London, Bates saw an opportunity to fill the void created by this failure. He secured, apparently without collateral, a loan of £20,000 from Labouchère and, with one of the scions of the Baring family, founded a partnership that attracted a significant portion of the American financial market in the British capital.

The Barings were not slow in assessing the talent of their young competitor, and two years after Bates went into business he was offered, at the age of thirty-eight, a full partnership in the House of Baring.

Bates became a naturalized British subject. His daughter Betts was received frequently at the court of the young Queen Victoria, and he, in the 1840s, was generally presumed to be the most influential American in London. It was through his skill that the Barings survived the panic of 1837. And it was to him that both the

British and American governments looked when arbitration of a number of bilateral financial issues was required.

In America Joshua Bates was celebrated by his countrymen not for his financial successes but for his philanthropies, the most important of which were instrumental in the foundation of the Boston Public Library in 1852. It was a landmark event in the extension of the American library movement, and Henry Stevens hoped, unsuccessfully as it turned out, to be the principal supplier of books to the new library. Stevens had long been a champion of free public libraries in England. In 1849 he was invited to testify before a select parliamentary committee of enquiry. And in 1852, when Bates was setting up his institution in Boston, Stevens was invited to Manchester, along with Dickens, Thackeray, and a host of dignitaries, to witness the opening of the first public library in the kingdom established under the Ewart Act of Parliament.

Free libraries were a boon to the people; they were also a new and ever-increasing market for Henry Stevens, who supplied many of the new books that these institutions required. Years later he was to write with pride to his sister, Sophie, "It strikes me that this is a great undertaking for a boy without any money to come green from Yankee Land and induce all these Libraries to purchase so largely of our literature &

Daguerreotype circa 1852–53 (Boston Public Library)

Joshua Bates, 1788–1864.   Unidentified daguerreotypist.

I flatter myself I am doing much for the Yankee by making their books known abroad. But it is not for me to feel big—I haven't time—I have to work too hard."

As his business thrived, Stevens devoted more and more time to the scholarly aspects of his calling. The venerable Society of Antiquaries bestowed a fellowship on him in 1852. He was the first American to be elected in the regular nonsupernumerary way. He became a corresponding member of the American Antiquarian Society, the Massachusetts Historical Society, and the New England Genealogical Society. The British Association for the Advancement of Science offered him a life membership, while both the British Archaeological Association and the Zoological Society of London welcomed him as a Distinguished Fellow.

When Joseph Henry, the first Secretary of the Smithsonian Institution, was casting about for a figure of distinction to represent its interests in Great Britain, his eye fell upon Henry Stevens. The principal duty of the Smithsonian's representative was to arrange the exchange of scholarly publications between the Institution and sixty learned societies in the kingdom. Stevens was the perfect appointee, for not only was he resident in England, but he was laying the groundwork for his massive *Bibliographia Americana* which he hoped Joseph Henry would publish. Thereafter, Stevens's letterhead frequently carried the title "Literary Agent in London of the Smithsonian Institution."

As his connections and reputation grew, Stevens was approached confidentially by wealthy individuals who desired his expertise in the selection and purchase of complete, handsomely bound libraries, to be used more for decorative than elucidative purposes. Nicholas Brown of Providence, William W. Corcoran of Washington, D.C., W. W. Gilbert of New York—they and others came to Stevens for this newest type of bibelot. It was a lucrative practice, though Stevens respected books too much not to resent the purpose for which they were being purchased. At one point he growled cynically, "Many of our rich snobs who have no books in their heads might without injury to their children have their house furnished with them."

One of those who purchased books en bloc from Stevens was George Peabody, the prince of merchant princes. It was Peabody, who once remarked that everything he touched "seemed to turn to gold," who was destined to succeed Joshua Bates as the premier American banker in England. And it was he who wore the laurels of the greatest philanthropist of his generation.

Stevens had known Peabody, a lifelong bachelor, for some years. They dined frequently together at Morley's Hotel, almost always in the company of Peabody's closest confidant, Horatio Gates Somerby, who was the first American genealogist to carve out a career for himself in London by tracing the pedigrees of those of his countrymen anxious to prove their noble lineage. When Peabody bought books from Stevens, it was not for his own shelves (Peabody never read anything more serious than a newspaper); rather it was for one of the numerous libraries in America that he was to endow. Peabody regarded books as just another of nature's commodities. Frequently he would ask Stevens, "How are books today?" as one might query the price of hogs. When, in 1850, Stevens purchased three thousand manuscripts of Benjamin Franklin in London, it was Peabody who accepted them as security for loans. (Stevens held the manuscripts for over thirty years.) But in spite of this blind spot, Peabody did have a profound respect for the personal enrichment that only a fine education could give. It was a luxury he lavished, not only on many of his younger relations, but also on tens of thousands of his compatriots through his significant donations to institutions of higher and advanced learning.

George Peabody's success in the world of finance was a classic Horatio Alger story. He began virtually with nothing, and by the age of thirty-two was an established mercantile baron in Baltimore and Washington. But the limitations placed on a dry goods merchant were too straitening for a man like Peabody, who was far more

Oil on canvas,
date unknown
62¼″ × 40″
(National Portrait
Gallery, Smithsonian
Institution)

George Peabody, 1795–1869. George Peter Alexander Healy,
1813–94.

interested in the manipulation of capital than in the development of endless inventories.

George Peabody was not a witty man. He was formal to the point of stiffness, and his reserved politeness could never be called charming. He carried his afternoon meal to work in a small metal lunchbox; and when not entertaining publicly, he preferred to dine in inexpensive chophouses. A fisherman, a devotee of whist, backgammon, and Scottish airs, George Peabody appeared more a character out of a story by Goldsmith than the business tycoon who stormed the British Empire. But in the world of finance, where integrity and reliability were the keystones to a man's reputation, Peabody was a rock of respectability. He lived alone, and he lived exclusively for his work: it was the most precise expression of his personality.

Peabody did not settle in England until 1837, when he was forty-two, but prior to that time he had visited Britain on five occasions, developing connections for his business interests. Gradually it became clear to him, as it had to Henry Stevens, that in Britain there existed a unique opportunity for a man of his talents. Thus began Peabody's transformation from merchant vendor to merchant banker, a road that was subsequently traveled by many famous American financiers, including the founders of Kuhn, Loeb and Co., J. W. Seligman and Co., Levi P. Morton, Henry Clews, and the redoubtable Junius Spencer Morgan.

In December 1838 a brass plaque went up on the door of 31 Moorgate, in the heart of the City of London, announcing that George Peabody and Co. had taken premises. Peabody was one of three commissioners appointed by the State of Maryland to market an $8 million bond issue abroad. It was not to prove an easy task, for American securities, in the wake of the panic of 1837, were a highly speculative investment. The whisper of default was in the air—indeed, between 1840 and 1845 nine states of the Union, including Maryland, did suspend interest payments.

The price of the Maryland bonds continued to drop, and Peabody was urged to sell at any figure that could be obtained. Finally, after much negotiation, he convinced Joshua Bates that the much-discounted bonds had reached a level where they could be considered a bargain by Baring Brothers; Bates certainly was not going to handle the issue as a patriotic duty.

It was a great coup for Peabody, who added to his reputation by magnanimously refusing the $60,000 commission which Maryland owed for his services. Peabody honestly believed that American investments were sound. And when interest was suspended on these same bonds, he began to speculate heavily in them, trusting that eventually interest would be repaid retroactively. Peabody bought for pennies what previously had sold for pounds. And when his prognostications proved correct, and Maryland did honor her commitments, he found himself not only an immensely wealthy man, but also one highly regarded by his peers for his sagacity and foresight.

George Peabody and Co. moved from Moorgate to larger premises in Warnford Court and began to compete seriously with the Barings for the ever-expanding American business that flowed through London. It was 1851, the year of the Great

Exhibition. In the huge Crystal Palace erected in Hyde Park, 40,000 square feet had been allocated to American exhibitions. But instead of being received as an exemplar of the greatness of the New World, the American section was held up as an object of derision. The United States stood alone as the only participating government unwilling to subsidize its exhibitors even to the extent of decorations, and the result was a motley display spread randomly over a huge space.

Punch noted with delicious malice, as the exhibition was being formed, "We could not help . . . being struck by the glaring contrast between large pretension and little performance . . . of the large space claimed by . . . America. . . . What was our astonishment . . . to find their contribution to the world's industry consists . . . of a few wine-glasses, a square or two of soap, and a pair of salt cellars! For a calculating people, our friends the Americans are thus far terribly out of their calculations."

Peabody, whose offices had become a visiting center for Americans in London, was personally shocked by this situation. Like so many nineteenth-century Yankees, he was hypersensitive to criticisms of America by sophisticated Europeans. But, on a more substantive plane, it was in his interest as a businessman that things American be as highly regarded as possible in England.

Eight weeks before the official opening of the exhibition, a confidential meeting was held with the American Minister, Abbott Lawrence, to ascertain if the Legation could remedy this highly embarrassing situation. Lawrence, however, was without funds, and so Peabody felt obliged to offer a loan to the Minister of almost $15,000 so that Hobbs's unpickable lock, Colt's revolver, McCormick's reaper, Hoe's printing press, and even Hiram Powers's *Greek Slave* might be suitably displayed. To the credit of the Congress, Peabody's loan was eventually repaid.

Having once again pulled his compatriots' fat out of the fire, Peabody celebrated the success of the American exhibition by hosting a great banquet at the London Coffee House, where Americans had traditionally gathered since the days of Benjamin Franklin. Henry Stevens supervised the decorations and later produced a presentation volume commemorating the occasion. Life-size full-length portraits of the Queen, her consort, and George Washington were hung side by side, draped with the flags of both nations. One hundred forty men sat down to dine with George Peabody, who rose at the end of the meal to give the traditional toast: "The Queen, God Bless Her!" Here was one American who was always sensitive to British national feeling.

The dinner attracted much favorable comment in the press. It was a marvelous public relations event, just the thing to attract popular attention, for Peabody never spent or gave money away quietly. The great banker had given a similar dinner at the Star and Garter Hotel in Richmond on the Fourth of July, as a celebration of Anglo-American cordiality. The first Duke of Wellington was guest of honor, and, as one observer noted, "Where the Duke went all could go. It was without exaggeration the affair of the season . . . duchesses waltzed with Governors of States, and members of Parliament flirted with Massachusetts belles, long past the small hours of the night; newspapers chronicled the wonderful success of the rich American's banquet; and on the morning of July 5, 1851, George Peabody's name was in the mouths of half the kingdom." Peabody's Fourth of July dinners became an annual event on the London social calendar. Invitations became a highly prized commodity, and as his business grew so, too, did the length of his guest list.

By the early 1850s George Peabody was beginning to sense his own mortality. He was getting fat and found it increasingly difficult to move about, as gout, rheumatism, and intestinal disorders made claims on his diminishing supply of energy. Peabody needed a partner, a colleague who could administer the business with the same integrity for which the firm had become so noted. He had to be an American with a mercantile background, able to assess knowledgeably the intricacies of the volatile commodities and currency markets, and, most important, he had to inspire absolute trust in George Peabody, that most private of men.

After much deliberation Peabody, in May 1853, finally extended an invitation to Junius Spencer Morgan, a forty-year-old Boston merchant who was then on tour in England with his family. Morgan was not a self-made man. He was the son of a wealthy West Springfield, Massachusetts, real estate speculator, but had parlayed his patrimony into a much larger fortune through his own efforts. This was just the sort of individual Peabody wanted, and in the summer of 1854 Morgan joined the firm as a full partner in their new premises at 22 Old Broad Street. The business of the company continued as before—merchant banking and the issuance of credits, the purchase of stock and the conversion of foreign exchange. Produce and other commodities, particularly railroad iron, were bought and sold. The only significant difference was the quantity of business which, under Morgan's aegis, increased tremendously.

As Peabody grew older and more feeble, Morgan took over most of the business entertainment that was required of the firm. At his mansion on Prince's Gate overlooking Hyde Park, and at his country villa, Dover House, near Roehampton, Junius Morgan laid the groundwork for the eventual transformation of George Peabody and Co. into the formidable House of Morgan, the most powerful of all American financial dynasties.

With the coming of the Crimean War, the market for American grain and cotton expanded enormously. In order to transport these raw materials from the hinterland to coastal ports where they could be shipped to Europe, the great railways expanded in all directions, fed by an ever-increasing supply of British capital exported through the countinghouses of George Peabody and Co. and their competitors. But when the war ended and European demand for American raw materials declined, the specter of depression stalked the land. Countless firms went bankrupt and, with nothing to deliver, many railways filed for bankruptcy.

Once again, Peabody and his new junior partner were faced with a choice. They had created a market for American securities in Britain and had made enormous profits by exporting British gold to the New World. If the integrity of the American market was to be maintained, the value of American stock, particularly railway stock, had to be defended. A run was on as British investors sought desperately to get out of American stocks before they bottomed out. The year 1857 was one of panic. Over £32 million in American debt was held by British investors, and, at the height of the crisis, Peabody and Morgan were paying out over £800,000 per day through the repurchase of American shares. Even the most impressive reserves could not resist such an onslaught indefinitely. Peabody extended quiet overtures to a number of private banks, asking temporary assistance until the crisis abated. With vulpine grace his competitors swooped down, offering short-term loans only on condition that Peabody wind up his banking business in London and return to America. Many thought that here was an ideal chance to destroy a firm which was disliked as much for its success as it was respected for its integrity.

Peabody and Morgan responded furiously by committing all of their personal resources to maintaining the value of American stocks and bonds, but by November

Oil on canvas, date unknown 43½'' × 33¾'' (J. S. Morgan)

Junius Spencer Morgan, 1813–90. Braga (?).

it appeared that even this would not allay public insecurity. In desperation Peabody turned to Thomson Hankey, Jr., the Governor of the Bank of England, whom he had cultivated since the early 1830s. In an action that was unprecedented, the bank announced that it was lending £1 million to George Peabody and Co., as a symbol of its confidence in the firm's solidity. This was the signal that was required. With the Bank of England behind him, Peabody had no trouble in securing ample credits from his correspondent banks in New York. And, when the panic of 1857 passed and the American economy began to recover, the millions of pounds' worth of stock that Peabody and Morgan had absorbed at incredible discounts rose again in value, making the two American bankers wealthy as Croesus.

From this low point the firm moved from strength to strength. During the American Civil War they placed their trust heavily in Union bonds and were rewarded with the fruits of victory, for by now the Barings had been completely eclipsed as the chief financiers in the American governmental market.

In the aftermath of the Franco-Prussian War, Morgan organized a consortium which courageously floated a loan of $50 million to the new Parisian government in the form of 6 percent bonds. His syndicate had gambled on the stability of the new regime and reaped enormous profits. In so doing, Morgan cut himself off from total dependence on the American market and rose in the world of international finance to a position second only to the Rothschilds. Andrew Carnegie came within his orbit as a trusting and valued customer. And, when Junius Morgan was instrumental in the refunding of the U.S. debt, perhaps the most important single event in his financial career, the great magnates and plutocrats of America gathered at a dinner in New York, in 1877, to do him homage for "upholding unsullied the honor of America in the tabernacle of the old world," as Samuel Tilden put it. It was the greatest testimonial ever given in America to a financier, and Junius Morgan stood *primus inter pares* because he and his partner had been skillful enough to seize an opportunity that only Britain offered and exploit it to the fullest.

George Peabody, who in 1859 was preparing himself for retirement, felt a strong sense of obligation to the two nations who had enriched him beyond any right of expectation. The thought had crossed his mind that now was the time to return to America, and he wanted to leave to the people of London, among whom he had dwelt so long, a lasting memento of his affection. He considered an elaborate scheme of drinking fountains for the metropolis but abandoned the idea as lacking distinction. Lord Shaftesbury, the great social reformer, urged Peabody to donate funds to his Ragged School Union for indigent children. Education was clearly a top priority, but Peabody saw, as few of his generation did, that an improved education would have little impact on the life of a child who was forced to return from class each day to the brutalizing environment of slum housing. Peabody did not have to read Dickens, Kingsley, and Ruskin to learn of the conditions in London's slums. They were everywhere to be seen, especially in the Tower Hamlets near his countinghouse in the City.

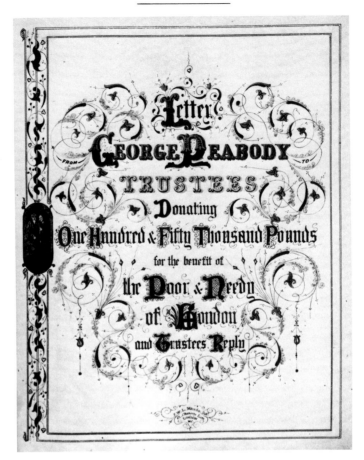

George Peabody's formal offer, to the Corporation of London, of £150,000 to build housing for the city's poor.   (Peabody Institute Library, Peabody, Massachusetts)

In 1842 a royal charter was granted to the Metropolitan Association for Improving the Dwellings of the Industrial Classes. It was the first private group organized as an expression of concern over the ever-expanding slums of the cities. Angela Burdett-Coutts and Sir Sidney Waterlow, the philanthropic consciences of the nation, were actively promoting the erection of model dwellings for the poor, arguing that they would not be charities but commercially viable investments if the right sort of tenant were secured. The cry of reform was in the air, and George Peabody, with his immense resources, was not deaf to the message.

The depression resulting from the panic of 1857 had virtually stopped all model housing projects in London by 1860. Yet the population continued to grow and, in certain sections of the metropolis, the conditions of the indigent deteriorated to a level of absolute despair. Thus when *The Times* of March 26, 1862, reported, "We have today to announce an act of beneficence unexampled in its largeness and in the time and manner of the gift," it signaled not only a revival of the housing reform movement but also the creation of the first of the great modern foundations, the Peabody Donation Fund. Peabody originally intended to endow the fund with £100,000, but by the time of the public announcement this sum had been increased to £150,000, and eventually to £500,000.

He was to take no direct hand in the administration of the money. Instead, five distinguished trustees, all old friends of the donor, were appointed: Junius S. Morgan, Peabody's business partner; Edward Stanley, fifteenth Earl of Derby, son of the Prime Minister and himself a distinguished foreign and colonial secretary; Sir James Emerson Tennent, Bart., a former Northern Irish Member of Parliament and mandarin of the Civil Service; Sir Curtis Miranda Lampson, Bart., an American by birth who made a fortune in the fur trade and who, for his work in laying the transatlantic telegraph cable, had received a baronetcy from the hand of Queen Victoria; and finally, as an ex-officio trustee, Charles Francis Adams, the U.S. Minister to the Court of St. James's.

Peabody had his own views as to what sort of "deserving poor" should be allowed tenancies in the Fund's buildings. They should be Londoners "by birth or residence" and were to be judged eligible without consideration of sectarian religious or party political affiliations. More important, it was to be understood at the outset that the Fund was not a charity. Those who were bereft of all income, the blind, the crippled, the mentally deficient—paupers of all types, were to be excluded as a matter of principle. Peabody's donation was aimed at improving the lot of the "working poor," of artisans of good conduct and demonstrable moral virtue who were attempting to keep body and soul together, while at the same time making their contribution to society in as respectable and sober a manner as possible. It was an eminently Victorian and utilitarian approach to a trying social question, in which the beneficiaries of patronage had to possess at least a modicum of self-respect so that they could appreciate what they were being given. The Peabody Donation Fund was not utopian; it could not save all of society and chose instead to aid that segment which arguably had the strongest chance of survival and whose contribution to the commonweal was deemed of sufficient importance to merit encouragement. How much of the New England Puritan showed in George Peabody is not hard to assess in the principles laid down in the creation of his housing policy.

What Peabody created, and what still survives today, was no less than the first large housing agency in Britain, operating completely independently of government on a noncommercial basis. It was an enormous undertaking, reflecting the strong sense of social responsibility felt by the donor and his trustees. The fact that an individual could attempt to solve such a problem did not go unnoticed in Parliament where, between 1868 and 1890, a number of bills were enacted specifically to deal with the problems of substandard environments in urban centers. Peabody's work was a catalyst which spurred government action toward the creation of a national housing policy. This in itself was a major political achievement.

The public response to Peabody's gift to London was swift. The Court of Common Council of the Corporation of the City of London granted Peabody the freedom of the City and commissioned a portrait of him to hang in the Guildhall. He was the first American to be so honored. The Lord Mayor of London held a great banquet in Peabody's honor at the Mansion House, and he was admitted as a Freeman of the ancient livery companies of Fishmongers and Clothworkers.

The Queen, through Lord John Russell, enquired privately of Peabody whether he would accept the honor of a baronetcy or perhaps the Grand Cross of the Order of the Bath. Both, however, would have required him to surrender his citizenship and declare allegiance to the Crown of Britain, which he could not bring himself to do. When the Sovereign, intent on honoring the philanthropist as best she could, enquired what sort of gift he would accept, Peabody replied that all he desired was a portrait miniature of the Queen, together with a personal note in her own hand. The royal letter arrived at the end of March 1866 and was bound by Peabody within Morocco boards decorated with the most elaborate of gold tooling and lined with watered silk. The royal miniature (or plaque) appeared soon thereafter, showing the Queen wearing the Garter, the Koh-i-noor diamond, and a jeweled cross presented to her by Prince Albert. It was set in a frame of heavy maroon velvet, inlaid with thousands of dollars' worth of gold, and Peabody was so pleased with the gift that he commissioned Daniel Huntington to paint a greater-than-life-size portrait of himself with the Queen's bounty set on a table at his side.

In America, Peabody's beneficence to museums, musical conservatories, lecture halls, free libraries, and universities was extensive. But it was in the aftermath of Civil War, when he gave $2 million to restore Southern education under the auspices of the nation's first true foundation, the Peabody Education Fund, that his

This box of solid gold contained the parchment declaration granting Peabody the Freedom of the City of London.   (Peabody Institute Library, Peabody, Massachusetts)

Watercolor on enamel, 1867 (Peabody Institute Library, Peabody, Massachusetts)

Queen Victoria. Set in gold and velvet, this portrait was commissioned by the Sovereign as a personal gift to George Peabody. F. A. Tilt, active 1866–68.

reputation as the founder of modern educational philanthropy was established. A chorus of praise was raised across the nation. Harvard, itself a beneficiary of a new museum, granted Peabody an honorary doctorate of civil law. The U.S. Congress, "in acknowledgement of his beneficial promotion of universal education," commissioned the New York silversmiths Starr and Marcus to design the most elaborate gold medal ever created in America; a bauble which displayed a profile of Peabody, three inches in diameter and a half-inch thick, set amid a display of allegorial figures and palm trees, all fashioned of solid gold. It was a moving testimony to a man who valued education so highly because, as Peabody wrote, "Deprived as I was, of the opportunity of obtaining anything more than the most *common education,* I am *well* qualified to estimate its value by the disadvantages I labour under in the society in which my business and situation in life frequently throws me, and willingly would I now give *twenty times* the expense attending a good education could I possess it, but it is now too late for me to learn and I can only do to those that come under my care as I could have wished circumstances had permitted others to have done by me."

Ever since his retirement, Peabody debated returning to the United States, where his name commanded as much awe as it did in England. But, although he did visit his homeland, Peabody could not break the chains that now bound him to England. And, as his health grew more delicate after the Civil War, it became more and more difficult to contemplate such a move.

In 1867 Oxford awarded Peabody an honorary doctorate of civil law. A subscription was raised to erect a statue of him on Threadneedle Street near the back of the Royal Exchange in the heart of London's financial district. William Wetmore Story, the celebrated American expatriate sculptor from Rome, was engaged to execute the work. Such a mark of respect from the City might well have been the supreme accolade for Peabody, for even after he was dead, his colleagues desired to have an ever-present physical reminder of his life and works.

But Peabody was more than just a man of the stock exchange and the banks. He had become a national possession—even pubs were named after him. And, when he did expire in 1869, the Dean and Chapter of Westminster offered space in the

Gold, 1867
8'' × 6'' (plate size)
(Peabody Institute Library, Peabody, Massachusetts)

The U.S. Congress presented this medal to Peabody in recognition of his gift of $2 million to promote education in the southern states.   Starr and Marcus Goldsmiths of New York.

Abbey for burial—the highest honor that can be conferred on any British subject, here offered for the first time to an American. But Peabody's will was specific; his remains were to be returned to the family plot in Salem, Massachusetts. Consequently, a temporary thirty-day burial—a lying in state—was arranged at Westminster Abbey, followed by the transference of the remains to America aboard H.M.S. *Monarch,* the newest and largest warship in the British navy.

On Friday, November 12, Peabody's casket, covered with a blue velvet cloth bearing his personal monogram in white silk, was borne with great dignity into a sepulcher to enjoy an honor "coveted by nobles and not always granted kings." As is common on such occasions, the great and powerful of the realm, led by William Gladstone, the Prime Minister, gathered to pay their respects, while outside the Abbey there assembled, in the words of the London correspondent of *The New York Times,* a crowd "more interesting than that within. The gaunt, famished London poor were gathered in thousands to testify their respect for a foreigner who had done more than any Englishman for their class, and whose last will contains an additional bequest to them of £150,000." They were the anonymous multitude who, for generations, would remember George Peabody's name best of all.

Wood engraving, in the Illustrated London News, *November 20, 1869 16" × 22½" (Library of Congress)*

Funeral of Peabody in Westminster Abbey. He was then carried to the United States aboard the H.M.S. Monarch, *the newest warship in the British navy.*

5

Expatriates Incarnate:
The World of Henry James

—

And the great domed head, con gli occhi
    onesti e tardi
Moves before me, phantom with weighted motion,
Grave incessu, *drinking the tone of things,*
And the old voice lifts itself
    weaving an endless sentence.

Such was Ezra Pound's reminiscent vision of Henry James. James—the Master of Manners both facund and fecund—the Passionate Pilgrim—the Expatriate Incarnate.

Out of Boston he came, flying to Old England from New; from what H. L. Mencken called "a Devil's Island of intellectual poor relations, eternally wearing out the English chemises and pantaloons of season before last." His choice was the Old World—"my choice, my need, my life." But it was a choice not made without trepidation.

No European writer is called upon to assume that terrible burden, and it seems hard that I should be. The burden is necessarily greater for an American—for he must deal, more or less, even if only by implication, with Europe; whereas no European is obliged to deal in the least with America. No one dreams of calling him less complete for not doing so. (I speak of course of people who do the sort of work I do; not of economists, of social science people.) The painter of manners who neglects America is thereby not incomplete as yet; but a hundred years hence—fifty years hence, perhaps—he will doubtless be ac-counted so.

Being an American in Europe was far from a curse to Henry James. It was, in his own words, "an excellent preparation for culture." For the American, liberated from the national prejudices, bigotries, limitations of the Frenchman, the Italian, the Spaniard, or even the Englishman, was free to pick and assimilate into his person whatever he chose from any culture. He could claim his aesthetic property wherever he found it.

Oil on canvas, 1908
39¼'' × 32''
(National Portrait
Gallery, Smithsonian
Institution; Bequest of
Mrs. Katherine
Dexter McCormick)

Henry James, 1843–1916. Jacques-Émile Blanche, 1861–1942.

James had known Europe since he was a child—his parents were blessed with the financial wherewithal to permit extensive travel. The young Henry, of intense sensitivity and acute observation, was determined to carve out a literary destiny for himself, suspended in a civilization far more ancient than his own. He tried France, but it was no good. He found the French eternally superficial and himself "an eternal outsider," and so on to England on December 10, 1876.

Like Washington Irving he toured the provinces. From the Welsh border through the Wye Valley. On to the Cotswolds—to Gloucester, Newport, Tewkesbury. And finally to the dreaming spires of Oxford, golden in summer term, where the now standard "indescribable emotions" overtook him as they had so many of his countrymen. He was tempted to remain forever "in the happy belief that all the world is an English garden and time a fine old English afternoon."

But the countryside, idyllic though it was, could never compete with London for James's emotional allegiance. He arrived with proper credentials, with suitable connections and letters of introduction, and the doors of creative society opened. James was introduced at a "banquet of initiation." He met the Pre-Raphaelites: William Morris, Edward Burne-Jones, Dante Gabriel Rossetti. He dined with the great John Ruskin, and Leslie Stephen, and the Catholic poet Aubrey de Vere. They were said to be avant-garde; yet they lived in the past. James found them, and so many others, fascinating. He viewed them and their womenfolk "as an artist and as a bachelor; as one who has the passion of observation and whose business is the study of human life." Here was the most acceptable of social roles, that of a passionate observer. For Henry James there could be no other. For him marriage was not a necessity—he felt no procreative urge—it was "only the last and highest luxury." James declared, "I shall never marry; I regard that now as an established fact, and on the whole a very respectable one; I am both happy enough and miserable enough, as it is, and I don't wish to add to either side of the account. Singleness consorts much better with my whole view of existence (of my own and of that of the human race), my habits, my occupations, prospects, tastes, means, situation "in Europe," and absence of desire to have children—fond as I am of the infant race."

Eventually, James would pay the price of loneliness for his solitude, yet for him there was no choice. When he was a young man, it was not the domestic bliss of family life that he coveted; nor was it the amorous embraces of a pretty young thing that he sought to possess. Rather, it was the literary conquest of London that Henry James set as his first and most important goal. He found it

.... difficult to speak adequately or justly of London. It is not a pleasant place; it is not agreeable, or cheerful or easy or exempt from reproach. It is only magnificent. You can draw up a tremendous list of reasons why it should be insupportable. The fogs, the smoke, the dirt, the darkness, the wet, the dirtiness, the ugliness, the brutal size of the place, the horrible numerosity of society, the manner in which this senseless bigness is fatal to amenity, to convenience, to conversation, to good manners—all this and much more you may expatiate upon. You may call it dreary, heavy, stupid, dull, inhuman, vulgar at heart, and tiresome in form. I have felt these things at times so strongly that I have said—"Ah London, you too are impossible?" But these are

Oil on canvas, 1858
30'' × 51''
(Museum of London)

A Summer Day in Hyde Park. For Henry James, London was "the most complete compendium of the world." John Ritchie, active 1855–75.

occasional moods; and for one who takes it as I take it, London is on the whole the most possible form of life. I take it . . . as one who has the passion of observation and whose business is the study of human life. It is the biggest aggregation of human life—the most complete compendium of the world.

At the end of a long day of writing, he could settle down in one of the private seraglios known as gentlemen's clubs, where he possessed honorary entrée. In sanctums sanctorum like the Athenaeum, "the last word of a high civilization," he found the stimulation of august company—though it was often asleep. And although the food left much to be desired, the library, with "such lounges and easy chairs," was a source of endless pleasure. How convenient and reinforcing London was for a "lonely celibate." How it catered to the needs of those who were most relaxed in exclusively masculine environs.

James was not blinded by romantic idealism to the horrific reality of Dickensian London. Rather he chose in his art and life not to confront it. His world was the world of what he called "the better sort," and if they were on occasion "too genteel," they were far more appealing than the lower orders who were too base or miserable for his observant but nonreforming pen.

By the middle of 1878, James was established in London as a writer of tales that appealed to British sensibility. Indeed, "There are times when I seem to myself to carry all England in my breeches pocket." Here was fantasy now transformed into fact.

Her name was Daisy Miller, and she was Henry James's discovery—the American girl "cut" by expatriate society in Rome. In a brilliant tour de force, he presented an international theme: the American abroad endowed with riches, curiosity, and naïveté. A class aggressive in its social ambitions and pretensions, unrepentantly insensitive to the hollow protests of those who objected to the commingling of the aristocracies of blood and wealth.

Out of the well of his keenly wrought memory for observed detail, James crafted a world of elegant fiction which did no less than articulately mirror the quest of an entire generation of his countrymen; a generation innocent and impassioned with a zest for embracing the sophistication of Europe. James watched and remembered everything: details of dress; modes of social courtesy; minute differences of accent, inflection, and vocabulary; and rituals performed repeatedly at tea, supper, and dinner. He studied society at leisure and play, and was intent on observing just how those blessed with money actually spent their time. Were they truly different from you and me? There lay the question. James himself dined out 140 times during the winter of 1878–79. It was all a part of his "Londonizing process," he told himself. Yet the very counting of his engagements as a measure of social success revealed a conscious and ever-present insecurity. Nevertheless, such gregariousness was not without its rewards. And in his richest, most productive period, James refined and restated his vision of society into resonant masterpieces of narrative, such as *The Portrait of a Lady, The Wings of the Dove, The Ambassadors,* and *The Golden Bowl;* and upon these an enduring reputation was founded.

"No man is more popular in London dining-rooms and drawing rooms than Henry James," wrote the essayist Justin McCarthy. James could do everything in a conversation except be commonplace. But the burden of observation weighed heavily on him and distracted him from personal self-development. "I am sometimes really appalled," he wrote in 1879, three years after his arrival, "at the matter of course way of looking at the indigenous life and manners into which I am gradually dropping! I am losing my standard—my charming little standard that I used to think so high; my standard of wit, of grace, of good manners, of vivacity, of urbanity, of intelligence, of what makes an easy and natural style of intercourse!" It was a process of acculturation that affected many foreigners in London. Yet, perhaps by endlessly delving into the life-styles of others, James found a suitable distraction from a growing emptiness in his own soul.

One thing is certain: the more he saw of Americans abroad and the more he wrote about them, the less he liked them.

The Englishmen I have met not only kill, but bury in unfathomable depths, the Americans I have met. A set of people less painted to provoke national self-complacency than the latter it would be hard to imagine. There is but one word to use in regard to them—vulgar, vulgar, vulgar. Their ignorance—their stingy, defiant grudging attitude towards everything European—their perpetual ref-

erence of all things to some American standard or precedent which exists only
in their own unscrupulous wind-bags and their own unhappy poverty of voice,
of speech, and of physiognomy—these things glare at you hideously.

By purging himself of those American traits he most abjured, James thought to
wrap himself in the cloak of the cosmopolitan. But it was never to be. Instead he
adopted a new parochialism based on the hierarchical values of a socially stratified
society. There, order and tradition were celebrated over mobility and innovation,
for the breath of democratic practice smelled rancid and was suspect.

In his critique on the work of Nathaniel Hawthorne, James recited the now
famous, if rather silly, litany of shortcomings which he found in the texture of
American life.

No State, in the European sense of the word, and indeed barely a specific
national name. No sovereign, no court, no personal loyalty, no aristocracy, no
church, no clergy, no army, no diplomatic service, no country gentlemen, no
palaces, no castles, nor manors, nor old country houses, nor parsonages, nor
thatched cottages nor ivied ruins; no cathedrals, nor abbeys, nor little Norman
churches; no great Universities nor public schools—No Oxford, nor Eton, nor
Harrow, no literature, no novels, no museums, no pictures, no political society, no sporting class—no Epsom nor Ascot!

He was not advocating that all this be incorporated into America. Far from it. For
James knew that, after all was said, a good deal remained in America, and what
remained was the American's "secret, his joke, as one may say."

James was speaking of less universal, more private passions, which explains his
personal devotion to the elitist life-style of the English upper classes. He was not a
political creature. But, as Hartley Gratten has written so wisely, James was "a
conservative son of a radical father, a man who positively idealized ancient institutions and customs hardened by usage into principles of conduct."

No wonder, then, that an artist dedicated to tradition should gravitate toward a
social and political system which enshrined conserving (conservative, if you will)
instincts as the best of all possible motives. These were demonstrated, no doubt, by
the evident success of British cultural imperialism which naturally followed in the
wake of Victoria's armies. Nowhere is James's attitude more clearly stated than in
his *English Hours* where he writes, "conservatism has all the charm and leaves dissent
and democracy and other vulgar variations nothing but their bald logic. Conservatism has the cathedrals, the castles, the gardens, the traditions, the associations,
the fine names, the better manners, the poetry." It was a sincerely expressed sentiment held by one who found it difficult to deal with a rapidly changing world and
who clung, however desperately, to those paradigms which bespoke the value and

salving grace of immutable tradition. American writers, from Washington Irving to T. S. Eliot, who chose England as their place of domicile, if not refuge, could well understand the spirit that moved Henry James. A spirit that yearned for distinctions, for differences between classes of men; that signified a variety of experience. T. S. Eliot was so right when he said, two years after James's death, "He had a mind so fine that no idea could violate it." James reveled in perceptions and sensations. Analytical constructs and carefully developed ideas based on principle: these were not the stuff and substance of his intellectual baggage.

It was in the autumn of 1885 that James began what was to be the first of several annual visits to the Worcestershire village of Broadway, in the Shakespeare country, fifteen miles from Stratford. Broadway, which James described as "the perfection of the old English rural tradition," nestled on the edge of the rolling Cotswold hills at the entrance to the fabled Vale of Evesham, reputed then and now to be the most beautiful village in all England, had become a gathering point for romantically inclined Americans in search of Elysium. It was an intensely quiet place, and in James's day still quite inaccessible, the nearest railway station being six miles away. The uniformly ancient houses gathered along a single meandering road stretching for about a mile, and the native population, still dressed in white sunbonnets and old-fashioned smocks, were highly reminiscent of another era.

The first American to settle in Broadway was the thirty-eight-year-old painter Francis Davis Millet, who had arrived in the hamlet with his family in 1884, on the recommendation of William Morris and the author Laurence Hutton. Millet, a son of Harvard (class of 1869), studied painting at the Antwerp Academy in the early 1870s with noted success. He was the first of his countrymen crowned by King Leopold with the Academy's laurel wreath and was also the first American to receive the coveted gold medal for excellence.

Millet was a creator of genre paintings. He specialized in domestic scenes of the seventeenth century. The idealized world of Cavaliers and Roundheads were his métier and Broadway the perfect backdrop for indulging his fancies.

At first the Millets lived at Farnham House, a Jacobean structure of some distinction, but eventually they moved on to Russell House, an even larger home, adding Pershore Grange, a third dwelling, for studio space. These were the sets for many of Millet's genre scenes, including his now famous *Between Two Fires* and *The Black Sheep.*

Frank Millet had a passion for old buildings—he was always renovating and restoring—opening derelict fireplaces; uncovering sealed windows; and recovering ancient beams. The movement for the preservation of ancient monuments was already a potent force in the land, no doubt spawned in reaction to the perceived philistinism of Victorian architects. But it had nothing to fear from Frank Millet who, like so many of his compatriots in Britain, was often more enthusiastic than his English brethren for preserving the ancient architectural heritage of the countryside.

Left: *Francis Davis Millet, 1846–1912. An inveterate traveler, Millet is seen here in his uniform as a war correspondent in Anatolia and Eastern Europe. George Maynard, 1843–1923. Oil on canvas, 1878. 60¼'' × 38½''. (National Portrait Gallery, Smithsonian Institution; Bequest of J. A. P. Millet)* Above: *Russell House, one of several Jacobean homes restored by the Millets in Broadway, Worcestershire. J. Jacques, Jr., dates unknown. Photograph, date unknown. 3½'' × 5⅛''. (Charles S. Millet)*

Oil on canvas, 1892 28¾'' × 36'' (The Tate Gallery, London)

Between Two Fires. Francis Davis Millet, 1846–1912.

Charcoal, circa 1889
14" × 10⅛"
(Yale University Art
Gallery; The Edwin
Austin Abbey
Memorial Collection)

Edwin Austin Abbey, 1852–1911. John Singer
Sargent, 1856–1925.

The Millets, who were financially comfortable, required a considerable amount of space in Broadway, not only for themselves but for the colony of creative spirits who gathered round them. The first and most intimate of these was Edwin Austin Abbey, who arrived in 1885 at the age of thirty-three and spent the next four years in residence with the Millets at Russell House.

Abbey was a Philadelphian by birth who, after an artistic apprenticeship at the Pennsylvania Academy under Christian Schussele, translated to the illustration department of *Harper's Weekly* in New York. There he emerged as one of the premier illustrators of his generation, and one of the great imaginative geniuses of the decorative page.

It was the Harper brothers who commissioned Abbey to create a series of illustrations to accompany the poems of the seventeenth-century bard Robert Herrick. When, in 1882, these were brought out as a separate deluxe volume, Abbey's international reputation soared.

Naturally, to soak up local color (the Brothers Harper were very indulgent of their illustrators), Abbey had come to England on what proved to be a lifelong excursion. He was introduced into London artistic society by the Anglo-American painter George Henry Boughton, at whose sumptuous Campden Hill home, West House, built by Norman Shaw, creators of all types of cultural goods gathered.

Boughton who, like Frank Millet, specialized in Puritan paintings, was never particularly good. But he was a fashionable raconteur who was eventually honored as a Royal Academician. There were few other homes in London where the obscure Abbey could meet the likes of Robert Browning, James McNeill Whistler, and Johannes Brahms, "the 'Hungarian Dances' chap," as Abbey called him, in such rapid succession.

Abbey and Millet, who also did work for *Harper's,* shared studio space in Bloomsbury's Bedford Square. And when they moved to Broadway, they were accompanied by Abbey's close friend Alfred Parsons, himself a noted landscapist, who took a neighboring house and remained a permanent fixture in the village.

There were endless visitors to Broadway during these years, some of great account and others of whom history has taken little note. But the magic essence of the place was well known. Henry James agreed with Burne-Jones that his "beloved Millets" had "reconstructed the Golden Age." It was not all rose leaves and lavender but was immensely stimulating as an exercise in consciously lived nostalgia. The resident Americans and their guests emulated their neighbors: Haymaking was celebrated annually according to local custom; meals were served alfresco when the weather was fine; and on memorable evenings in the big studio at Russell House, hung with tapestries and lined with carpets, there were impromptu concerts of

Photograph, date unknown 3¼" × 4½" (Archives of American Art, Smithsonian Institution)

The garden at Russell House in which John Singer Sargent painted Carnation, Lily, Lily, Rose. Unidentified photographer.

Schumann, Rubinstein, Grieg, and Lassen held amid the shining pots of pewter and brass which reflected in the glow emanating from the oversized fireplace. Truly, it was civilization brought into the wilds.

John Singer Sargent was another of those Americans who were drawn inexorably to Broadway. The compleat cosmopolite—it was said of Sargent that he was an American born in Italy and educated in France, who dressed like a German, spoke like an Englishman, and painted like a Spaniard.

In the Paris atelier of Carolus-Duran, the young Sargent, a "completely accentless mongrel," evincing "rather French, faubourg sort of manners," said Vernon Lee, imbibed the principles of Velásquez and Frans Hals that were to dominate his style until the end of his long career. And it was in the salon of the American expatriate Henrietta Reubell that Sargent first made the acquaintance of Henry James, who liked him exceedingly for his "remarkably artistic nature" and charm.

James was greatly taken with Sargent; so much so that he wrote to his confidante, Grace Norton, "The only Franco-American product of importance here strikes me as young John Sargent the painter, who has high talent, a charming nature, artistic and personal, and is civilized to his finger-tips. He is perhaps spoilable—though I don't think he is spoiled. But I hope not, for I like him extremely; and the best of his work seems to me to have in it something exquisite."

Oil on canvas, 1906
36" × 28" (sight)
(Galleria degli Uffizi,
Florence, Italy)

John Singer Sargent, 1856–1925. Self-portrait.

Preliminary drawing of Madame X. John Singer Sargent, 1856–1925. Pencil on paper, 1884. 12¾″ × 9⅜″. (Private collection; lent by courtesy of Hirschl and Adler Galleries, New York)

Oil on canvas, 1884 82½″ × 43½″ (The Metropolitan Museum of Art, New York; Arthur H. Hearn Fund, 1916)

Madame X (Mme. Pierre Gautreau).   John Singer Sargent, 1856–1925.

Sargent was equally impressed with James and they were often in one another's company. Little wonder, for, like James, Sargent had a penchant for the society of the beau monde. And in time he would paint the sort of women about whom James wrote so consummately.

James was taken to Sargent's studio on the Boulevard Berthier to see his portrait of the famous professional beauty, Mme. Gautreau, which, a few weeks later, enjoyed a *succès de scandale* at the Salon, when the critics and the public they led roundly damned it—*"détestable! ennuyeux! curieux! monstreux!"*

Such a reception was disheartening, to say the least, and James urged Sargent to come to England, "there being such a field in London for a *real* painter of women, and such magnificent subjects of both sexes."

A month after their parting in Paris, Sargent appeared in London in the spring of 1884 and was taken by James everywhere. They dined, went to the theater, visited the galleries. And with James at his side Sargent visited the studios of ten artists, including Sir John Everett Millais and the portentous President of the Royal Academy, Sir Frederick Leighton. Within a year of his arrival, Sargent was permanently settled in England, initially in the Tite Street studio recently vacated by his compatriot James McNeill Whistler. But he was not yet established. Some English critics found his bravura portraits too crude, lacking the familiar detail found in more finished works. But, like James, Sargent was not long in beginning his conquest of London.

Ned Abbey was one of the Americans with whom Sargent became intimate after his arrival in England. In the summer of 1885, the two left London for a boating trip up the Thames. At Pangbourne Weir Sargent noticed a group of Chinese lanterns hanging among the trees near a bed of lilies. He pointed them out to Abbey, remarking on the luminosity of the colors as they filtered the afternoon sunlight. It was all too perfect. The water was quiet and so Sargent, an avid swimmer since childhood, took a dive into an inviting pool only to severely injure his head on a spike that lay invisible beneath the surface. Abbey was very concerned and bundled his friend off to Broadway to convalesce. In so doing he added yet another member to the creative tribe encamped in the Cotswolds.

Henry James had best described the place when he wrote, "Furnished apartments are useful to the artist, but a furnished country even more so. . . . This is the great recommendation of Broadway: everything in it is convertible. Even the passing visitor finds himself becoming so; the place has so much character that it rubs off on him, and if in an old garden—an old garden with old gates and old walls and old summer houses—he lies down on the old grass (on a venerable rug, no doubt) it is ten to one but he will be converted. . . . It is delicious to be at Broadway and not to have to draw."

Edmund Gosse, another frequent visitor, recalled lovingly how, amid a little medieval ruin in the Millets' garden, he and James sat writing, while on the floor below Abbey and Millet were peripatetically attempting to paint between tennis and

*Pen and ink,
circa 1885
2″ × 3″
(Archives of American
Art, Francis Davis
Millet Papers)*

*John Singer Sargent, 1856–1925, painting Carnation, Lily, Lily,
Rose.   Self-portrait.*

cricket matches. Outside in the garden proper, Sargent and Alfred Parsons were
tilting their easels to catch the sun. Gosse recounted, "We were all within shouting
distance and not much serious work was done for we were in towering spirits and
everything was food for laughter."

The painting which Gosse recalled seeing on Sargent's easel was *Carnation, Lily,
Lily, Rose,* which found its inspiration in the quasi-oriental scene the painter had
witnessed at Pangbourne. The painting took its title from an old song and was
christened in honor of the painter's hostess, Lily Millet.

Sargent labored lovingly over the work. For no other painting did he make so
many preliminary sketches and drawings. A flower bed was cut at the back of Russell
House, and Sargent made the rounds of local nurseries gathering all the carnations,
roses, and lilies he could find. Two little girls, daughters of the illustrator Frederick
Bernard, were Sargent's models. He would stand each day for hours watching them
at play, and when the light of dusk assumed a favorable hue and the children struck a
particular pose, Sargent would shout "Stop as you are," and rush to his easel to
capture the moment. Only a few minutes of each day were possible for such painting, and when the children were absent from Broadway, the canvas was stored in the
Millets' barn.

This painting was the culmination of Sargent's impressionistic experiments at
Broadway and was by far the most artfully constructed of these works. The painter

*Oil on canvas,
1885–86
68½'' × 60½''
(The Tate Gallery,
London)*

*Carnation, Lily, Lily, Rose.   The most successful of Sargent's impressionistic Broadway canvases.
John Singer Sargent, 1856–1925.*

found it a "fearful difficult subject. Impossible brilliant colours of flowers, and lamps and brightest green lawn background. Paints are not bright enough & then the effect only lasts ten minutes." But when, in 1886, it reached the walls of the Royal Academy's annual exhibition at Burlington House, the glowing luminosity of Sargent's palette was dazzling when compared with the slick and rather silly Greco-Roman fantasies of Alma-Tadema and Poynter, or the cold and formal mythology of

*Engraving, in Oliver
Goldsmith's* She
Stoops to Conquer,
*1887
6³/₁₆'' × 9¹¹/₁₆''
(Library of Congress)*

One of Abbey's illustrations ("Am I in face to-day?") for a folio edition of Oliver Goldsmith's She
'Stoops to Conquer, *his most elaborate illustrated book.   Edwin Austin Abbey, 1852–1911.*

Leighton and the didactic homilies of Watts. Little wonder, then, that the English
critics found in Sargent's works something "bizarre," "audacious," "eccentric," or
"unfinished." Indeed, when considering the portrait of Mme. Gautreau, the Gallic
critics had reacted in exactly the same way.

Sargent's paintings could be seen not only at the Academy but also at the exhibitions of the New English Art Club which did so much to popularize the painterly
French cosmopolitan style in England. If his work was an acquired taste, it was
nevertheless one that was easily absorbed, for Sargent, particularly in his portraits,
knowingly captured the confident, if slightly inelegant, spirit of late Victorian England. His ability to encapsulate both the personality and the visage of his sitters was
simply too uncanny for him to remain on the fringe unrecognized. And thus, by
giving the public what it wanted, and in great profusion, Sargent was assured of great
success.

Ned Abbey's popularity as an illustrator in black and white was great from the
outset of his career. His illustrations of Herrick, of Goldsmith's *She Stoops to Conquer,* and his virtually endless series of drawings for Shakespeare's plays, which
occupied twenty years of his working life, were all recognized as classics in their own
time. But as a painter Abbey was a slow starter. It was not until he reached the age of
forty that, encouraged by Sargent, he put brush to canvas. Yet, once launched, there
was no stopping him as a prolific craftsman in oil, watercolor, and pastel.

Mary Anderson as Hermione. Albert Bruce Joy, 1842–1924. Pink plaster, date unknown. 27⅜'' height. (The J. B. Speed Art Museum, Louisville)

Mary Anderson, 1859–1940. John Singer Sargent, 1856–1925. Charcoal drawing, 1913. 18¾'' × 17½''. (José M. de Navarro)

Mary Anderson as Galatea. Napoleon Sarony, 1821–96. Photograph, 1883. 13'' × 7½''. (Library of Congress)

An Old Song.   Mary Anderson de Navarro modeled for the artist in this watercolor executed in her Broadway home, Court Farm. Edwin Austin Abbey, 1852–1911. Watercolor over preliminary sketch in pencil on paper, 1885. 27½'' × 47½''. (Yale University Art Gallery; The Edwin Austin Abbey Memorial Collection)

Abbey, a short elfin figure, was partial to tall, slender models of the feminine gender; they appear everywhere in his paintings. One of the most beguiling was the American actress Mary Anderson de Navarro, whose Broadway home, Court Farm, was the backdrop for several of Abbey's artistic fantasies.

Mary Anderson's career on the stage was meteoric. Almost from the moment she stepped onto the proscenium, audiences in America and England hailed her as *the* great dramatic beauty of her generation. She was painted and sculpted numerous times, her face being a frequent image at the Royal Academy's exhibitions. As Pauline in *The Lady of Lyons,* as Juliet, and as Galatea in W. S. Gilbert's *Pygmalion and Galatea,* and as the first actress to double as Hermione and Perdita in Shakespeare's *A Winter's Tale,* Mary Anderson stood within the charmed circle of superstardom. She was highly photogenic. One saw her picture reproduced countless times, not only in newspapers and magazines but on advertisements for soap and hourglass corsets as well.

But somehow it was all too intense an experience, and after she had had fourteen years on the stage her nerves gave out. Doctors recommended the quiet and moist climate of the English countryside as a palliative, and what began as a temporary retreat turned into a lifelong expatriation.

Mary and her husband, Antonio de Navarro, removed to England, where she became well known in society. Money was never a problem. Her husband Tony was a scion of a wealthy Basque-American family. His father was one of the fifty-two founders of the Equitable Life Assurance Society which put up everything from elevated railways to luxurious apartment houses in Manhattan. Consequently, for the second generation of Navarros, it was not a question of how to make money but rather how to lead a life of leisure *successfully,* without becoming bored for lack of achievement.

Puerile though such a question sounds, it was a situation that did confront a great many wealthy Americans who gravitated to England for social reasons at the end of the nineteenth century, only to find themselves hereditarily unprepared for a lifestyle which the English aristocracy had cultivated for generations.

It was a question that fascinated Henry James who, like Millet, Abbey, and Sargent, was close to the Navarros. How did people who did not have to work usefully spend their time? This was the crux of much of his correspondence with Tony de Navarro, who was sensitive enough to understand and to be vaguely embarrassed by the relative uniqueness of his position, for in many ways the Navarros were living examples of characters conceived in the fecund mind of Henry James.

Time passed pleasantly enough at Court Farm. Mary and Tony gave classes in woodcarving and embroidery. It was all part of the general revival of the folk-art movement in Britain. A distinguished pewter collection, now housed in the Fitzwilliam Museum at Cambridge, was assembled and written about. And there were numerous Catholic charities that required attention. Tony de Navarro was not only a Knight Commander of the Order of St. Gregory but was also a member of the Papal household as a "*Cameriere* with Sword and Cape." Their son, in turn, was the first Catholic prize fellow, since the Reformation, admitted to the high table of Trinity College, Cambridge.

Numerous attempts were made to lure Mary Anderson back to the stage, so memorable was her popularity. A syndicate of Americans went so far as to offer $100,000 plus a percentage of the gate receipts for a series of forty dramatic readings. This was a colossal sum of money for any actress. But nothing could tempt her out of retirement. She was content merely to act as the chatelaine of Court Farm and the model for her familiar, Ned Abbey.

In 1886 Henry James published an article about the friends he had made at Broadway. In Abbey he found "a certain refreshment in meeting an American of the first order who is not a pupil of 'Gerome or Cabanel.' " James thought it characteristically American that a talent such as Abbey's should be developed amid "the crowds, streets and squares, the railway stations and telegraph poles, the wondrous sign-boards and triumphant bunting of New York." Yet it never occurred to him how odd it was that none of these stimuli had the slightest impact on Abbey's art. James did not have to assert that Abbey had overcome his environment. It was clear to all that he lived completely, consciously, and passionately in the medieval past, where handsome people were ruled by codes of noble idealism. Where else could this have been done so successfully but in rural England, far richer than America in its sense of history, far removed from the plain vulgarity of city life, and much lower in its cost of living.

Abbey was an illustrator who produced consistently for the realistically inclined popular consciousness, and, in an age partial to the tales of Robert Louis Stevenson and Anthony Hope, he was an immense success. Abbey worked directly under the influence of the Pre-Raphaelites. In his art even the most minute of objects was wrought with precise detail. "What I'd like to do," he said, is "the representation of events not as they might be supposed *poetically* to have happened, but as they really might have happened."

Not trusting the conjurings of his own imagination, Abbey erected elaborate tableaux of models and props, creating a veritable *surmoulage* of history. He was a perfect romantic who was

so entangled and half-wedded to what must be more or less a conscious and therefore, not quite spontaneous variety of work, that I never know whether I do really see what I see or not; I mean, looking at an old window—suddenly—instantly, if it is suggestive at all, I don't see that window as it is, at all, but as it might have been with the people whom it was made for and the people who made it looking through it at each other. Everything old I see that way. A matter of habit, of course, but I lose all the pleasure a modern should have in the real aspect of real things, under the light. I suppose we can't be all quite alike.

Abbey was intimately acquainted with the buckles of shoes and the buttons of coats. He could have been a theatrical designer; indeed, for Mary Anderson de Navarro he did create a number of articles of clothing. But the characters depicted in his art were never mere masqueraders or harlequins on display. They did not wear their costumes so much as live in them. As he wrote, "If an illustrator is to show the manner and appearances of the people of the Middle Ages, it seems to me it should fairly *smell* of that time. I am picking up piece by piece a very valuable collection of accessories. I must have at least fifty complete costumes of various periods, mainly of the last two hundred and fifty years. These are nearly all original articles, or are carefully copied from originals which I have borrowed for the purpose."

The youthful camaraderie and playfulness; the unbounded optimism for the future of a world enveloped in relaxed elegance; of time that was an endless summer day; this was the perfection that crystallized in Broadway and lasted almost five years before its intensity was lost.

John Singer Sargent was off to America in 1887 and, again, in 1889, heralded by an epistolary paean from Henry James in *Harper's Weekly*. These were visits of discovery for one who had never seen the country of his ancestors until the age of twenty. But how they lionized him in Boston. Not since Copley had there been portraits from an American hand as glamorous as they were honest. One critic described them as possessing "an indefinable but palpable atmosphere of refinement, ease and—*tranchons le mot*—aristocracy, or whatever stands for it nowadays." It was an incisive comment, for Sargent's paintings, like those of Abbey and Millet, fell well within the mainstream of a school whose art was based on luxury, optimism, and the prosperity of the *haute bourgeoisie* and aristocracy. There was charm and temperance displayed in the absence of even the slightest suggestion of a struggle for existence so evident in early romantic portraiture. Such were the idealized self-conceptions of the Anglo-American beau monde.

Edwin Austin Abbey married the formidable Gertrude Mead of Boston, a Puritan who felt out of place at Broadway. It was far too bohemian for her tastes, and she did not sense the seriousness of purpose, in this American colony, which she felt was necessary to her husband's high calling. Consequently, in 1890, the Abbeys drifted away to Fairford in rural Gloucestershire, to a manor house called Morgan Hall, a refuge set in a park of twenty acres, which Henry James called "the most romantic place in this prosaic age." In the garden of the manor, Abbey built "a great empty place to work in"—a studio fully sixty-four feet long and forty feet wide. It was thought to be the largest artist's establishment in the kingdom. And well it needed to be, for there Abbey was to paint some of the dinosaurs of the late Victorian era, canvases and murals so large that they dwarfed all competitors when shown publicly.

The most grandiose of these creations was a series of murals 8 feet high and 192 feet long, painted for the Boston Public Library. In May 1890, Abbey and Sargent were approached by the architects Charles McKim and Stanford White who were looking for big names to decorate the library—Augustus Saint-Gaudens had already been retained to produce works of sculpture for the building. Abbey chose as his subject the quest of the Holy Grail, while Sargent, whose murals were almost as long, mapped out a plan to illustrate the progress of religious thought, using iconographic and intellectual motifs popular since the Renaissance.

Sargent moved into the Abbeys' home at Fairford for several months a year, between 1891 and 1895. There, in the enormous studio, the two artists worked side by side on the library's decorations. But the call of London and its cosmopolitan energy was too strong for Sargent. He had increasing numbers of portrait sittings which demanded attention. And eventually, the annual pilgrimage to Fairford had to cease.

Sargent took a lease on what was to be his permanent studio at 12 and 14 The Avenue, just off the Fulham Road in southwest London. There he continued work on his murals, which took a quarter-century to complete. He regarded them as his most important contribution to contemporary art, but belonging as they do to a classical tradition that was fast dying, posterity has found it difficult to agree with Sargent's own judgment.

With Sargent and Abbey gone from Broadway, Frank Millet found it increasingly difficult to remain, despite the presence of his wife and children. He was possessed of an all-encompassing wanderlust which drew him away from the village and from England for increasing periods of time.

Millet is remembered as a good, though by no means great artist. But he is celebrated as one of the first and most important promoters and administrators of the arts that America has produced. As a trustee of the Metropolitan Museum, and Secretary of the American Academy at Rome and of the American Federation of Arts; as Vice-Chairman of the (National) Commission of Fine Arts; and as Chairman of the Niagara Falls Commission and the Advisory Committee of the U.S. National Museum, Francis Millet, author, translator, and war correspondent, was a premier figure of his generation. He was one who thrived in the international art world, traveling extensively in celebration of a gypsylike existence. But the dice were thrown once too often, and when Millet boarded the luxury liner *Titanic* for a transatlantic crossing, it was to prove to be his last journey, his final pilgrimage.

As the nineteenth century reached its apogee, John Singer Sargent and Edwin Austin Abbey, both in their early forties, made their way up through the corridors of popular acclaim into the holy of holies of the artistic establishment, the Royal Academy.

In 1893 Sargent exhibited a portrait of Lady Agnew which created a notable sensation. No longer could any critic dismiss him as an ingenious but insubstantial revolutionary whose technique was at best a novelty. By the canons of realism then current, he stood first among equals. Indeed, no one could touch him.

The following year Sargent was elected an associate of the Royal Academy, and three years later he was accepted into the fold as a full academician. Leighton and Millais were dead. Poynter, Alma-Tadema, Orchardson, Herkomer, and Fildes—the

Oil on canvas, 1896 52½″ × 104¾″ (Yale University Art Gallery; The Edwin Austin Abbey Memorial Collection)

Richard, Duke of Gloucester, and the Lady Anne.   One of the most popular of Abbey's giant history paintings, it was the first canvas he exhibited after his election to the Royal Academy. Edwin Austin Abbey, 1852–1911.

fashionable society painters—adjusted to Sargent's lead, for he had become the most acclaimed of painters in the kingdom. What more suitable role could be found for one of the last magnificent exemplars of the formal representational tradition?

Edwin Abbey followed Sargent into the Academy as an associate in 1896 and became an academician two years later, in honor of which he presented a large silver skewer, once the property of Sir Joshua Reynolds, to the Academy's argent.

If there were those who wondered how an illustrator in black and white, who so recently had turned his attention to the rigors of oil, could be accepted into the pantheon of British art, they had only to look at the painting that Abbey sent to the Academy's annual exhibition after his election as an associate. *Richard, Duke of Gloucester, and the Lady Anne* was a masterful tour de force executed in the grand manner on a canvas over twelve feet long. It recounted the story from the first act of Shakespeare's *Richard III,* when the funeral procession of the late King Henry VI passed from the Tower on its way to Chertsey where the Lady Anne, in deep mourning, was confronted in her despair with the maniacal amorous attention of the hunchback usurper of the throne. The painting, accurate to the smallest of historic details, received a "perfect ovation" when it was first viewed at Burlington House. It was reproduced widely and for years after was recalled by Abbey as one of his most popular works.

The *Richard* set the style of Abbey's future history paintings, which presented lyrical works of the Establishment that united the official and the academic ideals of the English school. Abbey, a spiritual descendent of Benjamin West and Charles R. Leslie, carried on the tradition of Americans practicing in this highest of artistic genres. Little wonder, then, that when a giant group portrait was required for the

Oil on canvas,
1902–04
180″ × 108″
(Her Majesty Queen
Elizabeth II)

The Coronation of King Edward VII.   Edwin Austin Abbey, 1852–1911.

coronation of King Edward VII—a work alive with the rustle of ancient costume, the flash of brilliant jewels, the total magnificence of the King-Emperor regnant—it was to Abbey that the royal commission was extended. It was a final and perhaps supreme accolade to his achievement.

Honored with numerous gold medals, memberships in professional academies, and honorary doctorates, both Abbey and Sargent were passionately loyal to the Academy. They were active in the schools and served on numerous hanging committees, those bodies which sit uncomfortably for hours deciding what shall and what shall not be granted the official imprimatur of space in the annual exhibition.

At the death of Sir Edward Poynter in 1919, Sargent could have had the presidency of the Academy; it was there for the asking by acclamation. But this "sepulchre of dulness & propriety," as Whistler called him, shuddered at the thought. To Sir Arthur Cope he said, "I would do *anything* for the Royal Academy but that, and if you press me any more I should flee the country."

But, however strong their feelings for things Academic and English, both Sargent and Abbey were intense in their affection for America. In 1907 Sargent was offered a knighthood from the hand of the King, but it was refused as he was not, and had no intention of becoming, a subject of His Majesty. Abbey, too, was proud of his heritage and asserted that there were few of his countrymen "who would exchange his birth right for any number of official distinctions, no matter how much easier things would thereby be made for those of us who live here." But when the question of residence arose, as it frequently did, neither Abbey nor Sargent was inclined to return to America permanently. It was a question of environment, which was beyond the control of any artist. Abbey complained that an "atmosphere of art is the breath of life to an artist. Without it he can neither flourish nor grow—and how can there be an atmosphere of art in a country which practically prohibits the artists of all other countries from sending their work to that country—thus destroying the possibility of that ingathering from the whole world of all the best and latest thoughts, which would help to produce the art atmosphere in which alone the arts can flourish."

The death of the King-Emperor in 1910 was the last act of a romantic fantasy for England. The beau monde became pedestrian; the demimonde lost its fascination; and society's enthusiasm for representational realism in art was fast disappearing as the aesthetic beau ideal.

Ned Abbey continued to paint giant murals and paintings until his death, in 1911, at the age of fifty-nine. Isolated in a historic vacuum, he was virtually without competition. But after his death his work fell into fathomless obscurity from which it is only now beginning to recover. Perhaps if he had lived longer, he might have been witness to his own artistic demise.

Sargent, too, found it difficult to adjust to changing times. But for him there was greater malaise and frustration. As he grew older his enthusiasm for portraits all but disappeared. He was financially secure and cared little for the aristocracy who crowded into his studio to be entertained with music as he rushed at his canvas invoking his favorite incantation, "Demons! Demons!!" Their faces bored him, and their portraits increasingly found inspiration in the traditional formulaic poses, popularized by Reynolds and Gainsborough in the eighteenth century, that were now all too predictable. He could find in their visages none of the old magic and sparkle so redolent in the faces of individuals of achievement or of the nouveaux riches on the make.

To the Countess of Radnor he wrote, "Ask me to paint your gates, your fences, your barns, which I should gladly do but NOT THE HUMAN FACE." Even the numerous charcoal portraits which he executed quickly in lieu of oil were an increasing trial: "No more paughtraits whether refreshed or not. I abhor and abjure them and hope never to do another especially of the Upper Classes. I have weakly compromised and lately done a lot of mugs in coke and charcoal and am sick of that too, although occasionally the brief operation has been painless. I am winding up my worldly affairs in that line and now I shall be able to paint nothing but Jehovah in Fulham Road."

One of those whose portraits in charcoal and oil Sargent could never refuse to execute was Henry James, whose artistic sympathies and social parameters were so similar to his own. James, who like Sargent the painter lived off his talent, and who like Sargent his intimate friend externalized his solitary life *into* the products of his creative talent.

Just as Sargent recoiled in his middle age against the prospect of painting another portrait, so did James grow weary "of the whole 'international' state of mind." The

Charcoal on paper, 1912
16⅛″ × 24¼″
(Her Majesty Queen
Elizabeth II)

Henry James, 1843–1916.
John Singer Sargent, 1856–1925.

Anglo-American world which he had neatly dissected into compartments was melting together into a fused agglomeration. And James, like so many others, found himself swept along with the tide into a homogeneous pool where the only perspective that was civilized was that of the cosmopolitan whose *patria* was not tied to the irrelevancies of national boundaries:

> I can't look at the English-American world, or feel about them any more, save as a big Anglo-Saxon total, destined to such an amount of melting together that an insistence on their differences becomes more and more idle and pedantic; and that melting together will come the faster the more one takes it for granted and treats the life of the two countries as continuous or more or less convertible, or at any rate as simply different chapters of the same general subject. *And again,* I have not the least hesitation in saying that I aspire to write in such a way that it would be impossible to an outsider to say whether I am, at a given moment, an American writing about England or an Englishman writing about America (dealing as I do with both countries), and so far from being ashamed of such an ambiguity I should be exceedingly proud of it, for it would be highly civilized.

By the late 1880s the question for James was not so much how to write, but what to write. His place as a recognized novelist was secure. But, living as he did on current income, there was never enough cash on hand to provide a secure basis for the *haute bourgeoise* life-style to which he had been accustomed since childhood.

Consequently, when the actor-manager Edward Compton approached James asking if he would adapt his novel *The American* for the stage, the offer was instantly seized upon as a road to rapid affluence. For the sake of fame, art, and fortune,

Henry James, novelist, would attempt to become Henry James, playwright, for "Simplifying and chastening necessity has laid its brutal hand on me and I have had to try to make somehow or other the money I don't make by literature. My books don't sell, and it looks as if my plays might. Therefore, I am going with a brazen front to write half a dozen." But the theater was to prove a summit not easily conquered.

After a moderate success with *The American,* James devoted most of his time between 1890 and 1895 to the writing of a dozen plays, but he found it extremely difficult to persuade the financially conscious impresarios of London that his works were worthy of production. And it was not until George Alexander, the dandified hero of Piccadilly for whom Oscar Wilde had written *The Importance of Being Earnest,* agreed to produce James's original drama *Guy Domville,* that the prospect of success crystallized.

The play opened at the St. James's Theatre on July 5, 1895, with an audience far more distinguished than the cast. The world of literature and the world of art gathered, as if to a durbar, to pay court to the work of one of their own. Well-known faces could be seen everywhere: James's friends from Broadway—Sargent, Millet, and Alfred Parsons; the painters G. F. Watts, Frederick Leighton, Edward Burne-Jones, and George du Maurier; George Bernard Shaw's red beard was unmistakable, while H. G. Wells's mustache probably went unnoticed. The portentous Mrs. Humphrey Ward was present along with Edmund Gosse, W. E. Norris, and numerous members of the aristocracy who had long admired James.

But high in the gallery there was another audience, undistinguished and anonymous, who had never heard of Henry James and were only present to cheer the triumphs of beau Alexander. But *Guy Domville* was far too sophisticated a vehicle for the usual "chocolate box" entertainments, the light comedies with which Alexander was commonly associated. And it was not long after the curtain rose that catcalls, whistles, and other disturbances began to disrupt the play's progress. With the conclusion of the final act, there was a roar of sarcastic demands for "author, author," and James, in a moment of confusion, allowed himself to be led in front of the curtain. All hell broke loose as a withering tumult heaped verbal abuse onto the stage. The author's friends in the orchestra attempted to applaud the gallery into silence, but to no avail. And as the din rose, a crushed Henry James made his way backstage, "his face green with dismay." The play received encouraging notices from the critics and did run for exactly a month. But for a disconsolate Henry James, who walked home to Kensington that evening, there was an "unutterable horror of the theatre" which had finally, and in his mind most convincingly, rejected him.

James never lost his attraction to drama but, after the cataclysm of *Guy Domville,* he had to admit that it was not his spiritual métier. He would have to return to the novel; it was his only refuge and, as he confided rather theatrically to his notebooks, "It is now indeed that I may do the work of my life." It was a pity that he could not have lived to see an adaptation of his novel *Washington Square* triumph as *the* smash Broadway hit of the 1947–48 New York season.

But now it was time for escape. London, much as he loved it, was becoming unbearable for James. He desperately needed a respite, a refuge somewhere in the country where his spirit could be restored. And so it was that Henry James went for the summer of 1896 to the Cinque Port of Rye in Sussex, attended by his servants, and comforted by his dog, Tosca, and his newly acquired canary. Rye was an ancient place whose cobbled streets were lined by houses of Elizabethan vintage. There were no tourists; it was far too remote a place; and there James found that "the bliss of the rural solitude and peace and beauty are a balm to my spirit."

One place in particular struck the fancy of the novelist. It was a sturdy, ivy-covered red brick Georgian residence with Roman-arched bow windows, sitting at the curve of a steep incline leading to the parish church. James recalled having seen the very house, with its adjacent garden room, in a watercolor at the home of his friend, the architect Edward Warren, who told him it was called Lamb House and had for generations been in the hands of the family who had been mayors of Rye.

It was an enchanting, captivating house—one that James could not purge from his memory. And by the greatest of coincidences, when he discovered that it was vacant and available on a moderately long lease, the prospect of possession, of acting out his fantasies in a rural environ, of altering his entire way of life through a new commitment, hit James "a little like a blow in the stomach."

It was the eminently sensible thing to do. James could rationalize his position easily. He was too old to continue as a footloose expatriate, and it was practical to prepare a salubrious base for his old age. Lamb House could be a shelter against the

Left: *Lamb House. The picture that first attracted Henry James to this country retreat. Edward Warren, 1856–1937. Watercolor, September 26, 1895. 9⅜″ × 6¾″ (sight). (Houghton Library, Harvard University)*   Right: *Henry James at work in the garden room of Lamb House. Photograph, circa 1905–10. 7⁵/₁₆″ × 5⁷/₁₆″ (Houghton Library, Harvard University)*

*Photograph, 1906
(Roger Sherman
Warner II and Sturgis
Warner)*

*Henry James on the beach at Rye with
Mary Hooper Warner.   Roger Sherman
Warner, 1877–1940.*

turmoils of a turbulent world. Within its walls James could regulate his life according to the code he had assimilated. How well H. G. Wells recalled the table set in the front hall at Lamb House. On it there lay "a number of caps and hats, each with its appropriate gloves and stick; a tweed cap and a stout stick for the marsh, a soft comfortable deerstalker if he were to turn aside to the golf club, a light brown felt and a cane for the morning walk down to the harbour, a grey felt with a black band and a gold-headed cane of greater importance if afternoon calling in town was afoot."

Lamb House, which James took on a twenty-one-year lease in September 1897, became the physical prefigurement of the costumed life-style he created for himself. It was "really good enough to be a kind of little becoming, high door'd, brass knockered *facade* to one's life." Henry James was nothing if not acutely, almost tremblingly, honest with himself.

But, however appealing the physical attractions of Lamb House, James knew in the depths of his spirit that the place also held terrors. However many gorgeous afternoons and fine nights there were, the novelist sensed that he would experience most of them as a solitary anchorite trapped by an inconsolable loneliness. At least in London he could surround himself by those he held dear at almost any moment of the day. Such contact might be superficial, but it was much better than isolation in the hours after his writing and dictating had finished. There were servants, of course, but they were no company. James couldn't talk *with* them; they existed as it were in a separate world.

At times he was possessed of an almost desperate sense of isolation. His unhappiness rings tellingly in the eeriest of his Lamb House tales, *The Turn of the Screw*. There was only one solution that was partially satisfactory, and that was to fill the house with company. Invitations gushed forth from Rye, and the hatted figure of Henry James, standing waiting with his dog cart at the railway station, became a familiar one to the natives of the town.

Among those who came regularly were the young American men, the acolytes who sat at James's feet and called him Master. There was the twenty-five-year-old, New England, journalist William Morton Fullerton, a gifted child in the eyes of Henry James, who ended his days writing in French for *Le Figaro*. There was Henry Bennet Brewster, a Europeanized American of Mayflower descent whom James thought of as no more than his creation. "Know Brewster?" he once said. "Why I invented Brewster ten years ago." He died young, but James cherished the memory of "such a strange handsome questioning cosmopolite ghost." There was the blond sculptor, Hendrick Anderson, whom James met in Rome, but whose passage through Lamb House was of a brief duration. Between James and Anderson there was little spiritual communion, but on a physical plane James found him immensely attractive. In later years there was the young English writer, Hugh Walpole, whose reverence for the Master was said to have extended to an offer of physical intimacy—James is also said to have declined. There was Jocelyn Persse, whose mind James could not help but admire; and there was the Pennsylvania Quaker, Logan Pearsall Smith, more English than the English, the future author of *Trivia,* who delighted in speculating on the prenuptial suicides of male virgins in ancient Rome. Smith was one whose literary aspirations somewhat exceeded his gifts, but his critical standards were impeccable. He was never as close to James as he liked to pretend. But from the novelist, Smith did receive one memorable insight on the path of literary achievement. "My young friend," James said, "there is one thing that, if you really intend to follow the course you indicate, I cannot too emphatically insist on. There is one word—let me impress upon you—which you must inscribe upon your banner, and that word is *Loneliness."*

All of these young men were friends and some were confidants. But there was one who was closer to James than all others, and that was Jonathan Sturges, a well-known figure among the American community in England. A Princeton-educated cousin of J. P. Morgan, he was as familiar with Whistler's studio as he was with the divan at Lamb House. He was young, handsome, and wealthy, with dilettantish literary aspirations. But in childhood, poliomyelitis had crippled him completely below the waist. Here was someone who not only commanded James's affection and respect but could also be cared for, even mothered. Sturges was almost always there when James needed him. He was the boon companion of the novelist's years in Rye, and without him loneliness and bitterness might have seriously compromised the novelist's creative faculties.

All these young men had one thing in common for James—they provided distraction and support at times of mental stress. It was their presence and the presence of other friends that helped the novelist return to the discipline and comforting balm that was his craft. Theirs was the breath of human warmth which finally breached the self-protecting wall of icelike egotism within which James had shrouded himself for years. How ironic that almost all of them should have stepped out of the very cultural New England and Middle Atlantic milieu from which James himself had sprung.

By 1900 Henry James was ready to emerge from his hibernation. He discarded the beard worn for so many decades and felt generations younger. He could no longer bear the thought of staying in Rye all year and took rooms each winter in the Reform Club, his "perch" in London from which his social battery could be recharged.

For years James had written of the New World's discovery of the Old and of the effect of things English on America and his countrymen. But with the death of the Victorian era, he found it necessary to accept the fact that the cultural tables were turning. The Americanization of Great Britain could no longer be ignored, and it was a sight he found immensely distressing: "The Americans looming up—dim, vast, portentous—in their millions—like gathering waves—the barbarians of the Roman Empire." There was simply no escape. One could no longer get away. "The west is in the east, the east, by the same token, more and more in the west, and every one and everything everywhere and anywhere but where they, in the vernacular, belong." Henry James, who resolutely refused to give up his own romantic vision of England, resented, with childish petulance, the ever-increasing number of his compatriots in the country which he held dear. It was as if someone demanded that he now share his toy with others, and in so doing, the bauble had become tarnished and defaced.

Crayon, 1912
15½'' × 11''
(Princeton University Library)

Jonathan Sturges. The closest of Henry James's confidants. Albert Sterner, 1863–1946.

No doubt many had come to England sparked by the tales which James himself had written, but their very presence he viewed as a corrupting influence. It was "this overwhelming, self-defeating chaos or cataclysm toward which the whole thing is drifting . . . the deluge of people, of the insane movement for movement, the ruin of thought, of life, the negation of work, of literature, the swelling, soaring crowds, the 'where are you going?' the age of . . . the American, the nightmare."

But it was a two-edged sword, this newly revived transatlantic phobia. For James had come to realize that Europe—that England in its own way—had failed him, that there was something desperately shallow, not in his chronicle of the mannered society, but in the society itself. In his notes for *The Real Thing* (1892), he admitted in a somewhat perplexed manner that what he sought to depict was no more than "the little tragedy of good-looking gentlefolk, who had been all their life stupid and well-dressed, living on a fixed income, at country-houses, watering places and clubs, like so many others of their class in England, and were now utterly unable to do anything, had no cleverness . . . could only *show* themselves, clumsily, for the fine, clean well-groomed animals that they were, only hope to make a little money by—in this manner—just simply *being.*"

By 1903 the sixty-year-old James had been away from America for twenty-eight years and found that "Europe has ceased to be romantic to me, and my own country, in the evening of my days, has become so." And so he returned for a final communion with memories of his childhood and youth. From this voyage of rediscovery by a "reinstated absentee" evolved *The American Scene,* published in 1907. It ranks today as not only one of the great travel documents we possess but also as a quintessential interpretation of America—both pro and con—which only a native son, however long absent, could provide.

Here was New York, the city of his earliest memories, now transformed. His birthplace trumpeted "the power of the most extravagant of cities, rejoicing . . . in its might, its fortune, its unsurpassable conditions." One could not help but be proud of what had been achieved, but for James it was a pilgrimage whose passion was tinged with horror. James was, as George Santayana perceptively observed, a "classical" figure. He stood for the best that civilization could produce—beauty tempered by restraint; order regulated by moderation; composition based on the durable, the lasting. But this was not what he found in the commercial enthusiasm of America, where science and technology knelt as handmaidens to the altar of profit motive; where violence and plunder, both of the land and of basic human values, denigrated the quality of life to the extent that it was sufficient "to make so much money that you won't, that you don't mind anything." This, for James, was the ultimate perversion of liberty—the freedom to plunder—where the consummate, monotonous commonness of the pushing male crowd, moving in its dense mass— with the confusion carried to chaos for any intelligence, any perception; a welter of objects and sounds in which relief, detachment, dignity, meaning perished utterly and lost all rights.

But how narrow were the blinders James wore. For years he had successfully shut his eyes to the terrible effects that the Industrial Revolution had wrought on the face of Britain. Yet there he had been able to survive quite happily, securely ensconced in a tiny but dense, elite society where it was eminently possible to feel not only different but *better* than your neighbor, due to an endless series of social symbols whose underpinning was wealth masked by the qualities of breeding and style. No wonder that the only part of America where he felt truly at home was in the socially isolated island of affluence at Newport, where "the somewhat alien presence of leisure" held sway. No doubt the immaculate mugwump, H. L. Mencken, was manifestly unfair when he charged James with producing "painful psychologizings" which, "when translated into plain English, turn out to be chiefly mere kittenishness—an arch tickling of the ribs of elderly virgins—the daring of a grandma smoking marijuana." But there is something to wonder about in a large body of literature dedicated to an exhaustive analysis of leisured society. One cannot help but speculate on the sort of fiction Henry James would have created had he remained on the side of the Atlantic where he was conceived.

James's last years in England provided an emotionally refreshing denouement to his forty years of residence. On June 12, 1912, he stood in the Sheldonian Theatre at Oxford, attired in the robes of a Doctor of Letters, to hear the Public Orator of the University celebrate *fecundissimum et facundissimum scriptorem, Henricum James*. A few months later Edith Wharton, one of his closest friends, attempted to raise a large sum of money to be presented to him in honor of his seventieth birthday. It was an impulsive gesture which the embarrassed author forbade as soon as he learned what was afoot. But a presentation of sorts was not to be avoided, for James was now too eminent a lion to go unnoticed on such an anniversary. From a committee of three hundred donors, drawn from the pinnacle of English art, politics, and social life, there descended a commission to John Singer Sargent to paint a likeness of his old friend—a portrait that now rests in the English National Portrait Gallery. From this same committee James also received a symbolic "Golden Bowl," in honor of the best of his literary accomplishments, a gift which he acknowledged somewhat diffidently in a printed broadside sent to each individual who had subscribed to the honor of his name.

The Great War that erupted in Europe in 1914 was a holocaust that struck James to the quick. It seemed that civilization was about to be incinerated in a fire storm of madness. He was an old man, helpless to do anything. Mary Anderson came out of retirement to entertain the troops; John Singer Sargent was trapped in the Austrian Tyrol and continued to paint; but, for the first time in forty years of English residence, Henry James was made to feel an alien whose freedom of movement was subject to the controls of others. It was an unpleasant sensation for one who had come to think of himself as an Englishman in all things save one. But that one quality, the prize of citizenship, was something he had never been able to bring himself to accept: "Hadn't it been for the War, I should certainly have gone on as I was, taking it as the simplest and easiest and even friendliest thing, but the circumstances were utterly altered now."

Faced with new circumstances, James felt compelled to make a choice. On June 28 he wrote to his old friend Herbert Asquith, the Prime Minister, indicating his wish to become a subject of the Crown, "to testify at this crisis to the force of my attachment and devotion to England and to the cause for which she is fighting." The Prime Minister was delighted and quickly took steps to facilitate the application for naturalization. Exactly one month later Henry James incanted, *"Civis Britannicus Sum,"* and then added, "I don't feel a bit different."

James did not have long to live. Felled by a stroke in December 1915, he sank rapidly. But there was one more honor that he was still to receive. It was known that James was dying; but now that he was a British subject there was no obstacle to awarding him the Order of Merit, the rarest and highest honor that can be conferred by the British Crown on a man of letters. On the traditional New Year's Day honors list, in 1916, there appeared the name Henry James, O. M. And when Lord Bryce, the great proponent of Anglo-American unity, brought the insignia of the Order to the author's bedside, the old man was reported to have said, "Turn off the light so as to spare my blushes."

Finally, on February 28, 1916, he was gone, having died in the very block of flats where his friend Sargent would expire nine years later.

Henry James, who asserted twenty-four months before his death, "I am that queer monster, the artist, an obstinate finality, an inexhaustible sensibility." Henry James who, as T. S. Eliot said, was not a romanticizer of England out of fear or laziness but rather because "he was possessed by the vision of an ideal society; he saw (not fancied) the relations between the members of such a society. And no one, in the end, has ever been more aware . . . of the disparity between possibility and fact."

"TELL THEM TO FOLLOW, TO BE FAITHFUL, TO TAKE ME SERIOUSLY." That was the message of Henry James. It has not been forgotten.

Left: *The "Golden Bowl." Presented to Henry James by Edith Wharton and others in recognition of his greatest literary achievement. (Houghton Library, Harvard University).* Right: *The badge and insignia of the Order of Merit, presented to Henry James by King George V. (Houghton Library, Harvard University)*

6

The Grandes Dames:
Lady Randolph Churchill, Consuelo Vanderbilt, and Mary Curzon

In February 1902 a rather extraordinary advertisement appeared in the London *Daily Telegraph,* announcing to the advisers of heiresses that

> An English Peer of very old title is desirous of marrying at once a very wealthy lady: her age and looks are immaterial, but her character must be irreproachable; she must be a widow or a spinster—not a divorcee. If among your clients you know such a lady, who is willing to purchase the rank of a peeress for twenty-five thousand pounds sterling, paid in cash to her future husband, and who has sufficient wealth besides to keep up the rank of a peeress, I shall be pleased if you will communicate with me in the first instance by letter when a meeting can be arranged in your office. I beg you to keep this confidential. The peer will pay handsomely for the introduction when it is arranged.

The author of this missive was the fifth Marquess of Donegall, fast approaching his eightieth year, who was better known for his bankruptcies and alcoholic former spouses than for any achievement concomitant with his rank in society.

But the old boy did have something to sell. He was, after all, a peer of the realm six times over, who could offer a woman of substance a short marriage and a lifetime of social prestige. Small wonder, then, that ten months after taking out his advertisement, Lord Donegall was married in London to the elegant Violet Twining, a graduate of Wellesley College in Massachusetts, who is said to have agreed to support her new husband with an annual allowance of $40,000.

A marriage of convenience no doubt, but more than a few eyebrows were raised when, ten months after exchanging the hurly-burly of the chaise longue for the serenity of the nuptial bed (to paraphrase Mrs. Patrick Campbell), Lady Donegall produced a son, styled Earl of Belfast, who at the age of seven months succeeded his father as the sixth Marquess.

The Donegall marriage contract was by no means atypical for the times, though the age difference separating the bride and groom was quite extreme. The Anglo-American marriage had become a fixture of international society since the 1870s—Henry James had written about it and John Singer Sargent had painted its participants. And by the end of the Edwardian era, well over a hundred such alliances had been concluded.

The times were all too right for these events. The aristocracy of England stood on the threshold of its last great moment in history. Land, that most solid of assets, gave one position in society but scarcely any means of maintaining it in the face of declining rents and property values. Capital regeneration was necessary for many noble houses, and according to that time-honored precept "Do not marry for money but marry where money is," North America became the most likely of shopping arenas, for there fortunes were conveyed by inheritance not just to sons, as in Europe, but to daughters as well.

The new American plutocracy, far richer than most of its European counterparts, had consolidated its financial position at the end of the nineteenth century to such a degree that any material possession, however costly, was now well within its grasp. And predictably, once material passions were fully sated, new expressions, or symbols of achievements which distinguished one family from another, were eagerly sought.

How perfect a meeting of circumstances. For the British aristocracy, whose titles were thought to carry far more distinction than any of their European brethren, possessed just what the newly rich American wanted, a social preeminence based not simply on the speculative waves of finance but on the rock of primogeniture. If one's daughter were a duchess, one's grandson would without question be a duke. It was the most pleasant of certainties.

For the newly ennobled American peeress, entrance into the highest of social circles was not an impossibility. At the court of the reclusive Queen Victoria, the reins of social power were held fast in the hands of Albert Edward, Prince of Wales, that "corpulent voluptuary" as Kipling called him, who, in the words of Lord Granville, was loved by his people "because he has all the faults of which the Englishman is accused." In the Prince of Wales's circle, known commonly as the "Marlborough House Set" after his place of residence, "sweet women and dry champagne" were the order of the day.

The Prince had few official duties; the Queen, even in her dotage, saw to that. And so, with little of substance to do, life at Marlborough House was a constant party, full of glamour and glitter, but marred by a formal pomposity which bordered on the inane. Yet, for amusement and social advancement, there was no better place, and American women, so long as they were pretty, witty, and rich, were rarely denied admission, for the Prince was not nearly as socially fastidious about the pedigrees of transatlantic beauties as he was about those of his own female compatriots. "I like them," he said of American women, "because they are original and bring a little fresh air into Society. They are livelier, better educated and less hampered by etiquette . . . they are not as squeamish as their English sisters and they are better able to take care of themselves."

One great beauty to celebrate this rite of passage cynically recalled the general "classlessness" into which wealthy Americans were cast: "They were all supposed to be of one uniform type. The wife and daughters of the newly-enriched Californian miner, swathed in silks and satins, and blazing with diamonds on the smallest provocation; the cultured, refined and retiring Bostonian; the aristocratic Virginian, as full of tradition and family pride as a Percy of Northumberland or a La Rochefoucauld; the cosmopolitan and up-to-date New Yorker—all were grouped in the same category, all were considered tarred with the same brush."

She was in a position to know, for Jennie Jerome, the Lady Randolph Churchill, was fast within the Marlborough House Set and spoke with an authority based as much on experience as conviction.

She was one of three strikingly beautiful daughters (all of whom married Britons) of the fabulous Leonard Jerome, the proclaimed king of Wall Street and father of the American turf. But the destiny of the Jerome girls did not lie in the countinghouses or on the racetracks of New York. The family's instincts were far too cosmopolitan, and their social ambitions were international in scope. The Jerome women sparkled at the Parisian court of the Emperor Napoleon III, and when the Franco-Prussian War and its aftermath virtually wiped out that world, they fled to England for safety and for entertainment.

The London season traditionally ended in the first week of August, when much of Society gravitated to the tiny village of Cowes on the Isle of Wight where the three hundred members of the world's most exclusive sailing club, the Royal Yacht Squadron, kept court. Naturally enough the Jerome women were on the scene, and by 1873 their social position was sufficiently established to warrant an August 12 invitation from the officers of H.M.S. *Ariadne* to a ball given by the Prince and Princess of Wales in honor of the Czarevitch and Czarevna of All the Russias.

It was a memorable evening for Jennie, not only because of the splendor of the occasion, but because there she met and captivated Lord Randolph Churchill, the younger son of the seventh Duke of Marlborough.

Randolph Churchill, small and slim with a walrus mustache that did little to enhance his countenance, was an elegant, almost dandified, intimate of the Marlborough House Set. His polished manner bore all the marks of the assumed superiority of his class, but in the presence of Jennie's wit and beauty he found it impossible to remain aloof.

It was a love match from the outset. Jennie, both snob and sensualist, found in Randolph an ideal mate. He in return was prepared to suffer his family's disapprobation (for the Marlboroughs traditionally married into the high peerage), the blow to family pride being undoubtedly softened when questions of dowry were raised. Randolph's father, the Duke, was strapped for funds and had little to offer his

Left: *Jennie Jerome, Lady Randolph Churchill, 1854–1921. John Singer Sargent, 1856–1925. Charcoal on paper, date unknown. 14" × 10" (sight). (The National Trust, Chartwell)* **Right:** *Lord Randolph Churchill. Philip May, 1864–1903. Pen and ink, date unknown. 12" × 10". (National Portrait Gallery, London)*

younger son. It was insisted that "Miss Jerome takes the finance department under her own control," and Randolph agreed "that Jennie will have to manage the money."

Leonard Jerome was not as fabulously wealthy as everyone assumed, and, consequently, the negotiations over the marriage contract between his lawyers and those of the Duke were long, complicated, and messy. But eventually sums were agreed upon, and, in 1874, what was to be the first of a long series of Anglo-American aristocratic marriages was celebrated, the father of the bride presenting his daughter with an ornate lace parasol as an intimate remembrance of the occasion.

Lady Randolph Churchill discovered that the world in which she now moved was dominated by social rituals that seemed arcane at best: "Having been brought up in France, I was accustomed to the restrictions and chaperonage to which young girls had to submit; but I confess to thinking that as a married woman I should be able to emancipate myself entirely." She soon learned that this was not the case: "To go by oneself in a hansom was thought very 'fast' . . . not to speak of walking, which could be permitted only in quiet squares or streets. As for young girls driving anywhere by themselves, such a thing was unheard of."

The early days of the marriage were a constant gala. The Churchills were seen everywhere: at hunt balls and races; at pigeon shoots and regattas; at the opera, the ballet, the theater, and the new Four-in-Hand Coaching Club. Everywhere the Prince of Wales went so, too, did the Churchills, and it was whispered that their plethora of invitations was due not so much to Randolph's wit as to the Prince's devotion to Jennie.

Such constant intimacy was not uninterrupted, however. When Randolph's elder brother, Lord Blandford, went poaching among the Prince's mistresses and apparently impregnated the Countess of Aylesford whose tolerant husband was known as "sporting Joe," the Prince was furious and demanded that Blandford divorce his own wife and make the Countess an honest woman. Randolph felt obliged to defend his brother's all too frequently sullied honor and intemperately threatened to publish love letters between the Prince and Lady Aylesford. He even bragged to one close friend, "I have the Crown of England in my pocket." It has been suggested that Lord Randolph was less disturbed by insults to his brother's reputation than by the Prince's all too obvious attentions to Jennie, who did not object to cordial reciprocation.

Soon the affair became the talk of the Court. A duel was even suggested, but cooler heads prevailed, and the Duke of Marlborough was persuaded to accept the Vice-Royalty of Ireland, taking Randolph with him as private secretary. And so the Churchills went into temporary exile until their personae non gratae status was alleviated through a pragmatic apology by Randolph to the Prince.

At his wife's urging, Lord Randolph entered Parliament as a member for a family seat at Woodstock in Oxfordshire. And when he rose to make his maiden speech, overdressed and sporting an excessive amount of jewelry, members thought a new

Oil on canvas, 1913. 28" × 39½". (The Hon. Jacob Rothschild)

Dinner on Board the Yacht Vanderbilt *at Cowes, Isle of Wight. Jacques Émile Blanche, 1861–1942.*

Disraeli had arrived in their midst. Like Dizzy, Churchill was a captivating speaker whose effectiveness grew, with time, to dominate debates in the House. His biographer Robert Rhodes James has written, "When it was gay, he stirred it into laughter; when it was flippant, no one could exceed him in droll irreverence; when it was united and determined, he spoke with seriousness and moderation; and when it was angry, he fanned the flames until they spread into an ugly glow; when it craved a leader who would 'show them game,' Lord Randolph Churchill stood in the van."

He formed a new clique among progressive Conservatives and dubbed it the Fourth Party, whose credo was "Tory Democracy," which demanded social welfare and education, as a substitute for coercion, to quell the increasing troubles in Ireland.

In 1883, in their new, electrically lit house in Connaught Place, Randolph, Jennie, and their friends founded the Primrose League, named after Disraeli's favorite flower, a political-social organization with all the costumed trappings of a masonic lodge, wherein Conservatives of all classes could meet to discuss the issues of the day. Many dismissed it as just another attention-getting Churchill sideshow, but soon the League was counting its members in the millions. Lord Randolph's mother was made President of the Ladies Grand Council, and Jennie was installed as a Dame. It was the first effective attempt to involve women directly in English politics, and for Jennie, it was the most exciting of times: "I became a Dame President of many Habitations and used to go all over the country inaugurating them. The opening speeches were often quaint in their conceptions, a mixture of grave and gay, serious and frivolous—speeches from members of Parliament, interspersed with songs and even recitations, sometimes of a comical nature. The meeting would end with the enrollment of converts. A strange medley, the laborer and the local magnate, the county lady and the grocer's wife, would troop up to sign the roll. Politics, like charity, are great levelers."

"Trust the people and they will trust you" was the cry of Tory Democracy, and when Gladstone resigned as Prime Minister in favor of a Conservative administration led by Lord Salisbury, Randolph Churchill's power in the party was acknowledged by his appointment as Secretary of State for India. And, with the passage of time, he was elevated to the Chancellorship of the Exchequer.

But the "Wasp of Woodstock," as Randolph was known, had neither the time nor the energy to conduct his own parliamentary campaigns for reelection. And so the task devolved onto Jennie, who seized the opportunity with enthusiasm, dreaming that one day her husband would be Prime Minister.

She organized public meetings and delivered rousing speeches to the electors, first those of Woodstock, and later in campaigns in Birmingham. From door to door she canvassed every household, aggressively asking for the vote of everyone she encountered. Jennie's face was well known; she had become one of the famous "PBs"—Professional Beauties—whose photographs were sold in shops all over the kingdom. And wherever she went crowds gathered.

When her husband was successful at the polls, it was Jennie who publicly thanked his supporters: "I surpassed the fondest hopes of the suffragettes and thought I was duly elected, and I certainly experienced all the pleasure and gratification of being a successful candidate." Letters of congratulation were sent to Jennie, including one from the Prince of Wales who declared himself converted by her speeches. Even the Queen took notice of her activities, and in December 1885, because of Randolph's office, personally conferred upon her the Insignia of the Imperial Order of the Crown of India.

Lady Randolph's political successes, though a source of much personal joy, arose from the unhappiest of circumstances. Her marriage was falling apart as her husband, spending more and more time abroad with male friends, was incapable of maintaining his career. Thus Jennie, to keep up appearances, was forced into the political fray, a role she relished far more than the domestic occupations of mother and social entertainer to which society regularly assigned women of her time.

Jennie found solace with the Prince, Count Charles Kinsky, and with many other lovers. And while some speculated that Randolph's absences from England masked sexual indiscretions, no one knew at the time that he was slowly dying of syphilis contracted years before. His behavior in the House of Commons became increasingly erratic, marked by speeches interlaced with bursts of temper that bordered on the hysterical. At the very height of his power, Lord Randolph resigned office in the Salisbury cabinet, thinking, in a juvenile manner, that he could blackmail the Prime Minister into accepting his views on public policy. But it was a power play that failed miserably, and when Salisbury quietly accepted the resignation and his administration did not fall, Randolph Churchill moved out of the magic circle of power, never again to reenter it.

Photograph,
date unknown
6" × 8" (oval)
(Anita Leslie)

Lord Randolph Churchill's traveling photograph of his wife and their sons, Jack and Winston.   Unidentified photographer.

It was a mark of his alienation from Jennie that even she was not informed of his decision prior to the resignation. Like everyone else she read of her husband's futile gesture in the newspapers the morning after.

By the spring of 1894 Randolph Churchill was clearly losing his mind, and his public utterances had become an embarrassment of the highest order. Arthur Balfour, a future Prime Minister and one of Churchill's closest associates, noted sadly, "There was no curtain, no retirement, he died by inches in public."

The spectacular political career that Jennie had helped build for her husband lasted but six years. Like a meteor he rose and fell, and at 6:15 on the morning of January 24, 1895, Randolph Churchill died in his sleep at the age of forty-five.

Colored lithograph, in Vanity Fair; *June 11, 1896 14'' × 22'' (Richard Kenin)*

Cycling in Hyde Park.   A fashionable pastime for Victorian ladies of the nineties which Jennie helped popularize. Hal Hurst, 1865–?

His passing was more a release than a burden for his family, and Jennie, after a requisite period of mourning, plunged back into society with the zest of a woman liberated. The elegance of the eighties had given way to the naughtiness of the nineties. And wherever there was a fashionable avant-garde, there too could be found the irrepressible Lady Randolph.

"Ideas were in the air," observed Richard Le Gallienne. Everyone seemed "convinced that they were passing not only from one social system to another, from one morality to another, and from one religion to a dozen or none. . . . Our new-found freedom seemed to find just the expression it needed in the abandoned nonsense-chorus of Ta-ra-ra-boom-de-ay."

Queen Victoria died at the beginning of the new century, and "good old Bertie" came to the throne as King Edward VII. Jennie, along with his other close female confidantes, sat in a special box in Westminster Abbey to witness the coronation of her sovereign lord. It was a sign of the times, when mistresses could be publicly displayed at the most solemn occasions.

London became popular as a winter capital, reversing the old order of things. People began to let town houses for the summer and retreat to the countryside now made accessible by the motor car. The weekend country house party became a fact of life, and, as Jennie observed, "Mothers with broods of unmarried daughters find this kind of entertainment a better market to take them to than the heated atmosphere of the ball room."

People tended to live much more publicly than before. Everyone was interviewed, photographed, and publicly dissected. It seemed that privacy was no longer a desirable luxury, so intent was the upper class on maintaining its position that advertising now seemed necessary to sustain deference. Consequently, attendance at every flower show, bazaar, and hospital opening was now viewed as a public duty.

It was no longer sufficient to simply be rich and beautiful, for these were accidents of birth. One had to be, or at least appear to be, *earnest*. The fashionable woman attended lectures by Bernard Shaw and concerts of Wagner. Bridge and bicycling—one for the mind, the other for the body—became the craze and passion of Society. For the first time women were required to have views on political and social questions, and a revival of salons aping those of the Mesdames Geoffrin, Deffand, and Récamier, was an everyday occurrence. But how poor were these modern travesties—mere caravanserai by comparison.

If the average working man earned only a pound a week, if his family were forced to endure whole lifetimes in wretched disease-ridden slums, it was small comfort for him, no doubt, to know that he was no longer invisible to the upper classes. His numbers were now far too great. But Britain, despite a bloody nose in the Boer War, remained politically stable. And at the apogee of King Edward's reign, "more money was spent on clothes, more food was consumed, more horses were raced, more infidelity was committed, more birds were shot, more yachts were commissioned, more late hours were kept than ever before."

It was a time of extraordinary social restlessness. The desire for anything—for everything that was new caused traditions to tumble. Manners in particular were affected as old values were discarded. A nod replaced a ceremonious bow; an elaborate curtsy gave way to a familiar handshake among women. And, as Jennie herself noted, "The carefully worded, beautifully written invitation of fifty years ago is dropped in favor of the generally garbled telephone message such as 'will Mrs S. dine with Lady T. and bring a man.'"

It was an ironic commentary on the times that Edwardian society took great delight in holding magnificent fancy-dress balls at which famous characters of history were portrayed. Thousands of dollars were spent on costumes and jewels for these events. Some came dressed as their own ancestors, without the slighest hint of self-consciousness. Others opted for figures from ancient history—Jennie's favorite was the Empress Theodora. It was society playfully emulating itself. One ball had as its theme "British Society Beauties Dressed as Famous Men in History," at which Jennie appeared "as a roistering Spanish cavalier. She wore black silk tights, doublet and hose, a dark velvet cloak trimmed with gold; had a sword, a great diamond blazing in her black sombrero, with its drooping feathers; diamond buckles on her pretty shoes, and a black moustache waxed and ferociously curled, like the Kaiser's."

Such circuses were by no means infrequent. The time and seriousness that were devoted to their organization were ample testimony of how avid was the pursuit of diversion and pleasure by the Edwardians. It was as if they had nothing else to do but give public demonstrations of their opulence.

Life after Randolph was by no means sexually empty for Jennie. Her oft-kimonoed figure continued to attract numerous lovers. And even as she aged, young men cooed about her hoping for favors. She married twice more, to men so far her junior that they could have been her sons. "Of course, the glamour won't last forever," she told a friend, "but why not take what you can, and not make yourself or anyone else unhappy when the next stage arrives."

Beyond the bedroom her life was also immensely fulfilled, for Jennie was blest with great creative faculties. She wrote plays which opened in London's West End and received more than just polite notices. She was instrumental in organizing the National Theatre Committee and its Shakespearian Memorial Theatre Ball, held at the Albert Hall in June 1911, an event which was remembered as one of the last magnificent gasps of Edwardian opulence prior to the Great War.

A highly successful impresario, Jennie raised a fortune for the Shakespeare Memorial fund by recreating an Elizabethan city—a product as much of fantasy as of fact—in the great exhibition arenas at Earls Court. Therein the world of "Merrie England" was relived by the fashionables of society, who adored dressing up as medieval knights and their ladies. Even the fantastical excesses of Marie Antoinette at Versailles paled by comparison. For Jennie, like so many of her American compatriots, felt a strong desire to preserve the best of British cultural history, stronger than did many of the Englishmen she encountered, who took much of it for granted.

She founded and edited *The Anglo Saxon Review,* one of the most beautifully designed, if financially ill-fated, journals of the fin de siècle, in whose literary pages articles from figures as eminent as Henry James, Algernon Swinburne, Cecil Rhodes, and even the Prime Minister, Lord Rosebury, could be found.

The outbreak of the Boer War touched her personally, for not only her eldest son, Winston, but also her future second husband, George Cornwallis-West, were on active duty. Jennie, always the most enthusiastic of women, yearned to be in the

Jennie (seated) *surrounded by the cast of her play* His Borrowed Plumes. *The star, Mrs. Patrick Campbell* (back row, center), *later married Jennie's second husband, George Cornwallis-West. Photograph, in the* Tatler, *July 14, 1909. (Raymond Mander and Joe Mitchenson Theatre Collection Trust)*

thick of the fray. She adopted and promoted a plan to provide an American hospital ship to care for the wounded in South Africa. What better testament of the strength of the transatlantic commonwealth, she argued, than the creation of a uniquely American-funded vessel to aid the British nation in its fight for "the rights and liberties of the Anglo-Saxon people." She knew the war had its opponents, but the moral rights and wrongs of the issue were far outweighed by her dreams of standing near the battlefield as a modern Florence Nightingale.

Jennie's committee of wealthy American women in Britain organized all sorts of entertainments to raise the £30,000 deemed necessary to secure and outfit a suitable vessel. Jennie blithely circumvented all the red tape that an official governmental action would have entailed. She wrote to her distant cousin, Theodore Roosevelt, the Governor of New York, asking for aid. And when he was unable to oblige, she captivated Bernard N. Baker, the founder of Baltimore's Atlantic Transport Company, who was sufficiently smitten to not only donate one of his company's ships but to throw in a complete crew as well at a personal expense of at least £3,000 a month.

The vessel, christened the *Maine* in memory of the ship sunk in Havana harbor, was an old cattle transport requiring major conversion. American nurses were obtained through the good offices of Mrs. Whitelaw Reid, who had supplied staff for the Spanish-American War from her father's Mills School of Nursing. Jennie launched a frontal attack on both the Admiralty and the War Office, with whose respective heads she was on a first-name basis, and secured an official designation for the *Maine* as a British military hospital ship. This in turn entitled her to supplies and an escort to South Africa.

Lady Randolph sported a white nurse's uniform. It was as if her life were filled with one costume after another. She was immensely pleased with the success of her venture, as a gesture from her compatriots, "for the *Maine* is to be essentially an American women's ship. We are not only to aid the wounded, but are to show the world that American women can do the good work better than anyone else can do it." The new King was also pleased that one of his most intimate friends should be so usefully occupied, and invested Jennie as a Lady of Grace of the Order of the Hospital of St. John of Jerusalem together with the insignia of the Royal Red Cross.

The sovereign was also increasingly considerate to young Winston Churchill, whose career was to be Jennie's project of longest standing. Winston would be everything his father was, and a great deal more if Jennie could help it. She placed his books with publishers and saw to it that they received good notices from reviewers who were old friends and confidants. When the young man ran for Parliament, there was Jennie on the stump, haranguing the crowds and pressing the flesh with

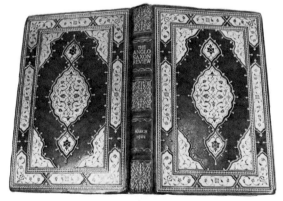

The Anglo Saxon Review. *Founded and edited by Lady Randolph Churchill, it was the most elaborate of all Edwardian periodicals. Vol. VIII, March 1901. (The Winston Churchill Memorial and Library, Fulton, Missouri)*

*Oil on canvas, 1906
87¼'' × 67''
(The Metropolitan
Museum of Art; Gift
of Consuelo Vanderbilt
Balsan, 1946)*

*Consuelo, Duchess of Marlborough, 1877–1964, with her younger son, Lord
Ivor Spencer-Churchill.   Giovanni Boldini, 1845–1931.*

more confidence than most seasoned campaign managers. When political dinners
were required for Winston to meet the powers within his party, it was Jennie who
acted the part of hostess. She was her son's alter ego, his ever-present mentor and
guide, and the font of all his social and political connections. Jennie lived a second
political life through Winston, and it is no small wonder that when, at the end of his
career, the great prime minister reminisced on his success, he ascribed it in toto to
the omnipresent efforts of his brilliant mother.

After the Great War, society was once again transformed by an overbearing desire
for speed, efficiency, and newness. Great banquets in private mansions gave way to
sophisticated dining in exclusive restaurants. New dances, like the Castle Walk and

Turkey Trot, became all the rage, and wherever the avant-garde of high bohemia played, there was the irrepressible Jennie.

She developed new acquaintances, like Scott and Zelda Fitzgerald, Igor Stravinsky, and James Joyce. No doubt it was necessary, for death was overtaking many old stalwarts of her crowd. But until the very end, in 1921, Jennie remained the elegant creature who had captivated Randolph Churchill a half-century earlier. She was one of those Americans whose penchant for all that was new left an indelible mark on the British social and political scene. And it is not hard to understand why, at the zenith of her career, Jennie was hailed by the press as "the most influential Anglo-Saxon woman in the World."

Jennie Churchill had not merely adjusted to England, she had seized it by the throat and demanded its obeisance. Her niece by marriage, Consuelo Vanderbilt, was not nearly as fortunate. Born into the family of the fabulously wealthy William Kissam Vanderbilt, the shy, eighteen-year-old Consuelo was forced into marriage with the ninth Duke of Marlborough by a mother whose social ambitions far exceeded those of her offspring.

In the cattle market of international marriage, Consuelo was a prime cut. She was brought, not to say bought, into London socially through the ministrations of Min-

Royal Visit to Blenheim Palace. The Prince of Wales is seated in the center, to the right; next to him is Mary Curzon; and Jennie and Consuelo are seated at the far left. Unidentified photographer. Photograph, November 1896 (Photograph courtesy the Duke of Marlborough)

nie, Lady Paget, and Consuelo, Duchess of Manchester, both Americans by birth who, being perennially short of cash, were rumored to be the organizers, for a hefty fee, of the most select and private marriage-through-introduction bureau in the realm. Both were leaders of British society, intimate with the Prince of Wales, and thus in a position to make just the right contacts necessary for brilliant, if not connubially happy, alliances. If ever there were characters who approximated Thackeray's Becky Sharp, they were these two redoubtable ladies.

It was at Lady Paget's home in Belgrave Square that Consuelo first met her future husband. Later he followed her back to America, and as she recalled, "It was in the comparative quiet of an evening at home that Marlborough proposed to me in the Gothic room whose atmosphere was so propitious to sacrifice."

After concluding a marriage contract highly favorable to himself, Marlborough agreed to a wedding on November 5, 1895. But the ceremony was moved up one day because the Duke discovered that Guy Fawkes Day fell on the fifth. Consuelo commented, "I could not understand why Guy Fawkes's attempt to blow up Parliament almost three centuries before should affect the date of our marriage, but this was only the first of a series of, to me, snobbish prejudices inspired by a point of view opposed to my own."

Consuelo soon learned that the Duke intended his wife to possess just as strong a sense of class-consciousness as he did. "My husband spoke of some two hundred families whose lineage and whose ramifications, whose patronymics and whose titles I should have to learn." And of course there was Blenheim Palace itself, the formidable seat of the Churchill family since the early eighteenth century, where Consuelo was to be mistress of numerous servants, each possessing his own distinct place in the hierarchy of the Duke's establishment. It was a difficult adjustment "from the prim monastic existence" enforced in the Vanderbilt household: "We slept in rooms with high ceilings; we dined in dark rooms with high ceilings; we dressed in closets without ventilation; we sat in long galleries or painted saloons and when guests were present no fewer than four changes of clothes were required for the various occasions of the day each centering around a vast repast."

Life was dictated by a highly formalized ritual. The mornings began with prayers in the chapel at 9:30 and, if one overslept, there was a mad scramble, "and I often had to run across the house to the chapel fastening the last hook or button, and ramming on a hat. At the toll of the bell housemaids would drop their dusters, footmen their trays, housemen their pails, carpenters their ladders, electricians their tools, kitchenmaids their pails, laundrymaids their linen, and all rush to reach the chapel in time."

Marlborough dressed his wife as one would decorate an expensive poodle. He carefully selected extravagant gowns from the designs of Jean Worth and matched them with precious stones and furs as a symbolic advertisement of his family's financial renascence. A small blackamoor dressed in oriental costume and turban was imported from Egypt to follow the Duchess everywhere as her page, and few

Watercolor, 1909
15½'' × 10''
(All Souls College,
Oxford)

"Once a Proconsul, Always a Proconsul." A caricature of George, Marquess Curzon of Kedleston. Max Beerbohm, 1872–1956.

were the days that passed when Consuelo was not reminded by the family that it was her primary duty to bear Marlborough a son and heir for, as the old Dowager Duchess bluntly put it, "It would be intolerable to have that little upstart Winston [Jennie's boy] become Duke." On that score, at least, the Churchills were to have little cause to complain, for Consuelo was born of fertile stock.

Yet Blenheim was by no means a prison. The Marlboroughs were frequently seen in public and, whenever the Duchess appeared, public men of all political persuasions flocked to her with attentive interest.

One house to which she was particularly drawn was that of George Curzon, the future Viceroy of India, and his American wife Mary, who was as fabulously rich as she was hauntingly beautiful—so much so that she was driven to complain, "People discuss my looks as though I were an oleographic."

She was the daughter of Levi Leiter who, as a partner of Marshall Field, had made a sizable fortune in the Chicago mercantile mart, and then retired to invest heavily in property, leaving a fortune at his death of between $25 and $30 million. Like Leonard Jerome, Levi Leiter had three daughters, all of whom married Englishmen, and on each he settled an extremely handsome sum.

Mary Leiter met the thirty-one-year-old George Curzon in a London ballroom (some say in Washington) in the summer of 1890, but it was not until five years later, after a two-year engagement, that the two approached the marriage altar.

George Curzon was punctiliously careful in all things, marriage not being the least of them. One newspaper described him as having "the complexion of a milkmaid, the stature of an Apollo and the activity of an Under-Secretary." His manner was formed in the grand style, with phrases drawn from classical allusions, and, like Gladstone, the majestically virile Curzon spoke to individuals as if they were a public meeting.

He was strikingly good-looking and, from his earliest days at Oxford, seemed marked down, at least by himself, for greatness. The oft-quoted rhyme (though itself a slight misquotation)

My name is George Nathaniel Curzon
I am a most superior person
My cheek is pink, my hair is sleek
I dine at Blenheim once a week

accurately portrays Curzon's own sense of self-worth. In constant pain from an adolescent accident and forced to wear a stiffening back brace which added to his haughty appearance, Curzon was convinced that his class was endowed with divine sanction to carry out the important work of state affairs. Words like "responsibility" and "duty" appeared on his lips on all occasions with perfect sincerity. And for those who came within his orbit, there was a compelling urge to believe that all that the charismatic Curzon stood for was the best in society.

Though his father was a peer, Curzon's upbringing had been essentially that of the mid-Victorian vicarage. His biographer Harold Nicolson wrote, of the family seat, "Its floors may well have been of opus alexandrinum and its columns of alabaster;

Oil on canvas, 1901
32'' × 28''
(Lady Alexandra
Metcalfe [daughter])

Mary Victoria Leiter, the Lady Curzon of Kedle-
ston, 1870–1906. Franz-Seraph von Lenbach,
1836–1904.

yet Kedleston was none the less a vicarage; there was more than a breath of Calvinism in the air; and Curzon's childhood was thus disciplined, narrowed, intimidated, uncomforted and cold." But though his early parliamentary career under Lord Salisbury's administration predicted high office in the future (Curzon was the youngest Privy Councillor in living memory), he was somewhat in need of adequate funds to support an exalted station, his father, Lord Scarsdale, being unable to provide properly for his son and heir. No doubt Mary Leiter's patrimony was an immense attraction, but there was more to her character that suited Curzon than just money. She was in every way the ideal mate for such an anointed creature.

Consuelo Marlborough recalled that Mary Leiter, after her marriage,

> had shed her American characteristics more completely than I was to find myself able to do. Wholly absorbed in her husband's career she had subordinated her personality to his to a degree I would have considered beyond an American woman's powers of self-abnegation. I was moved by the great love they bore each other. Her admiration for her brilliant husband's conspicuous attainments, for strong partisanship, her sympathetic understanding of his faults, the humor with which she accepted the secondary role he assigned her, even in the domestic duties usually delegated to women, were altogether admirable.

George Curzon was indeed an odd paterfamilias. His wife was excluded from virtually all the domestic arrangements of the house. He hired the servants; kept the household accounts; selected the colors for the walls of 1 Carlton House Terrace, the London mansion overlooking St. James's Park bought for them by Mary's father; fastened cork to the backs of chairs to prevent scraped walls; issued orders as to meals; and meticulously supervised every aspect of their domestic life.

His wife obediently accepted every foible, and Curzon crowed, "Give me a girl that knows a woman's place and does not yearn for trousers. Give me, in fact, Mary." It was enough to see her as a decorative emblem, pursued, admired, and adored, yet constant in her devotion to him. "For me," Curzon told friends, "the American flag is all stars and no stripes."

In the summer of 1898, Curzon was offered the supreme appointment in the gift of the British government, the viceroyalty of India. He was the first commoner to be offered the post, but was soon elevated to the Irish peerage (so that he might continue as a member of the House of Commons) as the Baron Curzon of Kedleston, a title he was to make famous. His wife, now a peeress of the realm, exclaimed with restrained humor, "Oh! the ladyships, I feel like a ship in full sail on the high seas of dignity."

India was the most brilliant jewel in the British imperial crown, and the Viceroy, as the living embodiment of the throne, took precedence over all other servants of Her Majesty on the subcontinent. In his person was invested the font of all honors,

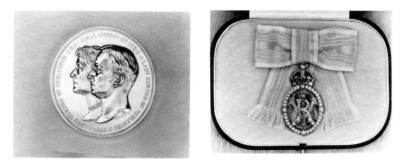

Left: *Medallion commemorating Lord and Lady Curzon's assumption of the viceroyalty of India. Allan Wyon, 1843–1907. Silver, 1899. 2" diameter. (The Rt. Hon. Viscount Scarsdale).* Right: *Insignia of a Lady of the Imperial Order of the Crown of India. (Her Majesty Queen Elizabeth II)*

as Master of the Orders of the Indian Empire and the Star of India. It was in the hands of the Viceroy—as *de facto* prime minister, president, and commander-in-chief—to direct, all but absolutely, the ship of state.

If Lord Curzon required a splendid reminder of the inheritance that was entrusted into his hands, he had only to wait for the afternoon of January 3, 1899, when the state carriage bore him and his Vicereine (or Vice-queen, as Mary preferred to think of herself) through streets lined with American and British flags to the entrance of Government House in Calcutta for the first time. Amid a tumultuous welcome sounded by the thousands of the city, Curzon surveyed his honor guard drawn from every regiment in India. Standing on foot, mounted on horse, perched on huge painted elephants, soldiers from across the face of the subcontinent, the Curzons saw them all—Punjabis and Mahrattis, Bengalis, Pathans, and the famous Nepalese Gurkhas. The tears that so frequently flooded the Viceroy's eyes on emotional occasions were very much in evidence: "I suddenly saw what had come into my hands, and what prodigies of energy and inspiration would be needed on my part to guide them."

That evening Curzon, dressed in his jacket of gold and crimson covered with the sashes of his office and a jeweled cloak of sky blue, and accompanied by his wife resplendent in her peacock gown and tiara, slowly descended into the great hall to receive the obeisance of the Queen-Empress's vassals and lieutenants. In the eyes of the Viceroy there could be nothing more glorious, for, in his own words, "All was novelty, brave hopes and high aspirations."

Mary Curzon was not nearly so enthusiastic, for "The lot of a Viceroy is one of absolute aloofness and everyone is in mortal funk of the august being. Being a Yankee I can't understand it but I manage to assume the necessary amount of awful respect for His X when we appear in public."

However real the responsibilities assigned to the viceregal couple, the amount of ceremonial required was absolutely staggering. At Calcutta, where the court was kept for the first three months of each year in a building ironically modeled on Curzon's own seat in Derbyshire, a personal entourage of almost nine hundred individuals, a bodyguard considered by many to be better outfitted than the Queen's own Household Cavalry, and a complete band which serenaded the Curzons during each meal were maintained. The Viceroy never left Government House without an escort of at least eighteen guards, outriders, and postilions, and for the servants of the house there was a special scarlet livery emblazoned with the golden viceregal monogram.

Every Thursday there was an official state dinner, with slightly less formal dinners on most other evenings. Each fortnight saw at least one dance which, together with state garden parties, balls, receptions, and levees for hundreds of individuals at a time, completely filled the social calendar which George Curzon so greatly relished.

It was monumentally expensive to run the viceroyalty. At the end of the first eighteen months of his appointment, Curzon calculated that he was more than £8,000 out of pocket, which is not surprising when one considers the lavishness of his entertainments. In one month alone, 3,500 meals were served to guests and residents at Government House. Clearly no such establishment could have been maintained without the constant support of Lady Curzon's personal fortune.

But the Vicereine was growing increasingly disenchanted as the months passed. "It's all very well for 'royalty,' " she complained, "they're born to it. They've been brought up to stand for hours and to walk for miles round exhibitions." It was not merely the endless socializing that demoralized her. As the weather turned hot each

Lady Curzon in her famous "Peacock" dress, worn at her husband's first levee in Calcutta. Jeakins, dates unknown. Photograph, date unknown. (Photograph courtesy Museum of London)

The Viceregal lodge at Simla, in the Himalayan hills. *(Photograph courtesy India Office Library and Records, London)*

April, the government and the court removed for six months to the viceregal lodge at Simla, a forty-eight hours' journey from Calcutta, in the Himalayan hills. There was a sense of escape in Simla. "I can live on views for five years," Mary wrote; but whenever government business took the Curzons away from their hilltop retreat, the lethal furnace of the Indian plain made life all but unbearable. In the autumn of 1900 Bombay was stifling. "Oh, the heat, the heat!" Mary complained, "I am getting more used to it, but dressing in it is simply awful, and with broad swift rivers running down all over you it is hard to appear dry and smiling at a daily dinner party."

Finally in 1901, ill health forced Mary Curzon to return temporarily to England. There was little magic or mystery in being required to remain forever gracious in the face of increasing pain. After an extended convalescence she did return to India to witness her husband's triumph, but it was to prove a fatal mistake.

In 1903 Lord Curzon staged at Delhi, the ancient imperial capital of the Moguls, a great durbar, or gathering, to proclaim the accession of King Edward VII as Emperor of All India. The external trappings of power, the flash of ceremony—these were the things that were closest to the Viceroy's heart. He was, for his time, the most brilliant of public relations men. Even the most minor details were given personal attention. To his superiors in London Curzon reported, "You would be amused at the questions I have to decide . . . the design of a railway, the width of a road, the pattern of a carving, the colour of a plaster, the planting of a flower bed, the decoration of a pole—all this along side big questions affecting the movement or accommodation of tens of thousands of people." Even the question of appropriate music was referred to the Viceroy. He rejected "Onward, Christian Soldiers" because he considered the lyric "Thrones and Crowns may perish—Kingdoms rise and wane" unsuitable for a celebration of the British imperium.

The durbar ceremonies lasted over a fortnight, but the chief occasion was the day of the Viceroy's proclamation of the King-Emperor's coronation. The Australian artist Mortimer Menpes was in Delhi on that day. He recalled that, by ten in the morning,

> The roads were thick with traffic of all lands—silver and gold carriages carrying the chiefs and their attendants in gold embroidered coats and turbans weighted with precious stones; smartly-equipped landaus and victorias containing British officers, civil and military, smothered with orders; judges; generals; governors and consuls; distinguished foreign visitors; representatives from Europe and the far West, Japan, Siam, Afghanistan, Burma, Baluchistan, and almost every part of the world; men on camels; natives in tightly-packed wooden carts; regiments of cavalry, British and native. It was one continuous stream.

In the horseshoe-shaped amphitheater twelve thousand guests sat expectantly, while outside the city walls thirty thousand men of the British and Indian armies awaited the arrival of the viceregal procession. The general splendor of the event was so all-encompassing that it took little imagination to transport one back through time to the court of the Mogul emperors. Only the presence of numerous still

From all over the Indian Empire, rajahs and maharajahs, princes and potentates gathered within the walls of Delhi in a great durbar called to celebrate the accession of the King-Emperor, Edward VIII, to the throne of India. (Photograph courtesy India Office Library and Records, London)

photographers, and even a motion picture crew, firmly set the occasion within the twentieth century.

A huge military band of some two thousand pieces began to play "See the Conquering Hero Comes," and, at eleven o'clock, into the arena marched, first, the Imperial Cadet Corps, followed by the ancient veterans of the Indian Mutiny, the men who upheld the Raj through heat, battle, and pestilence. They were greeted by a cheer so great that "women wept hysterically and strong men sobbed." Lord Curzon was never a man to underplay theatrical effect.

When the sun reached its crest in the sky, a shrill whine of bagpipes, fifes, and drums announced the arrival of the Viceroy's guard of honor, the Gordon Highlanders. The band struck up the national anthem, and the guests of honor, Their Royal Highnesses the Duke and Duchess of Connaught, arrived in a state carriage to take their place on the dais.

And then a moment of silence pregnant with expectation. In the distance a cloud of dust rose, stirred up beneath the hoofs of the Viceroy's bodyguard drawn from the regiment of the Fourth Dragoons. The viceregal carriage, drawn by four matched Arabian horses and escorted by outriders draped in gold and scarlet, passed through the gates of the imperial enclosure as a royal salute cascaded across the Delhi plain. Once seated on the viceregal throne, Curzon signaled his bandmaster, and, with a roll of drums and a flourish of trumpets, a royal herald in full livery followed by an entourage of thirteen attendants approached the dais, a silver mace held in his hand as a symbol of office. The proclamation of Edward VII was read out to the now silent throng. And when the herald concluded, a second flourish of

With a flourish of trumpets and the beating of drums, a royal herald proclaims Edward VII Emperor of all India. (Photograph courtesy India Office Library and Records, London)

trumpets was sounded; the royal standard was unfurled and, as the spectators rose in unison, the national anthem was slowly repeated.

The Viceroy delivered one of his predictable speeches, more a sermon than a statement of policy, glorifying the empire on which the sun never set. Most of the native rulers present evinced little comprehension of Curzon's rhetoric. They were there to pay court to the living icon of the King-Emperor. One by one they approached the dais, and Mortimer Menpes recalled seeing them all:

> First came the ruler of Deccan, His Highness the Nizam of Hyderabad, a loyal prince noticeable for the extreme simplicity of his dress. He was followed by the great Mahratta prince, the Gaekwar of Baroda, in a white dress with a red turban and most magnificent jewels. His is one of the richest states in India. Then came His Highness the Raja of Mysore, a man with very large dominions; the Maharaja of Kashmir; the Rajput princes; the Mahratta chiefs, the Sikhs; the Indian Mussulmans; a striking figure, Her Highness the Begum of Bhopal, who laid a jewelled casket at the feet of Lord Curzon; Pathan chiefs; Shans from Burma . . .[and on and on].

As a chapter in the ritual of the state, truly it was, in the words of one of Curzon's biographers, "the high noon of empire." But for the American Vicereine, who knew more of what it felt to be royalty than any of her compatriots, the durbar, gorgeous and imperial though it was, proved to be nothing more than a great trial and strain on her fragile health.

Shortly before the ceremony she wrote, "Every bit of my vitality is gone, and I am iller than I have ever been and simply can't get back to life. But I believe absolutely in my power of 'coming up to time' or 'answering my ring' as an actor does in the wings of a theatre. Some day, though, the bell will go and I shall not appear, as India I know slowly but surely murders women. But I suppose many humble and inconsequent lives must always go into the foundations of all great works and great buildings and great achievements." It was a moving and sadly all too accurate prognostication. Slowly, but irrevocably, life seeped out of Mary Curzon's body, and she died in London in July 1906 at the age of thirty-six.

Mary Curzon defined her life entirely in terms of its utility to her husband's career. She was never particularly happy either in England or India, where her role as a decorative object was constantly reinforced. But so long as the "great work," which her fortune had made possible for George Curzon, was carried out, there was a sense of contentment and accomplishment.

No doubt the degree to which Lady Curzon abnegated her personality was extreme, even for the times in which she lived. Consuelo Marlborough, for example, found it impossible to suppress what she regarded as American democratic traits in her personality. Eventually she divorced her husband to become an active figure in the women's rights movement: founding women's hostels (one of which she named after Mary Curzon), promoting institutions for women's education, writing articles, lecturing to public assemblies, and even successfully standing for political office as a Liberal member of the London County Council.

For any American heiress in the late nineteenth century, it was a great social coup to be accepted for love or money, or both, into the aristocracy of England. But the challenge was to avoid being transformed into an ornament, a mere bibelot valued more for her purchase price than for her intrinsic merit. A few were successful; a great many were not. But for those whose only ambition was social success measured in terms of courts and coronets, England was *the* central arena, where fact and fantasy were coeternal—one frequently mistaken for the other—and where individuals who were financially blessed could play at life in an endless costumed charade. This generation, prior to the commencement of the Great War, was certainly the last to enjoy such a timeless intellectual and emotional luxury, for theirs was a fragile world which could not survive unaltered amid the challenges and cultural chaos of the modern era.

Consuelo signing up as a member of the women's suffrage movement. Unidentified photographer. Photograph, date unknown. 9½" × 7⅜". (Library of Congress)

7

The Butterfly:
James McNeill Whistler

Fly away, butterfly, back to Japan
Tempt not a pinch at the hand of a man,
And strive not to sting ere you die away.
So pert and so painted, so proud and so pretty,
To brush the bright down from your wings were a pity—
Fly away, butterfly, fly away!

—Algernon Swinburne

He stood posturing in white duck trousers partially covered by a black frock coat—a "harmony" in black and white, as he called it. His hands were covered with yellow gloves, one of which held, ever so languidly, a wandlike walking stick, more an Elizabethan staff of office than a contemporary article of dress. His hair was a mass of black ringlets, save one precious white lock preened into prominence just above his forehead. And in one eye was a gleaming monocle, enhancing the ferocious grin that spread out below it—an amalgam, as one of his biographers observed, "of arrogance, aggressiveness, isolation and insecurity; of perfectionist, poseur, poet and prophet."

"Fame," he said, "even if artificial, is not only a balm, it is a tonic." And during his lifetime there was no one, not even the irrepressible Oscar Wilde, who had such a flair for self-advertisement as did James McNeill Whistler, the perennial Victorian outsider.

Some thought Whistler effeminate, so fastidious was he of his appearance. Few were those who saw that behind the strutting of the dandy was the perfectionist incarnate, who demanded as much finish in himself as he did in his art and his writing.

Scornful of the values that permeated the Victorian mind, Whistler was no acolyte to the rural idyll of the English countryside. A pure metropolitan who celebrated sensibility over sentiment, he was, as John Butler Yeats wrote in 1914, "a true artist, he lived in a world where the truth fully expressed is a truth murdered; his function not to represent but always to suggest. . . ."

Oil on canvas, 1897
67'' × 37''
(The Brooklyn
Museum; Gift of A.
Augustus Healy,
1909)

James McNeill Whistler, 1834–1903.
Giovanni Boldini, 1842–1931.

He could not explain his pictures. The viewer either understood, appreciated, and experienced them or not—there was no other course—for Whistler did not stare at nature, and "You must not stare at his pictures," said the critic Arthur Symons. His were the most unique of hands that could, with a stick of pastel, the point of a needle or pencil, or a brush dipped in oil or watercolor, create an art that was truly international. He founded no school in the real sense of the word, but left many followers convinced that he had taught them to *see* for the first time. For James McNeill Whistler, while ironically not a Briton, was no less than the greatest artist to emerge in England during Queen Victoria's imperium.

Like John Singer Sargent, Whistler was a cosmopolitan: born in America into a peripatetic family destined for expatriation, raised in the Russia of the Czars, artistically educated in France, and for years a practicing artist in England. There was little of the Yankee in Whistler; yet he resolutely retained what was only a technical citizenship, nostalgically reminding others that he was not only an American, but a West Point man to boot (despite the fact that he had been expelled from the military academy). But being an American in Europe, an American who never intended to return home from a self-imposed exile, had its purpose, for it reinforced the sense of alienation endemic to a personality which would dedicate *The Gentle Art of Making Enemies* to "the rare Few, who, early in life, had rid Themselves of the Friendship of the Many": how consummate a self-portrait.

George Washington Whistler was a paragon of respectability. A military man and a civil engineer, he fathered four children, three of whom survived, all as expatriates in England. Major Whistler hoped and expected that his children would be as estimable and God-fearing as himself. It was a reasonable expectation. His eldest son became a physician; his daughter the wife of the British artist-surgeon, Sir Francis Seymour-Hayden. But for his youngest son, born in July 1834 and christened the following November as James Abbott (to which he later added McNeill), conventionality was not to be the order of the day. Jimmy Whistler revolted against authority whenever and wherever he encountered it. A romantic of the first order, he denied what was an uncontestable birth amid the smoky chimneys of Lowell, Massachusetts, and placed his nativity instead in the more salubrious southern clime of Maryland. Somehow it was more agreeable in his mind's eye to be a southern gentleman than a bourgeois Yankee.

His removal to Europe in the 1850s, after a series of abortive apprenticeships in America, was eminently predictable. It was still the fashion to study art abroad—America remained, more or less, culturally impoverished, and the exotic appeal of ancient civilizations was hard to resist. But Whistler's pilgrimage was a far cry from that of Henry James. Rank, privilege, and leisure were foreign concepts to be despised. Creative genius—that was the only idol worth courting with revolutionary fervor.

First it was to Paris, with Courbet and Fantin-Latour as his intimates. Whistler read the amoral criticism of Théophile Gautier and discovered art inherent in the poems of Charles Baudelaire. From Fantin-Latour he imbibed the credo that the true artist made art out of nature rather than merely recording or idealizing God's handiwork. And through his friends Whistler learned of the techniques practiced at the atelier of Lecoq de Boisbaudran, wherein light, in its multifarious intensities, was the ultimate determinant of the quality of the artist's colors.

But if Paris was essential to the development of Whistler's aesthetics, London was equally important to the maintenance of his corporeal being. For when funds were short, food scarce, and creditors obdurate, it was to the British capital that Jimmy Whistler fled, to the warmth and succor of the Sloane Street home of his brother-in-law, Francis Seymour-Hayden.

Etching, 1859,
included in Sixteen
Etchings of Scenes
on the Thames and
Other Subjects,
1871
5⅞'' × 8⅞''
(Library of Congress)

Black Lion Wharf.   James McNeill Whistler, 1834–1903.

Etching, 1859,
included in Sixteen
Etchings of Scenes
on the Thames and
Other Subjects,
1871
5'' × 7⅞''
(Library of Congress)

Limehouse.   James McNeill Whistler, 1834–1903.

Oil on canvas, 1861
28'' × 40''
(Mr. and Mrs. John
Hay Whitney)

Wapping.   James McNeill Whistler, 1834–1903.

The Hayden home, set on the dividing line between the comfort of Knightsbridge and the splendor of Belgravia, was about a mile from the riparian towpaths of the Thames. It was the transparent magic of London's river, flowing quietly in sharp contrast to the grim urban crudities of the Industrial Revolution which bound it, that captivated Whistler's imagination. Hayden did not share these visions. He required the upriver tranquillity of Fulham and Richmond for his etchings, while Whistler plunged downstream from Chelsea to the noisy wharves, factories, and warehouses of Wapping and Rotherhithe whose dank and seamy realism defied idealization.

It was there that Whistler completed his *Thames Set* of etchings and drypoints that did much to launch his career as an artist in England. But of equal importance, it was on the wharves of dockland that he painted a "secret" work, as he described it in a letter to Fantin-Latour, which he called *Wapping.*

One of Whistler's models for the painting was Joanna Hiffernan, a remote young Irishwoman whose beauty, accentuated by a striking head of copper-colored hair, entranced the painter. Whistler painted Jo in deep décolletage, and when friends warned him that such immodesty could never be admitted to the walls of the Academy, he retorted that, if the painting were rejected on such grounds, he would open the bodice more and more each year until he was elected an academician who could hang it himself. It was not an opportunity he was ever to enjoy.

From 1860 to 1871, Jo became both his model and his mistress, and when relations with his brother-in-law deteriorated to the breaking point (two such opposite personalities could never have long endured under the same roof), Whistler took Jo with him to Paris in 1862 and there painted her as *The White Girl: Symphony in White No. 1*. The painting, which marked the commencement of his consciously formulated theory of color harmony, was refused at the Royal Academy that year; but the following season, after it was again denied entrance at the Paris Salon, Whistler took it to the now famous Salon des Refusés, where it attracted almost as much attention as Manet's *Déjeuner sur l'Herbe*.

It was the critic Paul Mantz who described the painting as a "Symphony in White." Whistler, who was receptive to the use of musical titles, from his readings of Baudelaire, adopted Mantz's description as his own and used it with variants on many subsequent works. Symphonies, harmonies, nocturnes, arrangements—he painted them all, perhaps the most famous being the portrait of the artist's mother entitled *Arrangement in Grey and Black No. 1*.

As he told Frank Harris, "One wants the spirit, the aroma, don't ye know. . . . If you paint a young girl, youth should scent the room; a thinker, thoughts should be in

Oil on canvas, 1862 84½'' × 42½'' (The National Gallery of Art, Washington; Harris Whittemore Collection)

The White Girl: Symphony in White No. 1. James McNeill Whistler, 1834–1903.

the air; an aroma of the personality. . . . And with all that, it should be a picture, a pattern, a harmony only a painter could conceive. . . . I sometimes say an arrangement in black and white or blue and gold, don't ye know."

In February 1863 Whistler leased, first, 7, and later, 2 Lindsey Row (now Cheyne Walk)—two small dwellings adjacent to the once fabulous Lindsey House straddling the Thames near the wooden piers of Battersea Bridge. These were the first of many Chelsea houses he was to occupy, all of which provided cheap rents and easy access to the river, his object of continuous devotion. It was there, the following year, that Whistler, plunging into new experiences, painted an impressionistic self-portrait of *The Artist in the Studio* with Jo and another model, dubbed "La Japonaise," grouped together in a study of grays and whites, intended to shock the academicians. Whistler wrote to Fantin-Latour that he intended it as a preparatory sketch for a much larger finished work, but, like so many of his plans, it was not brought to fruition.

Proximity to the Thames was not the only advantage of life in Lindsey Row. Whistler and his mistress found themselves within short walking distance of the bizarre Tudor House of Dante Gabriel Rossetti at 16 Cheyne Walk. And it was there, amid the curious human and animal menagerie collected by Rossetti, that Whistler first discovered the mannered bohemian world in which such exotics as Algernon Swinburne and George Meredith luxuriated.

Whistler, who spurned most friendships after a time, remained close to Rossetti through the years. And when the latter died in 1882, he remarked unaffectedly, "Rossetti was a king." Each delighted in the sparkle of an epigram and the punch of a

Terra-cotta, 1872
26⅛'' height
(National Portrait
Gallery, Smithsonian
Institution; Bequest of
Albert E. Gallatin,
1952)

James McNeill Whistler.
One of the few works of a fellow artist which
Whistler deigned to own.
Sir Joseph Edgar Boehm, 1834–90.

bon mot. And both shared a passion for all manner of the fantastic, which explained in part why Rossetti littered his house and garden with peacocks, gazelles, monkeys, and even a fearsome "Bull of Bashan," as christened by Whistler.

Rossetti was a collector of people and things. His acquisitiveness extended even to the dining table where, in his zeal for rare orientalia, especially the precious blue-on-white porcelain called Nankin, he had a formidable competitor in Whistler. Both artists are given credit for awakening public interest in the decorative arts of China and Japan, but by right the kudos must go to Whistler, who translated his passion not only into his life-style but also his art.

At 7 Lindsey Row, his rooms were marked with screens and lacquer. Shelves of blue-and-white porcelain separated by prints, fans, and kakemonos created a profusion of subtle color and pattern on flat-washed walls. At 2 Lindsey Row, delicate petals of flowers were painted on the dado of the staircase to accompany ships in full sail painted on the panels of the hall. Whistler covered his floors with grass matting or simply left them bare. His furniture was simple, and what Sheffield plate he bought was valued more for its form than its rarity. In all such things, he praised the light but ordered aesthetic of the Orient, a taste in sharp contrast with the riot of decorative excess so common in English homes touched by the neo-medievalism of William Morris.

Few works by his contemporaries graced Whistler's drawing room—one exception being a terra cotta bust of the master by Sir Joseph Edgar Boehm; a slight concession to vanity or perhaps a question of confidence.

In his studios, devoid of the usual bric-a-brac common to the workrooms of Victorian artists, Whistler produced a number of works that reflected his nascent disenchantment with the Gallic realism of Courbet. In *The Gold Screen, The Balcony,* and the *Princesse du Pays de la Porcelaine,* he deliberately created a japanized world whose beauty was foreign to his own life experience and consequently somewhat artificial in construction. In *The Lange Lijsen of the Six Marks,* a name drawn from Dutch descriptions of the "long ladies" seen on blue-and-white Chinese porcelain, Whistler wrapped his model (who is probably Jo) in Japanese drapery. But she hardly lives in it, as she sits perched on the edge of a chair, surrounded with a profusion of porcelain from Whistler's own collection, yet arranged in a manner that would never have been emulated in the houses of Tokyo or Canton.

The fact that the device was all too obvious did not seriously disturb the painter, for he was not out to paint Japan or China but rather merely to re-create, amid the soot of Battersea, the form and color of oriental detail, as if to say to the English, "This is foreign taste not yet acquired by your palate but well worth an investigation." Certainly it was not denied that Whistler's art was unique in its conception.

After a brief and rather unexplained trip to Valparaíso, where he embraced the techniques of impressionism before they appeared in the works of Manet, Degas, Renoir, and Monet, not to mention Courbet, Whistler returned to London in late 1866, emotionally repudiating the heavy realism that he had learned in Paris. To

Oil on canvas, 1864
36¼'' × 24¼''
(Philadelphia
Museum of Art; the
John G. Johnson
Collection)

Purple and Rose: The Lange Lijzen of the
Six Marks. James McNeill Whistler,
1834–1903.

Fantin-Latour he wrote in 1867, "All that he [Courbet] represented was bad for me.
. . . I must tell you that I am now much more exacting and hard to please than when I
threw everything slapdash onto the canvas, knowing that instinct and beautiful color
would pull me through. . . . Ah, my dear Fantin, what an education I am giving
myself! or rather, what a terrible lack of education I feel! With my own natural gifts,
what a painter I should be now if, vain and content with these qualities, I had not
turned my nose up at everything else!"

The new word in Whistler's vocabulary was *nocturne.* As a category of painting,
the nocturnes were not evocations of the river. Rather they were pieces of the night,
capturing the iridescent contrast of golden light sources against the gray and black
voids that nature provided between dusk and dawn. Solid forms became mere
suggestions of substance in Whistler's nocturnes, as he dutifully recorded the passage of evening's time.

In the early mornings, and on those nights when weather permitted, Whistler
embarked onto the Thames accompanied by the faithful Greaves brothers, Walter
and Henry, the former a devoted pupil, a Whistler manqué, though like all the rest
repudiated and venomously scorned in the end by the master. The Greaveses would
row until Whistler spied a view that he fancied. The order to stop was given, and out

Oil on canvas,
circa 1875
27'' × 53⅛''
(The Metropolitan
Museum of Art; John
Stewart Kennedy
Fund, 1912)

Cremorne Gardens, No. 2. James McNeill Whistler, 1834–1903.

came the brown paper and the black and white chalks for sketching. At times the mists were so heavy that Whistler composed his forms of buildings, bridges, and lights more by the intensity of feeling than the assuredness of sight, explaining, "As the light fades and the shadows deepen, all the petty and exacting details vanish; everything trivial disappears, and I see things as they are in great strong masses. The buttons are lost, but the garment remains; the sitter is lost but the shadow remains; the shadow is lost but the picture remains. And that, night cannot efface from the painter's imagination."

Often the boat would glide up the river a quarter-mile from Lindsey Row to Cremorne Gardens, the twelve-acre amusement park which, with its pagoda-shaped bandstand and open dance floor lit by gas lamps, its Venus fountain and marionette theater, its beer gardens and bowling alley, was to Victorian London what Vauxhall Gardens had been in the previous century, a sort of English Tivoli where, for a shilling, one could have fifteen hours of diversion.

Whistler loved Cremorne and went there often. He became its artistic bard, as Thomas Rowlandson had been of Vauxhall. And it was there that he created some of his most beautiful night pieces: *Nocturne in Blue and Silver: Cremorne Lights, Nocturne in Black and Gold: The Fire Wheel,* and, perhaps most famous, the controversial *Nocturne in Black and Gold: The Falling Rocket.* One admirer told the painter that on a boat trip up the Thames she observed patches of haze which, in her mind's eye, were reminiscent of a series of Whistler's. "Yes, madam," he dryly responded, "Nature is creeping up."

With the evolution of the nocturnes there also appeared, in 1874, the butterfly, the Whistler trademark of immortality that was to remain ever present on all his works. It was found in his paintings and etchings and even his handmade frames. It was on invitations to his famous Sunday breakfasts, where self-loving Britons first discovered the joys of American griddle cakes. He designed jewelry in the form of butterflies and printed them on the covers of his various catalogues and pamphlets. No name was necessary as a further embellishment. Jimmy Whistler was the butterfly, highly strung and always in animated motion.

In 1876 Whistler's mother noted, "My dear Artist son's summer has been spent in decorating a spacious dining-room for Mr. Leyland. It is indeed quite an original design." This was hardly an exaggeration, for what Whistler created survives as one of the great monuments of interior decoration of the Victorian era.

Frederick Leyland was an immensely prosperous owner of a shipping fleet, the Leyland Line, who was also an ample source of patronage for the entire Pre-Raphaelite movement. Like a Renaissance potentate who bought the art of Botticelli and Crivelli, Leyland purchased the creative outpourings of Millais, Rossetti, and Burne-Jones. Whistler, too, was the beneficiary of the magnate's largesse. Indeed, it was Leyland who first suggested that Whistler apply the word *nocturne* to his night pieces.

At his patron's country home, Speke Hall, near Liverpool, Whistler labored for months on commissions, some of which were never finished. For it was to Whistler's discredit that of all his patrons Leyland was the most financially liberal and, unfortunately, also the most ill-used.

In 1876 Leyland, requiring a larger establishment to house his collections, sold his house in Queen's Gate and moved around the corner into a twenty-year-old town house overlooking Hyde Park at 49 Prince's Gate. Leyland engaged the great architect, Norman Shaw, to redesign the interior, and made it a tempting commission by purchasing a magnificent gilt bronze balustrade, rescued from the demolition of Northumberland House, for use on his entrance hall staircase.

The balustrade, coupled with Leyland's collections of European inlaid cabinets, Chippendale and Louis XVI furniture, Beauvais tapestry, Genoese velvets, oriental carpets, and grand musical instruments were enough to transform any mansion, however unprepossessing, into a veritable palace.

Certainly the most attractive feature of the house was the positioning of three interconnecting living rooms on the second floor. When the walnut screens that divided these rooms were folded back, a gallery ninety-four feet long was created—it was a salon very much in the grand manner.

It was here that Leyland intended to display his remarkable collection of blue-and-white porcelain, together with Whistler's *Princesse du Pays de la Porcelaine* as a singular pictorial embellishment. But a problem arose as to how to reconcile Leyland's collections of oriental pots with the rich cordovan leather he had acquired at great expense for the walls. Thomas Jeckell, the original designer commissioned to do the room, produced a result that manifestly failed and, with hopes of making the best of a bad situation, Whistler was called in for consultation. But Whistler was much more than a consultant. He demanded, first, that the red flowers that decorated the leather and the red border of the room's vast oriental carpet be removed, as they clashed with the colors of his painting which was already in place. It was a case of a little color placed here and there, he told Leyland, and all would come right. But, when the artist had finished, even he had to agree with his horrified patron that the room now looked far worse.

Somewhat bewildered by what was happening, Leyland had no choice but to accept Whistler's assurances that the matter would be soon rectified, and retired to the country to await the result, which was to be, although a decorative tour de force, far removed from the owner's expectations. Whistler decided to smother the uncompromising Spanish leather with layers of Antwerp blue so that he might paint golden peacocks upon them. The Greaves brothers brought in pail upon pail of paint and endless books of gold leaf, all charged to Leyland's account. They gilded from morning to night until the room shone like a Byzantine altarpiece. Walter Greaves recalled, "I worked like a nigger and really in the way of decoration have done something gorgeous." Whistler was grown "quite mad with excitement." He told his biographers, the Pennells, years later, "I just painted on and on, without design or sketch—it grew as I painted. And towards the end I reached such a point

A panel from the Peacock Room, created by Whistler for Frederick Leyland.   *(Freer Gallery of Art)*

of perfection—putting in every touch with such freedom—that when I came round to the corner where I had started, why I had to paint part of it over again, or the difference would have been too marked. And the harmony in blue and gold developing, you know, I forgot everything in my joy in it."

The Peacock Room had become a public entertainment as word passed among the cognoscenti, and Whistler reveled in the attention. He even went so far as to have broadsides printed, as a kind of public invitation, and had them left in well-known shops, never mentioning that it was Leyland's house to whom the masses were being invited. After several months of labor he christened his creation:

HARMONY IN BLUE AND GOLD
THE PEACOCK ROOM.

The Peacock is taken as a means of carrying out this arrangement.

A pattern invented from the Eye of the Peacock, is seen in the ceiling spreading from the lamps. Between them is a pattern devised from the breastfeathers.

These two patterns are repeated throughout the room.

In the cove, the Eye will be seen running along beneath the small breastwork or throatfeathers.

On the lowest shelf the Eye is again seen, and on the shelf above—these patterns are combined: the Eye, the Breastfeathers, and the Throat.

Beginning again from the blue floor, on the dado is the breastwork, BLUE ON GOLD, while above, on the Blue wall, the pattern is reversed, GOLD ON BLUE.

Above the breastwork on the dado the Eye is again found, also reversed, that is GOLD ON BLUE, as hitherto BLUE AND GOLD.

The arrangement is completed by the Blue Peacocks on the Gold shutters, and finally the Gold Peacocks on the Blue wall.

Regardless of public attention, the ultimate question still remained: What would Frederick Leyland think when he saw the transformation of his drawing room? Whistler made light of the whole situation, telling the critic J. Comyns Carr, "Leyland, you see, Carr, is utterly ignorant of art. He's only a millionaire, and that a thing should be costly is the only proof that he has of its value. Well, let him spend his money on doing the thing as I tell him it has got to be done. I'll see that it doesn't cost too little." At which point he broke out in a malicious cackle of laughter. It was hardly an honorable way to treat a man who had been the most fulsome and patient of patrons. Perhaps Whistler was emotionally girding himself for the quarrel that he knew must now come.

Yet the Peacock Room was a truly extraordinary feat of decoration, and Whistler's pride was such that he arrogated to himself the accolade of a private view which he trusted would conclusively establish his reputation as the premier artist of his generation. To Leyland he wrote with scant regard, ordering him to remain at Speke

Hall: "These people are coming not to see you or your house: they are coming to see the work of the Master, and you, being a sensitive man, may naturally feel a little out in the cold."

Whistler did have his opening on February 9, 1877, but the day of reckoning with Leyland could not be postponed for long. When the owner of the Peacock Room finally did return to Prince's Gate, he was furious—Whistler had gone far beyond his instructions to make minor improvements, and not only was the cost extravagant, but Leyland's precious cordovan leather walls were completely obliterated beneath Whistler's gold and blue. How much! demanded Leyland, to get the artist out of his house. Whistler suggested two thousand guineas, though he owed at least half that amount to Leyland for advances on as yet unfinished paintings. Leyland would pay no more than a thousand—and it would be pounds not guineas; he refused to convey the traditional extra shillings normally given to professionals.

Whistler had no choice but to accept. He was, after all, legally on very thin ice. But he was to have his revenge. On the wall opposite the *Princesse* where two great peacocks were depicted in combat, Whistler retouched the panel so as to create a rich and poor peacock—the former covered in gold bullion while under its claws gleamed a pile of silver coins, the disputed shillings which Leyland refused to pay. Here was a permanent act of revenge which Whistler savored with glee. For, as he told a friend, "There Leyland will sit at dinner, his back to the *Princesse,* and always before him the apotheosis of *l'art et l'argent!*" Not everyone could have the joy of roasting a peacock any day of the week. This was Whistler's most intimate gift to Leyland. But the perpetrator would never have the opportunity of seeing his jape acted out. Mrs. Leyland had heard Whistler refer to her husband, his patron for a decade, as a parvenu. When next he called at Prince's Gate, he found that orders had been given to the servants not to admit him; for, insofar as Frederick Leyland was concerned, Whistler had enjoyed his final visit to the great room which he had created.

It was a classic Whistlerian dispute—not the first and certainly not the last. Such was the fine line that Whistler trod between genius and grotesque intractability. It was one of the many reasons that membership in the Royal Academy was never to be his. But Whistler was not the only painter placed beyond the academic pale. Many rival exhibitions had been held in competition with the Academy, but it was not until Sir Coutts Lindsay opened the Grosvenor Gallery that an institution sufficiently opulent and well-organized appeared to challenge seriously the primacy of the academicians. And, although commercial considerations eventually transformed the Grosvenor into a mere shadow of the Academy, hanging the overflow from its annual exhibition, in the early years after its foundation there was a quality of select specialty about its shows that was unique.

Sir Coutts Lindsay's inaugural exhibition opened in May 1877. Whistler lent three canvases, including his 1875 night picture of Cremorne, *Nocturne in Black and Gold: The Falling Rocket,* which was the only item he marked for sale. The crowds

*Oil on panel, 1874
23¾″ × 18⅜″
(The Detroit Institute
of Arts; the Dexter M.
Ferry, Jr., Fund)*

*Nocturne in Black and Gold: The Falling
Rocket. John Ruskin's criticism of this
painting led Whistler to sue him for libel.
James McNeill Whistler, 1834–1903.*

who flocked to the Grosvenor were considerable. Henry James came with the formidable "Mrs. Jack" (Isabella Stewart Gardener) on his arm. James appreciated many of the painters whose works were on view, but for Whistler he had slight esteem. James considered the nocturnes little more than "pleasant things to have about, so long as one regards them as simple objects—as incidents of furniture or decoration. The spectator's quarrel with them begins when he feels it to be expected of him to regard them as pictures. His manner is very much like that of the French Impressionists" with whom James had little sympathy.

The Times guffawed at the "vaporous" quality of Whistler's portraits, and an anti-American editorial in the weekly *London* sneered, "Mr. Whistler's brave attempt to enlighten the Britishers is lost to us. . . . But we can't despair, remembering as we do that the Whistlerian idea arose in the land of progress and Presidents, the land where Barnum blows and Whitman catalogues."

But there was one observer of the Grosvenor exhibition whose diatribe against Whistler crossed even the liberally established boundaries of legitimate criticism. John Ruskin, the august Slade Professor of Art at Oxford, was then in his fifty-eighth year. Some thought Ruskin merely eccentric, while others whispered that he was fast sinking into insanity. In either case he saw his responsibility to the art world in patriarchal terms, and devoted all his time, energy, and much of his personal fortune passing on to his selected flock a gospel of hard work and a simple life, which emotionally rejected the visual chaos created in England by the Industrial

Revolution. Ruskin dreamt of a utopian Elysium which he found prefigured in the nostalgic medievalism of Burne-Jones and William Morris. To him the supposed facility of Whistler's art was anathema.

For the elect, the Slade Professor preached from his pulpit at Oxford. For the masses, his word was disseminated in a pastoral newsletter christened *Fors Clavigera* ("fate bearing a hammer"), in whose pages only artists whose work was both "moral" and "finished" were worthy of praise. Rembrandt's art was frequently "licentious," quoth Ruskin. While Goya's *Caprichos* were "only fit to be burnt." And, as for Whistler, after seeing *The Falling Rocket* at the Grosvenor exhibition, Ruskin thundered in his public journal, "I have seen and heard much of Cockney impudence before now; but never expected to hear a coxcomb ask two hundred guineas for flinging a pot of paint in the public's face."

The gauntlet was down. Whistler sat in the smoking room of the Arts Club in Hanover Square with his old friend, the Anglo-American painter George Henry Boughton, who was thumbing through the current issue of *Fors Clavigera*. Ruskin's diatribe could not be missed. Boughton passed it expectantly to Whistler and later remembered: "Although I well knew how he rather enjoyed adverse criticism and made sport of the writers, I hesitated to call attention to this outburst. I shall never forget the peculiar look on his face as he read it and handed the paper back to me with never a word of comment, but thinking, furiously though sadly, all the time."

"It is the most debased style of criticism I have had thrown at me yet," muttered Whistler.

"Sounds rather like libel," his friend interjected.

"Well, that I shall try to find out," said the painter, as he lit a cigarette and rose to leave the room.

The case of *Whistler* v. *Ruskin* was an event of great notoriety. For the first time in English jurisprudence, the aesthetics of art and the rights of critics would go on trial. Whistler, claiming £1,000 in damages for libel, held that Ruskin's "falsely and maliciously published statements" had "greatly damaged his reputation as an artist" and thus seriously handicapped his ability to sell his paintings.

At first Ruskin was wildly, some say hysterically, excited about confronting Whistler in court. But his health was sufficiently precarious that, after five months delay, it was clear that the trial would have to go forward in his absence.

At 11:00 A.M. on Monday, November 25, 1878, in the crowded chambers of the Court of Exchequer, the presiding judge, Sir John Huddleston, motioned for silence. Ruskin's proxy, the artist Edward Burne-Jones, was there to defend "a national cause"; Whistler, the plaintiff, was also present, not only to vindicate his philosophy of beauty, but to ensure his very survival as an artist.

Both sides eloquently presented their cases, though Whistler was at a disadvantage due to the absence of his premier witness, Frederick Leighton, the new President of the Royal Academy, who had been summoned to Windsor to be knighted by the Sovereign. The central drama of the case was not enacted until Whistler, on the stand, confronted Ruskin's barrister, Sir John Holker, the Attorney-General, who rose to cross-examine.

Sir John, known for his verbal agility, attempted to pillory Whistler with sarcasm, but soon discovered that it was a most uneven match.

SIR JOHN: Did it take much time to paint the *Nocturne in Black and Gold?* How soon did you knock it off? (*Laughter.*)

WHISTLER: I beg your pardon. (*Laughter.*)

SIR JOHN: I'm afraid I was using a term that applies rather to my own work. (*Laughter.*) I should have said, "How long did it take you to paint that picture?"

WHISTLER: Oh, no! Permit me. I am too greatly flattered to think that you apply, to a work of mine, any term you are in the habit of using with reference to your own. Let us say then, how long did I take to "knock off"—I think that's it—to knock off that Nocturne. Well, as well as I remember, about a day. I may have put a few more touches to it the next day if the painting were not dry. I had better say, then, that I was two days at work on it.

SIR JOHN: The labour of two days, then, is that for which you ask two hundred guineas?

WHISTLER: No. I ask it for the knowledge of a lifetime.

The crowd of spectators burst into applause but were gaveled into silence by the judge, who, in his summing-up to the jury, made it clear that this was the sort of case that should never have been brought into court. Judge Huddleston held that if the jury were of a mind to award damages in recognition of libel, a mere farthing (one-quarter of a penny) might be the most suitable amount.

The jury retired for an hour, and then reported a verdict in favor of the plaintiff with damages set at the farthing recommended by the judge. Sir John, as a mark of his hostility to the presumed comic aspects of the case, refused to assess legal costs against Ruskin. This meant that Whistler would have to pay his own fees.

"That's a verdict for me, is it not?" he asked his attorney.

"Yes, nominally," was the reply.

"Well, I suppose a verdict is a verdict"—and to an American friend who offered sympathy, Whistler exhorted, "It's a great triumph; tell everybody it's a great triumph."

But it was a Pyrrhic victory at best. Whistler could verbally lambaste Ruskin in *Art and Art Critics*; he could wear the celebrated farthing on his watch fob as a mark of triumphant derision; but by taking Ruskin to court Whistler incurred substantial legal bills which were not subsidized by his friends as were those of his opponent.

"Alas for Jimmy Whistler!" wrote Rossetti in the aftermath of the trial. "What harbour of refuge now, unless to turn Fire-King at Cremorne? And Cremorne itself is no more! A Nocturne andante in the direction of the Sandwich Islands, or some country where tattooing pure and simple is the national School of Art, can now alone avert the long impending Arrangement on Black and White."

Rossetti's "Arrangement" was an unavoidable petition of bankruptcy. For years Whistler had piled up debts, not only with local tradesmen but also with clients who had advanced sums of money for paintings that were never completed. Frederick Leyland was, in this context, only a case in point. Even while preparations for the suit against Ruskin were in progress, Whistler was vastly increasing his indebtedness. He contracted with the architect Edward W. Godwin (whose widow he eventually married) to build, a few blocks east of Lindsey Row in Tite Street, a three-story house, faced in white Portland stone with a roof of green slate. The White House, as it came to be called, was remarkable for its lack of exterior ornamentation—a fact that produced considerable controversy with local planning authorities and architectural journals. It was an object of personal indulgence to Whistler in every way. Godwin constructed a forty-seven-foot studio at the top of the house; he had the door and exterior woodwork colored in peacock blue, and placed windows according to function rather than the dictates of popular convention or form. But, however unique an edifice it was, the house had cost a great deal more than Whistler could afford.

After a respite in Paris, Whistler and his second mistress and model Maud Franklin returned to London, and it was at the White House that he continued his futile game of cat-and-mouse with his creditors. On one notable occasion, when the Secretary of the Arts Club demanded £30 in back dues, Whistler suggested a payment in kind—perhaps one of his paintings, to which the exasperated official retorted in Whistlerian vernacular, "It is not a Nocturne in purple or a Symphony in blue and grey that we are after, but an Arrangement in gold and silver."

Whistler's White House in Tite Street. (Photograph courtesy Library of Congress)

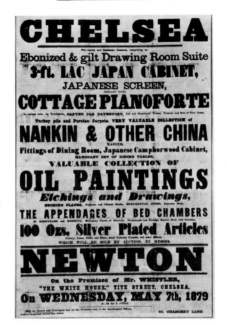

Poster advertising Whistler's bankruptcy sale at the White House. At Whistler's insistence his name, which appears on this poster, was deleted in later printings. (Library of Congress)

Early in May 1879, the financial roof fell in, and on Chelsea palisades and the walls of the White House itself, Messrs. Newton—Auctioneers announced that a bankruptcy sale would be held on Tuesday, May 13, at the premises of Mr. Whistler of Tite Street, who had filed a petition of bankruptcy with liabilities of over £4,600.

Whistler objected to his name appearing on the poster—he found it tasteless. And, consequently, a new broadside was printed with this pertinent information deleted. Always an aesthetic perfectionist, he ordered the bailiffs who were now in attendance to securely fasten down those posters which wind and rain had loosened on his walls. At such a time of crisis, there were still standards to maintain. Indeed, Whistler insisted on treating the matter as a great though savage joke. He sent out luncheon invitations, advising his guests, "You will know the house by the bills of sale stuck up outside." Knowing that he could not be held liable for debts incurred while under bankruptcy, Whistler continued an active social life. Stories of his famous Sunday breakfasts, with bailiffs in livery drafted into service as waiters, are legion. And no doubt there is much truth in the tales of paintings being spirited past these intoxicated guardians, for Whistler was determined to hide as much of his art as possible from his creditors, though in spite of his belligerence and arrogance it has to be admitted that many of the paintings were virtually unsellable at the time.

For his chief creditor, Frederick Leyland, Whistler performed a final act of perversity which, if nothing else, testified to the degree of strain and paranoia under which he functioned. When the owner of the Peacock Room and two others visited the artist's studio to ascertain what could profitably be sold, they found three canvases, all viciously caricaturing Leyland for whom Whistler's venom was unbounded.

One of these three, entitled *The "Gold Scab," Eruption in Frilthy Lucre,* still survives, and shows the shipping magnate as a peacock of unusually repellent aspect, scaled like a reptile in gold coins, perched on the White House which served as a piano stool, and making music. It was the last stab at one whom Whistler regarded as the source of all his difficulties, and was a regrettable testament of the aberrancy of a great talent.

On his last night in the White House, Whistler attended a costume ball at George Boughton's elaborate mansion on Campden Hill. He entered as Hamlet, dressed completely in black. But, far from being melancholy, he celebrated with great élan, speaking of the future rather than the past. Later that evening Whistler's neighbor, the cartoonist Carlo Pellegrini, happened to look out his window and spied the painter and his young illegitimate son, John Charles, placing a ladder against the front wall of the White House. While his son held a candle and steadied the ladder, Whistler climbed up to the lintel of the front door and there painted an inscription which he had first seen above the door of his friends the Lewis Jarvises at Sharnbrook—"Except the Lord build the house, they labor in vain that build it"—and to this he added with sardonic humor, "E. W. Godwin F.S.A. built this one." With this final injunction to posterity completed, Whistler descended from the ladder, bid his son adieu, and departed from England on the boat train to France, with Italy as his ultimate destination.

There was a kind of liberation in going through bankruptcy. Whistler, in his mid-forties, could now think of the future unencumbered by mountainous debts and the emotional catastrophes that seemed inherently to accompany them. A tempo-

Oil on canvas, 1879 73½" × 55" (The Fine Arts Museums of San Francisco, Spreckles Collection)

The "Gold Scab," Eruption in Frilthy Lucre. The most savage of all Whistler's caricatures of Frederick Leyland. James McNeill Whistler, 1834–1903.

Etching with drypoint, late 1870s, published in Venice, a Series of Twelve Etchings, *1880 7⅞″ × 11⅝″ (Library of Congress)*

Nocturne.   James McNeill Whistler, 1834–1903.

rary sojourn in Venice to create a series of plates for the Fine Art Society, modeled on the Thames set, seemed a good idea. Whistler had a chance to salve his injured pride and to sow the seeds of a life rebuilt.

When fifty-one Venetian etchings were shown at the Society in February 1883, a Whistler revival was clearly in the offing. With his natural gift for self-advertisement, Jimmy mounted an exhibition bound to attract attention. It was a Whistlerian ensemble in yellow. The gallery was painted primarily in yellow and filled with furniture upholstered in matching shades. Yellow flowers in yellow pots were amply in evidence. Even the gallery attendant was dressed in a livery which matched the walls, and admission to the private view was by a yellow-and-white butterfly, signed personally by the artist, who greeted his guests dressed in socks of the gayest primrose.

The catalogue, familiarly bound in brown paper, was much more serious. It is unlikely that any exhibition had been previously accompanied by such a document. Entitled *Mr. Whistler and His Critics,* it bore on its title page the epigraph "Out of their own mouths shall ye judge them," and was followed by an entry for each item on show, together with one of the many hostile comments Whistler had received in the past from well-known art critics. How appropriate that the quotation attached to the first etching in the show should read, "Criticism is powerless here." It was the consummate Whistlerian riposte. The Princess of Wales, who attended the opening with her husband, remarked to the artist, "I am afraid you are very malicious." No doubt it was true, but if Whistler had previously suffered at the hands of critics for being merely advanced in his artistic views, it was now his turn to attack: such was his renewed level of confidence.

He was once again becoming a public figure of some note, and not merely for his eccentricities. Of course, the great Whistler bons mots made the rounds of drawing rooms and dinner tables as before—when the Prince of Wales remarked that he knew Whistler, the painter's dry response was, "That's only his side!" But, in addition, the world of fashionable portraiture opened its door, at least partially, to Whistler. He painted a number of society beauties, including the redoubtable Lady Meux, who sat for no fewer than three portraits, while he lunged at his canvases like a champion swordsman with brushes as long as rapiers. But, of this side of his art, Whistler was generally cynical. He was once heard to remark, "Certainly the Englishwoman succeeds, as no other can, in obliging men to forget her sex."

Few men lived quite as intensely as James McNeill Whistler. If he was not painting furiously, then he was entertaining; and if his home was empty, then he was sure to be out and about at someone's table, trading puns with those he liked and hurling insults at those he despised. Like so many Victorians, he was an enthusiastic, though eclectic, clubman: the Arts, the Hogarth, the Fielding, the Arundel, the Beefsteak, and the Beaufort—not the best in social terms, but no doubt among the most interesting of such establishments—all claimed him as a member at various times. "I never dined alone for years," he once said. Life was not always a celebration, but one did have to keep moving at a frantic pace, else melancholy set in. In this respect Whistler and his compatriot Henry James had much in common.

Although the critics damned him, Whistler was not without acolytes, who were held in good grace so long as they paid obeisance to the Master. Oscar Wilde was one who initially paid court, acknowledging Whistler's primacy as wit, critic, and raconteur. But an intimate relationship could not long survive the sparring of two egos of such monumental proportions. Whistler worked hard to create an appearance of spontaneous wit, carefully keeping his best comments in reserve for use on just the right occasion. Wilde, on the other hand, was not only blessed with humorous fecundity but was also able to adopt almost any bon mot or pun he had heard from other sources as his own. It was this latter attribute that infuriated Whistler, who deeply resented the exploitation of his own wit in the cause of Wilde's reputation.

Pen, ink, watercolor, and pencil, date unknown
4¾" × 7¼" (sight)
(The Philip H. & A. S. W. Rosenbach Foundation, Philadelphia)

Whistler in his studio, painting three portraits of Lady Meux simultaneously by attaching his brushes to fishing poles. Sir Mortimer Menpes, 1860–?

How pleased Jimmy must have been to receive a telegram from Oscar, saying,

PUNCH TOO RIDICULOUS, WHEN YOU AND I ARE TOGETHER WE NEVER TALK ABOUT ANYTHING EXCEPT OURSELVES

for it allowed him to respond,

NO, NO, OSCAR, YOU FORGET, WHEN YOU AND I ARE TOGETHER WE NEVER TALK ABOUT ANYTHING EXCEPT ME

—and then delight in publishing the exchange in the press: so great was his need for public recognition of some sort.

After Wilde's lecture to the students of the Royal Academy, Whistler commented on the affair in so witty a fashion that Wilde was forced to respond, "Jimmy, I wish I had said that," to which his foil responded, in the famous *mal mot,* "You will, Oscar, you will"—and he meant it!

It was not simply a childish desire for justifiable recognition. Wilde borrowed as freely from Whistler's pronouncements on art as he did from his fund of humor, but there Whistler drew the line. If he was to preserve the integrity of his philosophy of aesthetics and protect it against callow prostitution, then it had to be codified and presented as his most significant arrangement. For years, Whistler had expressed himself in catalogues, pamphlets, and letters to the editor. But his artistic credo had to be different in every respect.

He elected to produce a public lecture, and engaged Prince's Hall in Piccadilly for the evening of February 20, 1885. Never known for his punctuality, Whistler assumed the same fault in his audience, and consequently scheduled the event fashionably late, at ten o'clock, so that his listeners might come relaxed from their dinner tables ready for an evening's entertainment.

After weeks of preparation, of arranging epigrams and memorizing lines, of trying out a few paragraphs on one friend and a few more on another, Whistler was ready. Never had an event of artistic importance begun so late in the evening, and long before the lecture was prepared, the "Ten O'Clock," as it was popularly known, had become the subject of speculation at the dining tables and in the smoking rooms of London's creative and social elect. Newspapers wondered whether "the eccentric artist was going to sketch, to pose, to sing, or to rhapsodize." But they need not have wandered so far afield, for Whistler sensed that "the air is just teeming with success—and the lecture is growing apace—and will be I need not deny amazing."

Those who entered Prince's Hall that evening did so with tickets designed by Whistler. They passed by posters of his own creation and took their seats to witness an event as yet unspecified. What they encountered was no less than an intellectual tour de force, the artist's verbal magnum opus. The gospel according to Whistler was mannered in the extreme. Part of its beauty lay in its elitist artifice and, as his biographer Stanley Weintraub has written, "In its polished, epigrammatical portions it was a prose etching; in its efforts at explaining the mysterious effect of art on the onlooker it became a prose nocturne."

Whistler presented a position, which he considered common to all great artists: they had to stand both as outsiders and exiles, whatever their society or locale, in order to produce that which time would judge as great.

> The master stands in no relation to the moment at which he occurs—a monument of isolation—hinting at sadness—having no part in the progress of his fellow men.

> He is also no more the product of civilization than he is the scientific truth asserted, dependent upon the wisdom of a period. The assertion itself requires the man to make it. The truth was from the beginning.

> So art is limited to the infinite, and beginning there cannot progress.

> A silent indication of its wayward independence from all extraneous advance, is in the absolutely unchanged condition and form of implement since the beginning of things.

> The painter has but the same pencil—the sculptor the chisel of centuries.

The Ten O'Clock was warmly received, and Whistler accepted several invitations to deliver it again to various groups. It also did much to enhance the artist's respectability and reputation for seriousness in the eyes of those who had previously dismissed him as being of no consequence.

Oscar Wilde, for one, considered the Ten O'Clock a masterpiece, but in reviewing it could not resist, amid sincere praise, poking fun at "a miniature Mephistopheles, mocking the majority." Wilde waxed enthusiastically,

> Mr. Whistler's lecture last night was, like everything else that he does, a masterpiece. Not merely for its clever satire and amusing jests will it be remembered, but for the pure and perfect beauty of many of its passages— passages delivered with an earnestness which seemed to amaze those who had looked on Mr. Whistler as a master of persiflage merely, and had not known him, as we do, as a master of painting also. For that he is indeed one of the very greatest masters of painting, is my opinion. And I may add that in this opinion Mr. Whistler himself entirely concurs.

The final line, undoubtedly clever, was not written in malice, but Wilde failed to appreciate not only how seriously Whistler took the lecture, but how abjectly he rejected criticism by those he regarded as practitioners manqués of art. Subsequent blasts were fired between the two, Whistler ending the friendship decisively in a letter to the *World*: "What has Oscar in common with Art? Except he dines at our tables, and picks from our platters the plums for the pudding he peddles in the provinces.

"Oscar—the amicable, irresponsible, esurient Oscar—with no more sense of a picture, than the fit of a coat—has the 'courage of the opinions'—of others!"

Whistler was never one to mince words, which explained in part why the Royal Academy never deigned to offer him the boon of fellowship; he had over the years simply offended too many of its members. Yet, while he evinced complete disdain for such bodies, he hungered for professional recognition from his peers. This was made amply clear when, in November 1884, the Society of British Artists, an ancient though hardly august organization of dilettantes and drudges, offered Whistler immediate membership by special dispensation of their rules. It was more than a fair trade, for the Society's somnolent exhibitions were suffering increasingly poor attendance, and they needed a star attraction as much as Whistler required a professional base. And so, at the age of fifty, James McNeill Whistler at last joined the artistic community, a fact which did not go unnoticed in the press. *The Times* reported acerbically, "Artistic society was startled by the news that this most wayward, most un-English of painters had found a home among the men of Suffolk Street, of all people in the world."

Whistler was not merely a new member of the Society; he was a presence who could not be ignored. Consequently, it was not all that surprising that, in the wake of his popularity resulting from the Ten O'Clock, he was, in 1886, elected to the presidency of the organization. Little did the Society know what turbulence they were in for over the next two years. There was much petty bickering during the first year of Whistler's presidency, but few members, however disgruntled, could ignore the immense increase in the Society's prestige. Not only did the Prince of Wales now grace their exhibitions with his presence, but in this, the year of Queen Victoria's Golden Jubilee, Whistler succeeded in obtaining the Sovereign's command that the Society should now be called "Royal," as a mark of Her Majesty's especial grace and favor.

It was a great coup. Whistler knew that many bodies were preparing formal addresses to the Queen on the occasion of the fiftieth anniversary of her accession, and he felt that his society should by no means be left out. But, rather than send one of the usual illuminated parchment scrolls so common to such occasions,

I took a dozen sheets of my old Dutch paper. I had them bound by Zaensdorf. Amazing! First came this beautiful binding in yellow morocco, and the inscription to Her Majesty, every word just in the right place, most wonderful. You opened it, and on the first page you found a beautiful little drawing of the royal arms that I made myself; the second page, an etching of Windsor, as though, "here's where you live." On the third page, the address began. I made decorations all round the text in watercolour—at the top, the towers of Windsor, down one side, a great battleship, plunging through the waves, and below the sun that never sets on the British Empire—What? The following pages are not decorated, just the most wonderful address, explaining the age and dignity of the Society, its devotion to Her Glorious, Gracious Majesty, and suggesting the honour it would show the Society to belong especially to Her. Then the last page. You turned, and there was a little etching of my house in Chelsea— "And now here's where I live!" And then you closed it, and on the back of the cover was the Butterfly.

This he accompanied with a personal gift of twenty-six etchings, comprising the *Second Venetian Set,* specially bound in a leather portfolio with the Royal Arms on the front cover.

As President of the now Royal Society of British Artists, Whistler attended all the formal ceremonies connected with the Jubilee at Westminster Abbey, Buckingham Palace, and at Spithead where a great naval review was held.

He also took it into his head to alter the sign which hung above the Society's door and recalled, "I treated it as I should a most distinguished sitter—as a picture or an etching—throwing my artistic soul into the Board." But he did much more than that. On a ground of royal vermilion he placed the Society's name in gold letters and added a golden lion and butterfly lying together: "a harmony in gold and red" he called it. But to others of the Society it meant much more. Whistler was trumpeting his dominance for all to see, and, for many, it was a bitter pill to swallow.

The President had made it clear that all decisions as to what would be shown at the Society's annual exhibition would be made exclusively by the hanging committee, which was dominated by his followers. He also decided, by fiat, that no longer would the Society's wall be covered with a hurly-burly of pictures. There must be adequate space between each work so that it might be appreciated. Thus, many artists long associated with the Society now found their works excluded from the annual exhibition, due to the personal objection of the President.

The crunch came in May 1888 just prior to the Society's summer exhibition. Eight members circulated a letter asking for a special meeting to demand Whistler's resignation. A gathering was assembled at which the President made a speech but refused to entertain an opposition reply. When some members attacked his eccentricities as being damaging to the reputation of the Society, Whistler put on his spectacles and, coolly surveying the hostile assembly, declared, according to one observer,

You know, you people are not well! You remind me of a ship load of passengers living on an antiquated boat which has been anchored to a rock for many years. Suddenly this old tub, which hitherto has been disabled and incapable of putting out to sea, to face the storm and stress of the waves, is boarded by a pirate. (I am the pirate) He patches up the ship and makes her not only weather tight but a perfect vessel, and boldly puts out running down less ably captained ships, and bearing a stream of wreckage in her wake. But lo and behold! her triumphant passage is stopped and by the passengers themselves. Unused to this strange and unaccustomed movement they are each and every one of them sick—ill. But good people you will e'en live to thank your captain. But then you talk of my eccentricities. Now, you members invited me into your midst as President because of these same so-called eccentricities which you now condemn. You elected me because I was much talked about and because you imagined I would bring notoriety to your gallery. Did you then also imagine that when I entered your building I should leave my individuality on the doormat? If so, you are mistaken. No, British Artists: I am still the eccentric Whistler whom you invited into your midst.

It was hardly a speech designed to mollify his critics. There were more special meetings at which motions of censure and expulsion were raised. And finally, by the time of the annual general meeting on June 4, Whistler found his position no longer tenable. A new President was elected and Whistler, together with a group of his followers, resigned in protest. "I am taking with me the Artists," he proclaimed, "and I leave the British."

Here was a declaration consistent with the old form, but it presaged something far more important. For, in the closing years of his life, Whistler developed a galloping hostility to all things English as represented by the Society which had rejected him. No painting of his hung in any English public gallery, though modern works by men of much less note were readily accepted at very attractive prices. This fact gnawed at him and produced great rancor. He would have sitters aplenty: Americans, Frenchmen, even Scots; but in the end would take on no English clients. His marriage to Trixie Godwin, the plump widow of the architect of his White House, was a moment of comparative happiness, but her untimely death, after a few short years, cast Whistler into a pit of deep melancholy. His health began to suffer seriously, and not even a sojourn in Paris and the transience of his briefly organized Académie Carmen could effect a cure.

Not that he was alone. In his last years there were many who gathered round the Master. William Heinemann, his publisher and friend, was always in evidence. The American multimillionaire Charles Freer, his most enthusiastic patron, could always be found. And then, of course, there were the Pennells, Joseph and Elizabeth, who clung to Whistler, styling themselves his most devoted companions, yet vulturelike in their hovering. They recognized in the painter a good thing, whose reputation could further their own careers, as indeed it did, and consequently were always in evidence.

Joseph Pennell was a Pennsylvanian who had studied art in Philadelphia under Thomas Eakins. His wife, Elizabeth Robins, a niece of the Gypsy-King, Charles Godfrey Leland, made her reputation as an art critic. They settled in England to

Firelight (Elizabeth Robins Pennell).
James McNeill Whistler, 1834–1903.
Lithograph, 1896. 7⅜″ × 5¹⁵/₁₆″.
(Library of Congress)

Joseph Pennell. James McNeill Whistler,
1834–1903. Lithograph, 1896. 6½″ × 5½″.
(Library of Congress)

produce quaint illustrated travel articles for American periodicals. And, as the golden age of illustration—of Abbey, Pyle, and Reinhart—prospered, they graduated into the production of popular illustrated books with titles like *Our Sentimental Journey, Canterbury Pilgrimage,* and *Our Journey to the Hebrides.*

But, however lucrative, these were matters of small moment when compared with the time they both invested in plumbing Whistler for information so that they might write an authorized biography. In essence, they were the last family unit Whistler possessed, and toward the end he became more and more dependent upon them.

When an exhibition of Joseph Pennell's lithographs failed to gain critical esteem, he looked around for a scapegoat. A convenient one was found in Walter Sickert, whose particularly ill-informed articles in Frank Harris's *Saturday Review* had made the mistake of asserting that Pennell's lithographs were not the genuine article because they were produced on transfer paper rather than on stone. Whistler himself had often produced lithographs via this method, and Pennell saw a chance to co-opt his dependent mentor in a legal suit which bore an uncomfortable resemblance to the Ruskin fracas of many years earlier.

Whistler attempted to avoid the unpleasantness of the matter. Such things no longer seemed so important to an aging man in ill health; yet Pennell pressed him enthusiastically. "But the case is as much yours as mine . . ." he argued. "Your reputation is involved. There will be an end to your lithography if we lose. You must fight." Pennell knew when he had the whip hand, and Whistler consented to enter

Pencil and wash,
date unknown
12¾'' × 10¾''
(Birmingham City
Museums and Art
Gallery)

*Mr. Whistler giving evidence in the case
of* Pennell *v.* The Saturday Review
and Another. *The last of Whistler's
celebrated court appearances in defense of
art. Max Beerbohm, 1872–1956.*

the lists. In spite of Frank Harris's apologetic attempts at conciliation, Pennell wanted his day in court, and it was granted. The case was a highly technical one, with experts on both sides much in evidence. When Whistler finally reached the stand, it was clear that Pennell's case was already made. The Master objected that "distinguished people like Mr. Pennell and myself should be dragged into court by an unknown authority, an insignificant and irresponsible person"—for Sickert, like so many of Whistler's former acolytes, had now been relegated to the dungheap of the artist's discards.

When defense counsel asked how, if Sickert was so insignificant and irresponsible, he could do any harm to Pennell and Co.: "Even a fool can do harm," rejoined Whistler, with a flash of the old sparkle. And it was then, with his testimony and cross-examination at an end, that Whistler slowly drew off his gloves, adjusted his eyeglass and said, "And now, my Lord, may I tell you why we are all here?"

"No, Mr. Whistler," responded the judge, "we are all here because we cannot help it."

Judgment was for plaintiff in the amount of £50. Such was Whistler's last and most successful appearance before the bar of justice.

It was through the entreaties of William Heinemann that Whistler consented, in 1900, to commission the Pennells to write an authorized biography of his life, and from that point on he was increasingly in their company. Yet Whistler rarely talked about the book. He suspected that the Pennells were attempting to make an Old Master of him before his time. He still wanted to be considered a contemporary, a modern of the first rank. One recalls the story of the lady who joined the painter's name with Velásquez as the only two artists she venerated. "True, true, dear lady," responded Whistler sadly, "but why drag in Velásquez?"

For the Pennells it was a magnificent opportunity. Mrs. Pennell wrote of her husband, "He loved Whistler, believed in Whistler's art, and was steadfast in his loyalty." No doubt much of this was true, and in the end the Pennells did produce what is considered by many still to be the definitive life of the painter. But their two-volume *Life of Whistler,* followed by *The Whistler Journal,* were not without flaws.

The Pennells regarded themselves and Whistler as "real Americans." Yet they were that strange breed of Yankee who had to live abroad to feel fulfilled. Unlike Henry James, who made every attempt to assimilate English culture, the Pennells obdurately resisted any such encroachment on their lives.

To be abroad marked one as a sophisticated exotic, and there were commercial possibilities in such a mask which could be exploited back home. But the more profound reason for the Pennells' expatriation was their fear of an America in transformation which was beyond their control. When the Pennells visited the United States, Elizabeth wrote that "the old long, lean, lanky Uncle Sam was as lost as the needle in the haystack; in his place, a fat, podgy, unhealthy Samuel of Posen." Pennell himself put it more bluntly. On a visit to Chicago in 1910 he found "Mr. Pork Packer and 2,916,418 and ½ jews, niggers, slovaks, dagos, irish, sicilians, scandinavians and one supposed native American—preserved in a bottle in a freak museum." Henry James's experience was not so different, but he put it a trifle more tactfully.

The Pennells were violently and unashamedly anti-Semitic and, it seemed, anti-everyone else who were not "native" Americans. When Elizabeth Pennell finally returned to settle in the United States, she found herself "a stranger in my native land." In the house where she stayed, there was an Irish chambermaid, a Greek waiter, and a Dalmatian handyman. Her boots were blacked by an Italian, her gowns pressed by a Pole: "All America during my absence has been turned, not into the melting-pot some call it, but the dumping ground, the refuse heap of Europe. The longer I am in my native land, the nearer I seem to get to the inevitable day when we real Americans like the Indians shall have our reservations and when our successors will come to pay their quarters to stare at us as curiosities." When they came to write Whistler's life, the Pennells transmitted much of their venom into his mouth so as to co-opt him into their happy band. And, in so doing, they placed a stain on what otherwise was a commendable personal memoir.

On July 17, 1903, James McNeill Whistler died, and was buried at Chiswick near the river which had been so intimate a part of his life. The police expected a large crowd at the cemetery, but by the time the procession had wound its way from Chelsea, there were relatively few who gathered at the gravesite. His pallbearers were distinguished—the collectors Vanderbilt and Freer; the artists Abbey, Guthrie, Lavery, and Duret. Three his compatriots; one each a Scot, an Irishman, and a

Frenchman. No English—an ironic, yet predictable, tribute to one who at the end consciously wished to expire outside the Establishment of English art.

A strange unknown man, dressed in "blue monocle, red coat, blue shirt, orange flower in buttonhole, fur cap, long fur edged gloves," came leaping over the gravestones as the funeral service concluded. A macabre and rather disturbing figure—surely not the last of the Master's arrangements or harmonies?

Whistler knew unquestionably that his own artistic ideals were at variance with the conventions of English painting, which he held in utter contempt. And it was this disenchantment with established mores that dominated every other aspect of his life. As Frank Harris noted, "He despised the materialism of the race, the courage that was usually self-interested and all too seldom chivalric." He had a clear conception of himself as an Anglo-Saxon who preferred London to all other places (the Pennells had not failed to note this correctly); yet he never missed an opportunity to rail at English foibles when they smacked of the philistine and rewarded greedy mediocrity.

"'Tis well with every land to be at odds," wrote Shakespeare in *Timon of Athens,* a view Whistler would no doubt have accepted, if only as a necessary fait accompli. Others would follow, and some would see in him a model, an exiled genius whose struggle was well worthy of emulation.

You had your searches, your uncertainties,
And this is good to know—for us. I mean,
Who bear the brunt of our America
And try to wrench her impulse into art.

So wrote Ezra Pound, who was, perhaps surprisingly, Whistler's most devoted and exacting of followers.

8

The Assimilated:
The Astors, Emerald Cunard,
and Chips Channon

"America is good enough for any man who has to make a livelihood, though why travelled people of independent means should remain there more than a week is not readily to be comprehended." So pronounced William Waldorf Astor, a financial titan who fled to England in 1890, regarding it as "a country fit for gentlemen to live in." Astor, who confessed, "I die many deaths every day," was a paranoid misanthrope of the first order, who ascribed his lack of political and social success in the United States not to his own shortcomings as a man, but to flaws inherent in the American democratic system. Astor considered America "the poor man's country," where wealth was despised as a pernicious menace to the popular institutions of government: "It is democratic and virtuous to be poor and aristocratic and un-American to be rich."

His was a unique and rather remarkable misreading of his country's history. But, in a state of high dudgeon, Astor made his position clear: "I never wished to live at Brookdale [sic] where Hawthorne went to learn that wealth is nothing nor should have I been content at Walden with the contemplation of nature and a daily plate of Thoreau's bean soup." On the contrary, he was so little a Diogenes that it seemed to him a truism that through wealth alone could the greatest pleasures of life be obtained in education, travel, and the refinements and embellishments of one's home.

William Waldorf Astor lived in the past. A few hundred years—a few thousand; the difference was only speculative. To define him as a political conservative was an understatement. His grandson Michael Astor wrote, "In politics and outlook he would have made the late Cardinal Segura, Bishop of Seville, the most reactionary prelate of his age, look like an evangelist." But politics were never the operative core of Astor's life. Spiritually he was a romantic, who indulged his fantasies in a variety of ways. He wrote egregiously overblown novels with titles like *Sforza, a Historical Romance of the Sixteenth Century in Italy*; *Valentino, a Story of Rome*; and

Oil on canvas, 1898
47¼" × 36½"
(The Viscount Astor)

William Waldorf Astor, first Viscount Astor, 1848–1919. Sir Hubert von Herkomer, 1849–1914.

Pharaoh's Daughter and Other Stories, a collection which contains lines like "Tush fool! Think you to bandy reasons with a Czar?"

Determined to act out his dreams, Astor created magnificent environments which stood as backdrops for a life dominated by rituals contrived in emulation of his idea of an English medieval baron. In 1893 he purchased Cliveden, a Buckinghamshire seat of the Duke of Westminster, which had been rebuilt by Charles Barry in 1850 vaguely in the style of a Roman villa. Cliveden, which Henry James considered "a creation of such beauty and distinction that the mere exposure of one's sensibilities and one's imagination to the effect and the 'message' of such a place (in itself) becomes a duty if the opportunity arises." Astor filled the house with medieval armor, crossbows, and halberds; with objects of devotion such as Tudor prayer books and crucifixes; and with a variety of large Roman marbles. From the Villa Borghese he purchased an entire stone balustrade some 200 yards long, complete with fountains and statues, and transported it en masse to England where it was installed along the back of the house.

While extending the gardens and vistas of the estate, Astor was determined to enjoy his pleasures in cloistered privacy. A high stone wall, topped with broken glass, reminiscent of those which surrounded the medieval colleges of Oxford and Cambridge, was erected around Cliveden, within which dwelt this most eccentric of millionaires, known to his neighbors as "Waldorf by name and walled-off by nature."

Cliveden, the Berkshire estate of the Astors, which abounded with costly treasures, including an entire balustrade from the Villa Borghese.   (Photograph courtesy The National Trust for Places of Historic Interest or Natural Beauty, London)

But Astor was not an absolute recluse. Determined to make his mark on England, he purchased the *Pall Mall Gazette* and promptly turned it from a Liberal to a Conservative newspaper. How surprised the new proprietor must have been when most of the staff immediately resigned and organized the *Westminster Gazette.* Yet Astor remained undeterred, and hired as his editor the flamboyant Harry Cockayne Cust, a thirty-two-year-old member of Parliament, who was heir to the Barony of Brownlow and a central figure of that most select of late Victorian salons known as "The Souls," whose members constituted the intellectual elite of the aristocracy. Cust was an individual of immensely independent temperament, who had little use for Astor's ideas but greatly valued his fortune. H. G. Wells, the one-time literary critic of the *Gazette,* recalled that Cust assembled a brilliant staff with "the highest of spirits and with a fine regardlessness of expenditures—for was not Astor notoriously a millionaire?" And while the relationship between editor and proprietor was frequently explosive, under Cust's three-year leadership the *Pall Mall Gazette* did become a leading Tory evening paper. The *Pall Mall Magazine,* which Astor founded as an outlet for his own literary productions, emerged as a leading literary monthly, with frequent articles by Wells, Kipling, Robert Louis Stevenson, and Alice Meynell. And the *Pall Mall Budget,* which Astor purchased along with the *Gazette,* retained its popularity as a leading home weekly. The end result of all this was that Astor, almost overnight, had placed himself within the ranks of the leading

Lansdowne House, Berkeley Square.   The London mansion rented by Astor.
(Photograph courtesy Royal Commission on Historical Monuments, England)

molders of public opinion in England. This was capped by his additional purchase of *The Observer,* the great Sunday newspaper, to which the proprietor attracted the editorial services of J. L. Garvin, perhaps the most distinguished journalist of the day.

For $25,000 a year, Astor rented the palatial Berkeley Square mansion, Lansdowne House, as his London residence, wherein he existed in what was described as "solitary state." But, to run his instant newspaper empire, he decided to build the most extraordinary private office building that London had seen for years.

The Astor Estate Office, or Astor House as it was commonly called, was erected, and still stands, on the Thames next to the legal chambers of the Temple. It was designed by the great Victorian church architect, John Loughborough Pearson, who was a perfect choice because he treated the building, according to Astor's requirements, much more as a sanctum sanctorum for the summoning of lackeys than as a place for the conducting of routine public business. It was yet another environment in which Astor's fantasies could be acted out.

Astor House was described as a Tudor "casket built entirely of Portland stone," on whose roof was set an enormous beaten copper weather vane of the caravel *Santa Maria,* in which Columbus discovered America. W. S. Frith executed two bronze lamp standards to flank the stone steps that rose to the main doorway entrance. Today they are regarded as among the finest examples of high Victorian sculpture.

*The Great Hall in Astor House, the mock medieval office building
erected by Lord Astor on the north bank of the Thames. (Photograph courtesy Smith and Nephew)*

Once within the vestibule, a visitor was instantly made aware of the strong literary
associations which Astor had inculcated into the building. As one approached the
staircase across a floor geometrically inlaid with marble, jasper, porphyry, and onyx,
one encountered a series of seven beautifully carved figures, the masterpieces of
Thomas Nicholls, representing the major characters in Alexandre Dumas's *The
Three Musketeers.*

Ascending the staircase, one reached a gallery on the first floor, supported by ten
pillars of solid ebony, on whose capitals were set more statues, by Nicholls, of
characters from novels by James Fenimore Cooper, Washington Irving, and
Nathaniel Hawthorne.

At the south side of the gallery, visitors passed through a large mahogany door
designed in Renaissance style, inlaid with nine silver gilt panels, by Sir George
Frampton, of heroines from the legend of King Arthur—and then into the Great
Hall where William Waldorf Astor kept court. "There is no more curious room in
London," declared one architect, "than this hall which was intended by its creator to
be a sort of temple of culture and expresses in a curious way his own tastes in art &
literature."

It is a massive room, seventy-one by twenty-eight feet, with a ceiling rising over
thirty-five feet. Astor paneled the Great Hall in pencil cedar, which he surmounted
with a frieze containing fifty-four carved portraits of figures close to his heart, such

as Voltaire, Henrietta Maria, and Machiavelli. And on top of the frieze, he placed twelve gilded wood statues of figures from Sir Walter Scott's *Ivanhoe,* which were lit, east and west, by stained-glass windows depicting Swiss landscapes in the rising and setting sun.

London took note of Astor's new position in society. The aristocracy attended his lavish, though infrequent, receptions, but there was always an undercurrent of hostility to one branded, or so they thought, with the mark of the nouveau riche. Even the radical politician John Burns, who had little to say in defense of the English upper classes, said, in reference to Astor, "I can stand a decent duke or a militant marquess, but I can't endure the miserable and ungentlemanly conduct of a new millionaire."

However grandiose his gestures, Astor found it impossible to make friends. He committed social gaffes of immense rudeness, and when, as an expression of his ultimate contempt for America, Astor donated the battle flag of the U.S.S. *Chesapeake,* made famous in the War of 1812 by Captain Lawrence's command, "Don't give up the ship!" to the Royal United Service Museum, there were many Englishmen who regarded the gesture as in execrable taste.

But Astor was unmoved. In 1899 he formally adopted British citizenship, and though crowds surged up Broadway to burn an effigy in Times Square of "the most hated American living," Astor relentlessly published, in his journals, expensive but highly questionable genealogical pedigrees that showed his ancestors were no less than Spanish Counts of Astorga, the blueness of whose blood was presumed an excellent recommendation for social acceptability. When the American press jeered at his presumptions, Astor passed a rumor that he had died of pneumonia and sat back to read his obituaries. Unfortunately, even they were not as conciliatory as he might have hoped.

Now that he was a British subject, Astor saw no obstacle why he should not become an aristocrat in fact, as well as in spirit. A "modern knight who wielded his cheque-book as a sword to win a patent of nobility in England," Astor began a concerted campaign to ingratiate himself with the government. He donated nearly $100,000 to the Boer War effort and like sums to Oxford and London universities. Cambridge received $50,000 as did four London charities.

In 1903 Astor purchased Hever Castle, the reputed birthplace of Anne Boleyn. Any nobleman worth his salt naturally had a castle, and Astor wanted the most famous one available. He was reported to have spent $10 million restoring Hever. The course of the River Eden was altered to create a lake. A new deer park was laid out, and a new bridge, power house, model farm, Italian garden, and mock-Tudor village were erected to entertain Astor's guests. Full-grown trees and huge rocks were imported to mask the castle from public eyes. And, as at Cliveden, a great wall was erected, this time with enormous electrically operated gates which could admit the favored and shut out the intruder at a moment's notice.

The model village was connected to the castle by a subway. Its piggeries were finished in costly oak, while, in the cowsheds and dairy, Italian tile mosaics were laid by craftsmen imported specifically for this purpose. No seat could compare with Astor's, and to it he invited those whom he wished to impress. But still no peerage was forthcoming, and Astor began to spend more and more time at his Italian villa, overlooking the Bay of Naples near Sorrento, where another million dollars was spent "re-creating an estate which a gentleman of the second century might well have enjoyed."

On Empire Day in 1911, the cream of English aristocracy gathered for a great costume ball at Claridge's Hotel. When clocks struck midnight, into the throng marched William Waldorf Astor wearing a peer's robes of state with a motto attached to his coronet: "499: just one more vacancy." Here stood a "mock peer in tinsel" making a final bid for ennoblement. It was an act spawned either from an immensely sophisticated sense of humor or from the depths of virtual desperation.

But Astor was fortunate. For, when the Great War broke out three years later, he was given an opportunity to demonstrate patriotic munificence. In the opening weeks of the conflict, he donated $125,000 to the Prince of Wales's fund, $180,000 to Lord Rothschild's Red Cross Fund, and $25,000 to Queen Mary's fund for women. Many bequests followed, including $125,000 for officers' families and an additional $100,000 to the Red Cross in 1915.

For the first time in his life, Astor began to receive a good press, and the end result was that, when the New Year's honors list for 1916 was released, it was announced that William Waldorf Astor had received a patent of nobility.

Hever Castle, the birthplace of Anne Boleyn, purchased by Astor as part of his campaign to become a peer. (Photograph courtesy Gavin, second Baron Astor of Hever)

Four months later he stood in crimson robes trimmed in ermine, amid his fellow peers in the House of Lords, to hear the Clerk of the House chant the familiar litany, "George V by the Grace of God of the United Kingdom of Great Britain and Ireland, of the British Dominions Beyond the Seas, King, Defender of the Faith, to all lords spiritual and temporal and all others our subjects whatsoever to whom these presents shall come, greeting:—know yet, that we of our especial grace, certain knowledge, and mere motion do by these presents advance, create and prefer our trusty cousin, William Waldorf Astor, to the state, degree, style, dignity, title and honour of the Baron Astor of Hever Castle in the County of Kent on this sixteenth day of April, 1916." And so, among "a host of English cotton-spinners, soap magnates, tobacconists, journalists and successful brokers," as Charles Beard described the upper house, Astor took his place as the first native-born American to be ennobled in England since the founding of the republic.

The following year he was elevated in the peerage to the rank of viscount, and spent a considerable amount of time designing the intricacies of his coat of arms. It was all that was left to an old man, whose health was fast failing, in virtual isolation.

In October 1919 Lord Astor died alone, not in the created magnificence of one of his great houses, nor in the affectionate bosom of his family, many of whom he had alienated. Instead he expired, as Michael Astor described it, "in a house in Brighton, imprisoned behind the locked doors of his lavatory." Even the chimera of a romantic exit was to be denied him; no doubt he would have described it as the final indignity.

The death of the first Viscount created consternation in his family. This was especially true for his eldest son and heir, Waldorf, who, in the absence of a law permitting renunciation of titles, was forced to give up a promising career in the House of Commons for the eternal somnambulism of the House of Lords.

Waldorf Astor had bright political ambitions, and both the intelligence and money to see them realized, but his position was inextricable. The only question that remained was, Who would take his place as the member of Parliament for

Lord Astor's coat of arms prepared, on his elevation to the peerage, by Charles Athill, the Richmond Herald at Arms. (Manuscripts and Archives Division, The New York Public Library, Astor, Lenox and Tilden Foundations; Astor Family Papers)

Oil on canvas, 1908
59¼'' × 39¼''
(The National Trust,
Cliveden)

Nancy Langhorne, Viscountess Astor, 1879–1964.
John Singer Sargent, 1856–1925.

Plymouth? The answer was to make British political history when it was announced that the new Viscount's wife, Nancy, would contest the seat for the Conservative party. Thus began one of the most provocative political careers of the twentieth century.

Nancy Langhorne was a Virginia beauty who married Waldorf Astor in 1906, after escaping to England to recover from a disastrous alliance with a confirmed alcoholic. Henry James declared that she was "full of possibilities and fine material though but a reclaimed barbarian, with all her bounty, spontaneity, and charm, too."

She was a capricious creature whose infectious enthusiasms could hardly go unnoticed by those who came within her orbit. Nancy was not a snob in the real sense of the word. She took the possession of great wealth for granted but refused to alter her personality to suit fashionable tastes in Britain. One thing she never did was to take the English upper classes as seriously as they took themselves. "You can't be a snob if you're a Virginian," she once declared, "because *we* can't imagine anyone being above us."

The Astors lived in the grand manner: at Cliveden, in London's St. James's Square; at Rest Harrow; at Sandwich; at Plymouth; and at a shooting box in Scotland—they migrated as occasion warranted. During the social season in the capital, there were frequent Astor receptions for anything up to one thousand people. Dinner parties for fifty or sixty were commonplace. And, at least twice during the year, their London mansion was the scene of a brilliant ball for five or six hundred.

An army of servants was in constant attendance—forty or fifty gardeners and a dozen stablemen for Cliveden, together with maids, cooks, footmen, and butlers of all descriptions. It was the most opulent of existences. Even the simplest occasion became a grand affair. One visitor to Cliveden recalled a summer invitation to tea: "Tea did I say? It was more like a Bedouin encampment. There was a table for tea, a table for cakes, a table for children, a table for grown-ups, a table for more grown-ups, and generally a nomadic group coming and going somewhere in the neighborhood of Nancy herself. Cushions, papers, people were mixed in a noble disarray. Nancy presided over the whole affair like a blend between Juno at the Siege of Troy, and one of the leading Valkyries caracoling over an appropriate battlefield."

Things were never stuffy at the Astors during Nancy's reign. Rather there was a Ruritanian quality of high bohemia, for Lady Astor was a literary and political lion-hunter who was far more pleased to banter with George Bernard Shaw and Ramsay MacDonald than to discuss needlepoint or fashion with Lady X, Y, or Z. John Singer Sargent, who drew Lady Astor twice, was surprisingly the only artist who was an intimate member of her circle. But their relationship was nothing if not proper, Sargent's life being, as his compatriot Logan Pearsall Smith wrote, "one of the greatest vacuums in the universe."

No one remained indifferent to Nancy Astor. "She either charmed or repelled," wrote one observer, who remarked that Nancy traded on her immense charm twenty-four hours a day. How could anyone remain serious about a point of discussion while watching Nancy "fan herself with a dinner plate, and push back her diamond tiara as if it had been an old hat."

But her enthusiasms had a darker side as well. Nancy Astor was a highly opinionated woman whose views, once formed, rarely changed. Under the influence of that dynamic duo, G. K. Chesterton and Hilaire Belloc, she came to believe that there was a conspiratorial Jewish plot against civilization. Lady Astor was never the most virulent of anti-Semites, yet the stain of religious bigotry was more or less a permanent part of her personality. So, too, was her contempt for Catholicism nurtured by Philip Kerr, the future Marquess of Lothian and wartime British ambassador in Washington. Kerr, a Catholic apostate, converted Nancy to Christian Science and turned her to the cause of ardent proselytism. But it was for Communists and their socialist fellow travelers, as Lady Astor saw them, that her most intense venom was reserved. And God save those individuals of left-wing sympathies who also happened to be Catholics or, even worse, Jews. They only confirmed her worst fears about the world for, as her biographer, Christopher Sykes, has written, there were two interdependent sides to Nancy's character. She was "the zealot, the missionary, impelled by love, who longed to help those she met, and the bigot, the woman of overbearing self-will, determined at all costs to get her own way, who at times entertained unusual and unnatural fears about the world and its wickedness."

On October 26, 1919, Lady Astor sent a telegram to the Conservative association of the Sutton Division of Plymouth, to announce that she would contest the seat being vacated by her husband's reluctant promotion to the House of Lords.

She was not the first woman to stand for Parliament. Seventeen of her sex were candidates in the general election of the previous year when women were first allowed to run. And one, the fiery Irish nationalist, Countess Markievicz, was elected for Dublin on the Sinn Fein ticket while serving one of her numerous sentences in Holloway Prison. But the revolutionary Countess, along with the seventy-three other members of her party who achieved election to the House of Commons, refused to take the mandatory loyalty oath to the King and was consequently disqualified from office.

And so it fell upon Nancy Astor to genuinely attempt to become the first woman actively seeking a place in the highest popular council of British government. She entered the lists with gusto, the *Daily Herald* of October 27 announcing, "Peer's Wife Enters To Fight Against Workers At Plymouth."

At the meeting of the Conservative association, where she was adopted unanimously, Lady Astor made it clear that she was not prepared to be simply a genteel substitute for her husband: "If you want an M.P. who will be a repetition of the 600 other M.P.'s, don't vote for me. If you want a lawyer or if you want a pacifist, don't elect me. If you can't get a fighting man, take a fighting woman. If you want a Bolshevist or a follower of Mr. Asquith, don't elect me. If you want a party hack, don't elect me. Surely we have outgrown party ties. I have. The war has taught us that there is a greater thing than parties, and that is the State."

Lithograph, 1919
6¾" × 8½"
(Richard Kenin)

Campaign broadside for Lady Astor.
Bowering Press, Plymouth.

She scorned the idea that a candidate had to look dowdy in order to curry favor. Dressed in the height of fashion, decked with pearls, Lady Astor drove about Plymouth in an open landau carriage, covered in red, white, and blue rosettes and driven by a huge, top-hatted coachmen in full livery. And wherever a group of people was seen standing together, that place became the site of a spontaneous campaign meeting, with Nancy standing in her carriage thundering, "Mr. Gay, the Labour candidate, represents the shirking classes, but I represent the working classes."

There was an ever-present sense of fun in the campaign, which was conducted much more along American than British lines. Over the years the Astors strove to create a special relationship with their constituents at Plymouth, which was rare in English politics though commonplace in the United States. And in the end it paid off, for on election day when the Town Clerk of Plymouth read out the results, the American Viscountess was elected with a comfortable majority of over five thousand votes.

At 3:35 on the afternoon of December 1, 1919, Lady Astor entered the chamber of the House of Commons dressed in a respectful suit of black, her head covered with a tricornered felt hat. She carried no purse, only a blue slip of paper, her election writ. At 3:45, the resonant voice of the Speaker of the House rang out, "Members desirous of taking their seats will come to the table."

It was a moment of high drama, of history in the making, as the first woman member to be seated in the British Parliament crossed the bar of the House. Flanked by two former Prime Ministers, Lloyd George and Balfour, both wearing full morning dress, Lady Astor advanced up the aisle of the House, pausing on three occasions to bow ceremoniously toward the Speaker's chair. Having surrendered her writ to the Clerk of the House, Lady Astor, a Bible in her right hand, swore the oath of fidelity in a smooth Southern accent that was not loud but carried throughout the chamber. She then signed the roll, shook hands with Mr. Speaker, and

The announcement of Lady Astor's election victory, November 28, 1919. The defeated Liberal and Labour candidates are on her left and right; Lord Astor appears at the far left. Photograph, in The Sphere, *November 29, 1919. (Astor Archives, The Library, University of Reading, England)*

retired from the House. Twenty-four years later she merrily recalled the occasion for the BBC: "I was introduced by Mr. Balfour and Mr. Lloyd George, men who had always been in favour of votes for women. But when I walked up the aisle of the House of Commons I felt that they were more nervous than I was, for I was deeply conscious of representing a cause, whereas I think they were a little nervous of having let down the House of Commons by escorting the Cause into it."

Nancy Astor served continuously in Parliament from 1919 until her retirement in 1945. She stoutly maintained, in her first campaign, that she was not a sex candidate. But, upon arriving in Westminster, Lady Astor soon found that the mantle of leadership of the cause for women's rights devolved upon her as a matter of course.

As a radical teetotaler, she chose the cause of prohibition as the subject of her maiden speech. It was not a popular issue; indeed, Lady Astor's career was full of lost causes. But, when she rose to address the House for the first time, members heard a voice dominated much more by emotional conviction than by a pragmatic desire to make political capital. Lady Astor opposed, on principle, the abolition of restrictions on drinking which had been in force since the outbreak of the Great War. But her reasons were unique: "I do not want you to look on your lady member as a fanatic or a lunatic. I am simply trying to speak for hundreds of women and children throughout the country who cannot speak for themselves. I want to tell you that I do know the working man, and I know that, if you tell him the truth about drink, he would be as willing as anybody else to put up with those *vexatious* restrictions."

Though politically a nominal Conservative, Lady Astor was eclectic in her ideology, arguing that it was "reactionaries who make revolutions." In regard to women's and children's rights, she always stood in the van, urging reform of the legal conditions governing guardianship; advocating more appointments for women in the Civil Service and on boards of enquiry where women's interests were at stake; promoting the supply of milk to the indigent and the suppression of prostitution. Equal opportunities for women accompanied by equal pay was one of her battle cries. And when, in subsequent years, other women joined her as Members of Parliament, Lady Astor went so far as to attempt the organization of a genuine women's party that rejected the conventional ideologies of all the established political organizations.

Tact was never one of her major virtues. Relying on her position as a woman, Lady Astor railed at her opponents in a personal manner that would never have been tolerated in a man. "I don't know whether I have become a force in the House of Commons as much as a nuisance," she said in 1921. The answer was that Nancy Astor, the political gadfly, did not always produce instant results—she only once initiated successful legislation in the real sense—but her influence in the long term was by no means nugatory.

It was the unmitigated abrasiveness of her manner, so evident in parliamentary and committee debates, that raised the hackles of many members, who found the very presence of women—much less aggressive women—an intrusion into the councils of government. Winston Churchill, the Secretary of State for War, was one of those who refused to hide his dislike for the "American virago." The Duchess of Marlborough recalled a famous incident when both Churchill and the Astors were staying at Blenheim Palace. Throughout the weekend the two politicos argued tenaciously over government policy, which climaxed during one breakfast when Nancy exclaimed: "Winston, if I was married to you I'd put poison in your coffee."

To which Churchill replied: "Nancy, if I was married to you, I'd drink it!"

On another occasion she accosted Churchill in the corridors of the House of Commons and demanded to know why he always treated her with such pointed lack of gallantry. "Because," he replied, "I find a woman's intrusion into the House of Commons as embarrassing as if she burst into my bedroom when I had nothing with which to defend myself, not even a sponge."

Nancy responded in a drawl, "Winston, you're not handsome enough to have worries o'that kind."

By 1930 Lady Astor had seen her best days in Parliament. Her influence, such that it was, steadily declined though her vitality masked this situation from the general public. Nancy frequently spoke before she thought. She was not a fascist, much less a Nazi, but her irresistible urge to speak immediately and over-confidently on any and every question without prior deliberation did convince many that there was something dangerous in her political philosophy, and this, too, contributed to her decline in public esteem.

A rumor arose in the mid-thirties that there existed a Cliveden Set, a group of powerful right-wing Englishmen who sought to influence British policy toward an accommodation with Hitler, and Nancy Astor was placed directly at the center of the conspiracy. Her greatest mistake was never to deny it effectively. The English Left lambasted her from pillar to post and were, surprisingly, joined by the British fascists who denied that Germany could ever make friends with the nasty "powers of money and the Press" symbolized by Cliveden.

So poor had Nancy Astor's political instincts become, and so extreme her views, that she did not see the storm that was gathering about her. In May 1937 she made a speech on the need of an Anglo-German pact as a bulwark against communism. It was by no means a novel argument, but a month later, while on a visit to America, she grotesquely elaborated her views at a press conference, which convinced everyone that an anti-Semitic harridan was in their midst. *The New York Times* reported,

Lady Astor voiced a warning that the backers of anti-German feeling were overplaying their hands, and declared that if the Jews were behind it they were going too far, and they needed to take heed. "I am pro-Jew and have always been a Zionist," Lady Astor declared, "but anyone who reads the papers can see what is coming; it will react against them. And I tell all my Jewish friends the same thing. I am against Communism which may also be partly responsible for this sentiment. Communism is the most horrible thing in the world today. I

"Where Our Foreign Policy Comes From." *The Cliveden Set was a name which conjured up images
of Nazi sympathizers gathering at the Astor family home. At the center of this alleged conspiracy
stood the uncowed figure of Nancy Astor. David Low, 1891–1963.*

hate all dictators and it is appalling to see this propaganda playing into their
hands.

To one of her son's German friends she volunteered the view that Hitler was
quite right to rearm, as the Reich was surrounded by hostile Roman Catholic
powers. Fortunately, the young man could only believe she was in jest.

Such publicly stated views, combined with an ill-timed gesture of hospitality to
the Nazi Foreign Minister von Ribbentrop convinced many people that the criticisms leveled against Lady Astor were true or else her judgment was now so poor as
to border on irresponsibility.

By 1942 there were those who questioned the wisdom of allowing her to continue as a member of the House of Commons. At least one trade union local went on
record demanding her internment for treasonous behavior. Nancy did little to allay
public fears. On one occasion she actually went so far as to warn the House, publicly,
that the BBC was being infiltrated by Roman Catholics bent on subversion, a charge
she leveled frequently at the Foreign Office.

Two years later her eccentric behavior reached a point where her husband demanded in no uncertain terms that she retire from politics. In essence, their marriage was at stake, for Lord Astor was deeply upset that his wife might soon become
a laughingstock, and saw quite clearly that her influence in Parliament was at an end.

*Emerald, Lady Cunard (Maud Burke), circa
1872–1948. Marjorie, Marchioness of
Anglesey, 1883–1946.*

It was a bitter blow to leave Parliament, which had been the hub of her existence for a quarter-century, and Lady Astor was never truly to forgive Waldorf for imposing his will upon her.

"I am an extinct volcano," she cried to reporters on the New York docks in January 1946. But there was enough brimstone in the old system still to cause people to sit up and take notice. Nancy had read that former Vice President Henry Wallace had spoken of the century of the common man. She disagreed completely, "It isn't the common man who is important, it is the uncommon man. You Americans like to quote Abraham Lincoln as a great common man, but you've had only one Lincoln." It was a statement reminiscent of another oft-quoted "Astorism": "The Socialists believe in equality: the man who starts from scratch and gets on the top they now tell us is a public danger. I suppose they want the man who starts from scratch and just keeps on scratching."

She was the most freewheeling, unabashed politician of her generation, who was either hated or loved but certainly never ignored. She was one of a kind—a genuine original. And while one could debate ad nauseam her utility to British political life, few would argue that, as a source of provocative stimulation, she was of immense value.

There were those, however, who found Lady Astor appalling on all fronts and, in the case of one particular individual, the feeling was genuinely mutual. Few were the women whom Nancy Astor disliked as much as Lady Cunard. It was a passion she shared with Queen Mary. Unlike Nancy, "Emerald" Cunard (she found her given name, Maud, somewhat common) was definitely of a type. She was the American society hostess determined to conquer London. Yet Henry James, in all his imaginative wisdom, could never have conjured a character quite as extreme as the formidable Emerald.

The transformation of Maud Alice Burke into Emerald, Lady Cunard, was a classic case of money marrying money. Maud Burke was the honorary niece of Horace Carpentier, an instant California millionaire sprung full grown from the Comstock Lode. Little Maud, "the yellow canary," was heiress to the Carpentier fortune and, thus endowed, launched herself on international society, determined to make an advantageous match.

After failing to capture the Prince André Poniatowski, grandson of the last King of Poland, by unilaterally announcing their engagement in the press, Maud settled, in 1895, at the age of twenty-three, for Sir Bache Cunard, whose grandfather had founded the great steamship company.

Sir Bache, twenty years her senior, found his chief diversions in the pleasures of the hunt, the paddock, and the kennel. At his country seat, Nevill Holt, a sprawling architectural pile near Market Harborough in Leicestershire, Maud found little that appealed to her highly strung personality. Everything was much too quiet, pedestrian, and boring—all in an upper-class way, of course.

It did not take long for Maud to remove to London, first to Carlton House Terrace, and then to a large corner house in Grosvenor Square, long a mecca for wealthy American expatriates, from whence she rarely ventured back into the country.

London, and more particularly Mayfair, was her milieu. It was the gathering point, not just for the wealthy and highborn, but also for the creative genius of the artistic Establishment. And to both groups Maud, rechristened Emerald, made her pitch. Swathed in emeralds, diamonds, and pearls, with innumerable rings on her clawlike hands, Emerald, dressed in the extreme height of fashion, with theatrical makeup more reminiscent of the pantomime stage than the London drawing room, set out to re-create a salon along the lines made fashionable in the previous century by Mme. Récamier.

At the outset, much of Edwardian society found her high-pitched machinations repellent, but by 1907 her position was sufficiently established, through social allies, that the author Maurice Baring could say that the time had arrived when he could resign with honor from "The Society for Prevention of Cruelty to Lady Cunard."

But even those who detested her had to admit that Emerald possessed a certain attraction. Virginia Woolf caustically referred to that "ridiculous little parakeet faced woman . . . but not quite sufficiently ridiculous" whose London house, draped in gold, silk, and marble, was dreadfully overdone. But, nevertheless, she had to acknowledge that Emerald "no doubt has her acuity, her sharp peck at life," with an "astonishing competence in the commerce of life."

She was not merely a socially ambitious snob whose ruthlessness was matched by her charm and unabashed wit. At the same time Emerald was an attentive, though eclectic, patron, not only of the established arts, but of all that was avant-garde. Ezra Pound and Wyndham Lewis were just as likely to be seen at Lady Cunard's as was the "libidinous old gargoyle," George Moore (whose passion for Emerald was unabating), or Sir Thomas Beecham whom Emerald, in turn, endlessly pursued.

It was variety that Lady Cunard celebrated. She did not require equal numbers of men and women at her soirees. Her guests were invited "for conversation, not for mating." If men were not important, they at least had to be amusing. And if women were not beautiful, they had to compensate with intelligence—mere money was never a sufficient passport. Richard Aldington was advised by H. G. Wells to cultivate the fabulous Emerald, for "If you want to meet the Prime Minister and the Archbishop of Canterbury at lunch, she can do it." Indeed, there were few other places in London where politicians and financiers could readily mingle on equal terms with the outstanding musicians, poets, painters, and, occasionally, even actors of the day.

At the zenith of her career, when all London was aware of her extensive support of the British National Theatre and Opera Companies, the poet Colin Hurry wrote one of his popular *Premature Epitaphs* in her honor:

> *Speak deferentially*
> *Here of the dead*
> *Tread reverentially*
> *Bare now your head*
> *Sculptor, musician*
> *Painter or bard*
> *That owe your position*
> *To Lady Cunard*

Emerald Cunard's parties were never mere social occasions; they were theatrical events. She frequently arrived slightly late, making an entrance with, in Roderick Cameron's words, "an extraordinary walk, like a temperamental racehorse being led into the paddock . . . stamping also it might be called a doe."

But however coveted an invitation to Lady Cunard's, she had the reputation of an enfant terrible whose banter only lightly covered a streak of maliciousness. Emerald thrived on verbal badinage, and woe to any guest of hers whose hide was not particularly thick.

Poor Michael Arlen was introduced by his hostess as "the only Armenian who has not been murdered," while the Russian Grand Duke Dimitri was presented loudly to her guests as "the murderer of Rasputin." When Somerset Maugham, who always retired early, attempted to leave one of Emerald's parties, she objected: "But you can't go now the evening has just begun."

"I daresay, Emerald, but I have to keep my youth."

*Oil on canvas,
date unknown
20" × 40" (sight)
(Sir Rupert
Hart-Davis)*

*George Moore sitting with Lady Cunard in her Grosvenor Square draw-
ing room.   Sir John Lavery, 1856–1941.*

"Then why didn't you bring him with you?" she replied dryly. "I should have been delighted to meet him."

To one well-known demimonde whose sex life was far from discreet, Emerald advised, "You should go on the stage, my dear. Then we could all know you."

Her life was a succession of bons mots but, as a prefigurement of the times, she struck just the right chord. One child of the sun, Harold Acton, gushed effusively:

> It is difficult to telescope so many flawless occasions when poetry melted into music and music crystallized into poetry again, evenings when nothing in the world mattered but the purest art, whose essence was all around us like the fragrance of cassia. We bridged the space separating past from present, dream from reality, invisible from visible. The *cafferi* clock made our time more precious and we enjoyed an entrancing ballet of the hours. Here life was thoroughly spent not economised. Lady Cunard had created an ideal setting for a synthesis of the arts. One could only abandon oneself joyfully, inhaling the luxuriance of sight and sound until one was lapped into silence. The pretentiousness that paraded in other "literary" houses was absent: there was never a false note.

Emerald's era was a time when sensibility and sentiment became confused; when verbal strychnine was laced with saccharin; when it was debonair to utter cant and pass it off as wisdom. In the twenties there was a desperate longing to recapture the gaiety and ease of society as it had existed before the Great War, but somehow it was all terribly forced. Emerald and her coterie of aesthetes could gather for all-night revels at smoke-filled meccas like the fabled Embassy Club where, above the din, the new phrases "I couldn't have liked it more" and "I couldn't care less" rose and fell amid endless embraces and shouts of "Darling!" Such places were perfect for individuals like Lady Cunard, who was so afraid of being alone that, whenever her house emptied, she instantly retired to the telephone to continue "meaningful" conversations. But, in the end, it was a life much closer to a Noël Coward farce than a Scott Fitzgerald novel. For, beneath the elaborate attempt to manufacture a romantic existence, there was very little of the stuff of intellectual or even emotional commitment. Instead, it was a life dependent on the ethereal cotton candy of endless socializing, where one simply kept moving, smiling, and endlessly talking, so as to avoid the silences that implied instantaneous boredom and isolation. To the writer John Lehmann, Emerald once admitted, "No man, John, has ever said to me 'I love you!' But I have had letters—I have had *letters*!" That was all that lay behind her mask of fantasy, a fantasy that acted out the dreams of an entire generation of her compatriots.

If Emerald Cunard did have goals in life, they were unquestionably social ones. And, as for so many affluent Americans in England after the Great War, this meant acceptance into the circle of the Prince of Wales, the "once and future king" Edward VIII. In many ways it was a re-creation of the Marlborough House Set which had enclosed the Prince's grandfather, His Late Majesty Edward VII. In her mansion Lady Cunard created a refuge for the heir to the throne where, at intimate gatherings, he could relax with a social set quite different from the foreign princesses and lanky debutantes who fluttered in and out of the Court of George V.

Daphne Fielding reports one memorable occasion when, at Lady Cunard's, the Prince sat down to lunch next to the erratic painter, Wyndham Lewis, who proceeded, true to form, to play with a small pistol on the table in front of him. Was it to be an occasion of suicide or royal assassination? Emerald took no chances. Quickly picking up the gun she remarked, "Oh what an elegant object, is it loaded with black pearls?" (an apparent reference to the *Duchess of Malfi,* Emerald's favorite play) and promptly deposited it in her purse.

This was just the sort of occasion that the Prince's mother, Queen Mary, frowned upon. She was convinced that the unconventionality of the Cunard circle was having an appalling influence on her son, and consequently held the lowest sort of opinion of such a hostess. But disapproval at Court was of little concern to one who was playing for higher stakes. George V was rapidly becoming an old man, and when he died there would be a new sovereign in Buckingham Palace who would no doubt receive Lady Cunard with especial grace. Emerald was intimately aware of the Prince's growing fondness for the American socialite Wallis Simpson, and is said to have taken an active hand in promoting the relationship by providing a quiet venue where the two could meet. How perfect should Britain have an American Queen!

Emerald envisioned a role for herself close to the throne. She would be Mistress of the Robes at the Court of Queen Wallis: it was not a dream entirely of her own creation; no less a figure than the irrepressible Henry Channon, M.P., had discussed the probability with her.

Henry Channon—his friends called him "Chips"—was the masculine equivalent to Lady Cunard. Born and raised in an atmosphere of prosperity in America, he spent his adult life within the fold of the English aristocracy, acting out dreams of kings and courts while consciously purging himself of what he regarded as a pernicious heritage.

Younger than Emerald by a quarter-century, temperamentally there was in Chips a little of Henry James and a great deal of Evelyn Waugh. Educated at Oxford, married to Lady Honor Guinness, eldest daughter of the fabulously wealthy second Earl of Iveagh, Chips decided at a young age that his spiritual home was England. He wrote, "I have put my whole life's work into my anglicization, in ignoring my early life." For in England, "where women are all sirens and men are all gods," he could play at being a gentleman in a world of large country houses and London society where rank, wealth, and privilege were the primary qualities by which a man was judged.

Toward America there was nothing but antipathy. "The more I know of American civilization," he wrote as a very young man, "the more I despise it. It is a menace to

Oil on canvas, 1938
60″ × 40½″ (sight)
(Paul Channon,
M.P.)

Sir Henry "Chips" Channon, 1897–1958, with his son, Paul. James Gunn, dates unknown.

the peace and future of the world. If it triumphs, the old civilizations, which love beauty and peace and the arts and rank and privilege will pass from the picture. And all we will have left will be Fords and cinemas. Ugh!"

Who, then, were his heroes? Why, no less than the Ludwigs of Bavaria, on whom he became an authority. How predictable that Chips and Emerald Cunard should be the closest of friends—two rococo figures in an age fast purging itself of traditional romanticism. In 1927, when he inherited the estate of his grandfather, Channon, whose maintenance was already secure, wrote with glee that he now belonged "definitely to the order of those who HAVE—and through no effort of my own, which is such a joy."

Chips was one of those individuals who, although emotionally committed to a social outlook that was both superficial and elitist in the worst sense of the word, was far too intelligent not to critically assess the ultimate reality of his position. Privately he produced self-deprecating analyses, as if in anticipation of the criticism of others. It was an act of self-protection, but nevertheless does reveal more of the psychology of the real man than any public action. He referred to himself as a "rake grown old before his time." A man often disappointed in companionship who found true friendship impossible. A character out of a Disraelian novel for whom drunkenness was dull but sobriety prosy; for whom literature grew stale and sexual intercourse no more than a source of fatigue; for whom wealth was surfeiting but poverty as an alternative far too debasing, for Chips was always more concerned with the spending of money than the making of it:

> Sometimes, I think I have an unusual character—able but trivial; I have flair, intuition, great good taste but only second rate ambition; I am far too suscepti-ble to flattery; I hate and am uninterested in all the things most men like such as sport, business, statistics, debates, speeches, war and the weather; but I am riveted by lust, furniture, glamour and society and jewels. I am an excellent organizer and have a will of iron; I can only be appealed to through my vanity. Occasionally I must have solitude; my soul craves for it. All thought is done in solitude; only then can I be partly happy.

The Channons' London home at 5 Belgrave Square became famous in the 1930s as one of the last places in the capital where life in the grand manner was still carried on. Harold Nicolson remembered a house "all Regency upstairs with very carefully draped curtains and Madame Récamier sofas and wall paintings. Then the dining-room is entered through an orange lobby and discloses itself suddenly as a copy of the blue room of the Amalienburg [Palace] near Munich—baroque and rococo and what-ho and oh-no no and all that, very fine indeed." There Chips and his guests ate off gold plate from a service originally made as a wedding present from Napoleon to his sister, Pauline Borghese: "It bears the Borghese arms with the French Imperial Crown, and very grand it looks."

The famous rococo dining room in the Channons' house at 5 Belgrave Square, decorated in emulation of the Amalienburg Palace. (Photograph courtesy Country Life)

His marriage to Lady Honor Guinness also provided Chips with a ready-made occupation. Without too much difficulty, he was elected, in 1935, as the Conservative Member of Parliament for Southend, a seat that had been held continually by her family since 1918. It is a seat which is held today by Channon's own son, Paul.

In the House of Commons, Chips was a well-known social figure, though as a political power he never approached the influence of his compatriot, Lady Astor, whose own career had long passed its peak. Chips treated the House more like a gentleman's club, and on that basis he was readily received: "No one now enjoys the House of Commons more than I. I am truly bitten by it. The first week I was shy but flattered, then I had a fortnight of doubt and of boredom, but ever since I have loved every minute of it. I like the male society. It reminds me of Oxford or perhaps of the private school to which I never went." But if in Parliament Chips was a self-proclaimed nonentity, in Society he was a power and reveled in supping with all the royals.

On November 18, 1936, he confided to his diary, "We were invited to eleven dinner parties tonight. The Iveaghs, while amused by our royal activities, are nevertheless impressed. Their gangster son-in-law from Chicago has put their daughter in the most exclusive set in Europe!" Nineteen thirty-six was also the year of the abdication. And Chips's ability to hobnob with the royal family was not just a sign of social preeminence; it had become a matter of national politics. Channon, like Emerald Cunard, cast his lot on the side of the anticipated new regime, as society divided into Cavaliers and Roundheads on the issue of the King's proposed marriage. He wrote, "The Simpson scandal is growing, and she, poor Wallis, looks unhappy. The world is closing in around her, the flatterers, the sycophants, and the malice. It is a curious social juxta-position that casts me in the role of Defender of the King. But I do, and very strongly in society, not for loyalty so much as for admiration and affection for Wallis, and in indignation against those who attack her."

Throughout November and early December the crisis over "the King's matter" reached a critical point, and it appeared for a time that the whole institution of monarchy in Britain might be compromised, so set was Stanley Baldwin's government against accepting Mrs. Simpson on the throne. As it became clear that either the Sovereign or Mrs. Simpson would have to go, those like Chips and Emerald who were among the most intimate members of the King's party were no longer socially invulnerable. At a "pompous manqué dinner" at Emerald Cunard's, an anonymous piece of venom was passed to the hostess which began, "You old bitch, trying to make up to Mrs. Simpson, in order to curry favour with the King." Chips noted that Emerald was both frightened and yet rather flattered. He saw clearly that he and his wife would soon be "out of the royal racket having backed the wrong horse, but I don't much mind." Yet when Edward VIII finally announced his abdication, so that he might marry the woman he loved, Chips lost his temper with "any Roundhead I could see, and hurled abuse at them in my royalist fury." Emerald Cunard wept bitterly, "How *could* he do this to me?" She took it as a personal slap, which was perhaps the most remarkable of her many fantasies.

Nancy Astor, on the other hand, had not supported Mrs. Simpson with enthusiasm, and when the abdication was proclaimed she personally broadcast in the early hours of the morning, to the United States, assuring her compatriots that the British government had not rejected Mrs. Simpson as an anti-American gesture. There were real fears in high government circles that the Americans would be deeply offended, which explains in part why, when the new King George VI came to the throne, Lady Astor was invested with the insignia of the Order of Companions of Honour which she wore with her robes of state to the Coronation in Westminster Abbey. Chips was also at the ceremony, as a Member of Parliament, and so taken was he with the splendor of the occasion that in the evening he confided to his diary, "I must really try and be a Peer before the next Coronation."

But romantic dreams of donning the crimson and ermine of the British aristocracy could scarcely be indulged in the late 1930s as Europe careened toward the holocaust of war. Like so many affluent Americans resident in Britain, Chips was far more frightened of communism than of the rising Nazi horde. His political views, in the words of the historian Robert Rhodes James, were "vehemently conventional." This was a polite way of explaining a pro-German perspective in rational terms. Like many of his class, Chips was a zealous advocate of the appeasement policy of the Chamberlain government. He supported the Hoare-Laval pact over Abyssinia; saw Franco as the savior of Spain; and, most important, argued that Mussolini and Hitler, whose historic cultures he greatly admired, be left alone. At Lady Astor's, Chips attended "a grand Disraelian 'do'—diamonds, superb wine, and all the 'dips' and 'pols'. The function will be criticised, since there is already talk of a so-called

'Cliveden' set which is alleged to be pro-Hitler, but which, in reality, is only pro-Chamberlain and pro-sense."

While Emerald Cunard and Nancy Astor entertained von Ribbentrop in London, Chips, a high churchman, joined with them in seeing a Jewish conspiracy behind every anti-Nazi declaration. Latent anti-Semitism had always been fashionable among the English upper classes. And for Americans who attempted to assimilate into that culture, to purge themselves consciously of their own native heritage out of a passionate Anglophilia or a profound sense of national inadequacy, it was not unusual for the most unattractive sides of the English aristocratic temperament to be the most readily absorbed. Such was the nature of the transatlantic chameleon. But again, although Chips's emotional attitudes guided his everyday activities, he was far too clever not to know what was really happening. He embraced the credo of the romantic with all his heart, but could not ignore the fact that "England is on the decline, and that we shall dwindle for a generation or so. We are a tired race and our genius seems dead . . . after twenty years my infatuation is wearing off—and I am tiring of England, perhaps of the world. But English life remains [for me] the only possible existence."

All too quickly the world of Chips Channon was dying. Many of the great mansions of the capital, including Londonderry House and Holland House, were being closed, and it was unlikely that they would ever open again. Even Emerald Cunard was attempting to sell her house.

"It would indeed be the end of a chapter were that to go," mused Chips, "however, I have had twenty years of splendour, fun and life—the Twilight of the Gods, it was worth it and nothing matters now—I have Gibbonian apprehensions."

His fears, however rhetorically expressed, were not misplaced.

Lady Astor robed as a peeress of the realm for the coronation of King George VI, 1937. (Photograph courtesy Valentine Museum, Richmond, Virginia)

9

The Captains of Commerce and Journalism:
Gordon Selfridge and Ralph D. Blumenfeld

—October 14, 1917—The cannons were over eighty miles away on the plains of the Essex coast; yet their boom-boom-boom could be heard distinctly without interruption. Ralph David Blumenfeld, RDB as the newspaper reading public knew him, sat writing in the garden of his half-timbered Tudor house near the village of Great Easton, the very garden in which H. G. Wells set many of the conversations of *Mr. Britling.* It was a familiar routine for one of the lions of British journalism, a regular course of business stretching back over twenty years. But the holocaust had changed everything, and, as he conjured his editorial columns for the London *Daily Express,* Blumenfeld reflected on the comparative frivolity of the world he had known in England prior to the Great War: "We used to agitate ourselves over freak dinners, over yacht races, over Derby winners and Mr. Bernard Shaw's lampoons on society. We found food for excitement in quarrels between Lords and Commons and Mrs. Pankhurst's lady rioters. We thought the end of all things had come when Sir Edward Carson's Ulster Volunteers marched unmolested along the wondering streets of Belfast, and we filled our papers with columns of the Kaiser's vows of friendship for the rest of the world." It was a cold douche, this war, which had awakened John Bull from a long sleep. The corpulent Edwardian gastronome had forfeited his place to a modern St. George out to slay the Hunnish dragon for King and country. England could never be the same again, wrote RDB, for the agricultural population had glimpsed a future that had no workhouse at the end of it: "Our youths are going to grow up with a chance to do things. The women who have come out into the world and gained a peep at it will see to that. That horrible ogre, Tradition, lies in the dust. Butlers are not going to bring up their boys to be butlers merely because their fathers before them were butlers. Since the son of a butler can be an officer in the Army, if he is good enough for the work, it has dawned on the people that there is a chance for everyone who will take it."

This was good wartime rhetoric, laced with a tinge of Blumenfeld's Yankee realism, composed not for just a few friends but for the eyes of a nation. Yet it was by no means an absolute manifesto of the true believer. RDB was far from a utopian socialist; indeed he was a founder of the Anti-Socialist Union, who, more than most, nostalgically venerated the old ways and styles. And among the great journalists of his generation it was his voice, an American voice ironically, that gracefully chided the British against moving too quickly toward a Shavian future lest they sacrifice much in the body politic that ought to be conserved.

Born and raised in rural Wisconsin, a child of German-Jewish refugees who fled from the continental revolution of 1848, Ralph Blumenfeld gravitated, as a young man, to New York, possessed of an all-consuming passion to become a great journalist—the man who charged the emotions and molded the opinions of thousands, not just once but every day of the year. Blumenfeld was a classic reporter with a natural gift for language. He served an apprenticeship with the United Press and was such a success that he became its special correspondent: first, at the Democratic Convention which nominated Grover Cleveland for the Presidency; and later, at the 1887 Golden Jubilee celebration of Queen Victoria's accession to the throne.

Blumenfeld was a lover of spectacle, and his reportage in the early days often veered toward the sensationalistic; he knew what the people wanted and gave it to them in abundance. After leaving the United Press he went briefly into the employ of the New York *Journal,* but was soon spotted and brought onto the staff of the *Herald* at the express instructions of its fabled proprietor, the "Commodore," James Gordon Bennett, Jr.

From his mansion on the Avenue Champs-Elysées in Paris, Bennett ruled the *Herald,* and his other publications, with a highly capricious though unmistakable fist of iron. Blumenfeld was an immediate favorite of the Commodore, who cabled him one afternoon with the news that he had been appointed temporary news editor of the New York *Evening Telegram,* the night edition of the *Herald,* "a job requiring a cold head and heavy fist in dealing with a gang of hickory-faced reporters, all of them I think much older than myself and with more worldly guile at their disposal." Through mere motion, Bennett delighted in manipulating his employees. A year after his first promotion, Blumenfeld was informed that he was to take a steamer to France the very next morning to receive personal instructions from the Commodore, who received callers much in the manner of an Eastern potentate. "When you return to New York," he told Blumenfeld, "you will be managing editor of the *Telegram*! But you will be a *Herald* man just the same. Your code name in the *Herald* code for cables will be 'Activity.'"

It was by no means a misplaced label. For, after briefly returning to New York, Blumenfeld found himself cast in the role of an international shuttlecock, bouncing back and forth across the Atlantic for interviews with his sovereign lord, which was no mean feat considering the time that was still required for a voyage from the New World to the Old.

In September 1890, Blumenfeld arrived in Paris but remained only a few moments. "Please go to London today," Bennett ordered. He was losing £1,000 a week on the London daily and Sunday editions of the *Herald,* and "I want you to conduct the funeral, so to speak." Blumenfeld had the option of saving the Sunday edition if he wished, but Bennett did not want to be bothered with details. He warned RDB, "If you go on with it and lose a lot of money I will hold it against you. If you make a lot of money I'll give you a third of the profits—but you'll not make it. . . . But whatever you do don't worry [me] about it. I hate the very name of London now."

Blumenfeld exceeded his proprietor's expectations and, after a few months, with a circulation of over 60,000, actually reported a small profit on the books. At which point a telegram arrived from Paris.

> CONGRATULATE YOU ON HAVING MADE A PROFIT AT LAST. STOP THE PAPER AT ONCE. CLOSE THE OFFICE. DISMISS EVERYBODY.

The formidable Mr. Bennett was nothing if not unpredictable.

Blumenfeld stayed on as the London correspondent of the *Herald,* a position of no small importance, for London was the great diplomatic and political center of the

Photograph, circa 1904 6″ × 4¼″ (Sir John [Blumenfeld] Elliot)

Ralph David Blumenfeld, 1864–1948. This studio photograph was taken about the time he became editor-in-chief of the Daily Express. *Unidentified photographer.*

world. But, in order to operate effectively, he was forced to adjust radically his methods of gathering news.

In America the personal journalism of Charles Dana, Wilbur Story, and the Commodore's father, the elder Bennett, so marked by adjectival assaults and political harangues of interminable length, had been replaced by the cyclone of sensationalism of the Brothers Pulitzer and the eminently base William Randolph Hearst. It was in this latter school that young Ralph Blumenfeld had been educated, but in England he found things were quite different. *The Times* was pontifical; the *Morning Post* snobbish, with information about duchesses and advertisements about butlers; the *Standard* was commercial; the *Daily News* purely literary—what came to be called *highbrow*; and the *Daily Telegraph* just a trifle vulgar because it printed things which others did not—"London Day by Day as it were." Front pages were full of dull advertisements and announcements that scarcely bore reporting. Indeed, there was an utter absence of information concerning just what the peoples of the world were doing outside their respective houses of government.

The British press was hallmarked by respectability and, as Blumenfeld saw it, "Respectability demanded not only that a newspaper *be* dull, but that it *look dull* as well." Not surprisingly, he found most British reporters "as a body were unoriginal and lethargic," for they had never had to cope with the master of the New York *Herald*.

But the rules of the game demanded a new demeanor from the *Herald*'s London correspondent if he were to successfully fill his long weekend cables with the personal opinions and political pronouncements of the great. Consequently, off came the tweed suits, the light flannel shirts, and the bowler hat, to be replaced by the essential frock coat, the white linen shirt, and the top hat of finest silk. One could not loiter about Parliament hoping to buttonhole a leading member, as was common in Washington. Instead, a polite letter had to be sent at least ten days in advance, asking for the favor of an interview, which was frequently refused, unless the great man had something in particular he wished to make public.

After three productive years in London, Blumenfeld, at the age of thirty, found himself an established figure in the British journalistic fraternity, a *Wunderkind* of consequence, the influence of whose newspaper could not be ignored. Once again, however, the capricious hand of James Gordon Bennett was felt on his shoulder. Summoned peremptorily to France, RDB was informed that he was to return to New York to supervise the construction of Stanford White's new *Herald* building, a copy of the town hall of Verona, which Bennett proposed to erect uptown between Broadway and Sixth Avenue on Thirty-fifth Street, in competition with Joseph Pulitzer's much-publicized skyscraper near the Brooklyn Bridge.

Walking with Bennett along the Promenade des Anglais at Nice, Blumenfeld strongly objected to the location of the new building. He couldn't understand the logic of so radical a move, particularly to a site held under a thirty-year ground lease which would revert to the original owners. "The wholesale newspaper distributors will not go so far uptown for their supplies and we shall miss many ferry and railroad connections," he told the Commodore. There followed the retort: "Never mind Blumenfeld, thirty years from now the *Herald* will be in Harlem and I'll be in hell!"

The building, topped by its owl, was put up and, when it was completed, the newspaper's city editor boldly announced that the address of the new premises was "Herald Square, New York." No official permission was sought. It was a magnificent case of assumption, closely emulated by Adolph Ochs when he erected *The New York Times* building on Forty-second Street.

RDB returned to London, his task completed, but Bennett had other things in mind. The Commodore had decided that, while Blumenfeld had an appreciable acumen for the business side of newspapers, he really did not understand what constituted news. He told Blumenfeld this in no uncertain terms and ordered him back to New York. It was really too much for one who had proven himself on numerous occasions. Blumenfeld returned to Manhattan only to close up his affairs, and promptly resigned his post at the *Herald* in a terse cable to Bennett. The two men never met again, though a rapprochement of sorts was effected some years later.

Blumenfeld could easily have gone to another New York newspaper, but England was now in his blood and, for him, there was no other place but London.

Rather than direct his attention to the construction of sentences and paragraphs, RDB began to think in terms of dollars and cents, and of pounds, shillings, and pence. It had not escaped his notice that the British newspaper industry was desperately old-fashioned in clinging to slow, costly, and cumbersome methods of hand-typesetting for each daily edition. Always a great believer in the advantages of mechanization, Blumenfeld saw in this blind spot a chance to score a financial success by promoting the use of linotype machines, which were already common in America.

From the Empire Typesetting Machine Company of New York, he secured European manufacturing rights, and proceeded to set up a factory in Batley, near Leeds. The whole venture was an enormous success. British newspaper proprietors were quick to see the advantages of Blumenfeld's product, and within a short time a minor revolution had been effected in English pressrooms. RDB envisioned a new Golconda "of safes full of golden sovereigns and a steam yacht for myself as well as a sailing contraption to challenge the New York Yacht Club." He was even tempted to join the elite ranks of newspaper owners when Bowchier Hawksley, Cecil Rhodes's solicitor, offered to sell him not only the *Observer* but also the *Sunday Times* for £5,000 "There was, of course, not much lock, very little stock, and you could not see the barrel"—so he backed away from it. Years later he recalled how William Waldorf Astor's investment in the *Observer* had netted him, every year, "a most picturesque profit," while other owners could not make it go. Blumenfeld was not wistful about an opportunity lost. He sensed that, although he had been fortunate in his first business enterprise, it was not a life which best suited him. Eventually there would have to be a return to the pressroom, for "I had printer's ink in my veins."

But, although he seemed unaware of it, Blumenfeld was of a type. He was the new man of a new century, the American carrying the technology of the Western colossus to older civilizations. The weight of the commercial pendulum was shifting, and American influences could no longer be ignored in Europe.

Andrew Carnegie was one Briton who saw the unmistakable trend in things. One October day in 1900, he descended on London from his Scottish castle to do some shopping with RDB as company. Carnegie was annoyed with London's shopping methods which he declared all wrong. "Just look at the jumble in the windows," he said, "so much stuff that you cannot take it all in. And when you go into a shop they treat you most indifferently. You are scowled at if you ask for goods out of the ordinary, and you are made to feel uncomfortable if you do not buy. These shop people drive away more people than they attract. That's all wrong. . . . What London wants is a good shaking up."

It was a prophetic comment, for what London's retail trade was about to experience was no mere tremor; it was an earthquake which bore the name of Harry Gordon Selfridge. "Mile a Minute" Harry, who frequently thundered, "There is no room here for yesterday. Ours is today and tomorrow and next year!" was the titan

*Oil on canvas,
circa 1935
44½'' × 38''
(Selfridge's Ltd. of
London)*

*Harry Gordon Selfridge, 1858–1947. Sir William Orpen,
1878–1931.*

of commerce, whose flair for advertising and marketing technique transformed the face of the British commercial scene.

After his arrival in London, Selfridge became one of Ralph Blumenfeld's most intimate friends. Born in Ripon, Wisconsin, a bare thirty miles from RDB's native Watertown, he was no mere trader dealing in goods across a counter. As Blumenfeld wrote, "His mind was fully aflame with what he called the Romance of Commerce." His greatest heroes were the German Fuggers and merchant princes of Venice, Genoa, and Florence. To be a Medici; to command caravans and direct ships; to live in palaces like oriental despots; to roam the world in a golden galleon—these were the dreams of Gordon Selfridge, one of the great showmen of his generation.

When asked why, in mid-life, he expatriated himself to England, Selfridge's reply was an accurate summation of his romantic philosophy: "The Scot roams the civilized and uncivilized world. And he doesn't wait until he is more than forty, as I did, before he sets forth upon his wanderings in search of adventure. He regards the continents of the world as the natural market places where, if he is to be successful and do things worth doing, his feet must be firmly planted. Why, therefore, do so many still consider it strange that an American merchant should have the audacity to leave home and unfurl the American flag of commerce over shopkeeping London."

His life could have been created in the mind of Horatio Alger. Selfridge was a relatively poor, fatherless child who, on finishing high school, applied for admission to the U.S. Naval Academy; but his application was rejected on the grounds that he was simply not tall enough to satisfy the Academy's entrance requirement. It was a traumatic experience, and thereafter Selfridge harbored an irrational hostility to men taller than himself. Anyone over six feet tall was automatically debarred from an executive position that would bring him into contact with "the chief," as Selfridge liked to be called. To compensate for his presumed lack of height (Selfridge was five-foot-eight), he took to wearing boots with built-up Cuban heels and high stiff collars which threw his head back like that of a soldier on parade.

With the gates of Annapolis firmly closed against him, the fifteen-year-old Selfridge entered the Chicago department store of Marshall Field as an apprentice, where his career was truly meteoric. With his genius for merchandising, by the age of twenty-five Selfridge was in a position to demand and receive from Field a junior partnership in the store. He introduced the then revolutionary tactic of holding special sales to attract large crowds and, with a showman's eye, he began to dress Marshall Field's windows in a flamboyant manner which had never been seen before. In essence, much of modern department store display began in the fertile mind of Gordon Selfridge.

The dandified Selfridge adored display in all manner of things, including himself. And, as his share of the profits rose from 3 to 10 percent, he allowed himself little accoutrements as marks of distinction. His dress had always been impeccable, and now, in his buttonhole, a fresh orchid of exotic hue appeared every day. This nicely harmonized with the carefully wrought gold chain that hung from his pince-nez. His manner, particularly with women, had always been courtly and formal; now it bordered on the exquisite, for were not the ladies of Chicago the ultimate source of his new prosperity? Selfridge's office was the grandest in the building, decorated with the finest period furniture and rarest oriental carpets selected from stock. Marshall Field's own inner sanctum could not bear comparison, for Selfridge was a believer in the creation of total environments. And it was intended that those who crossed his threshold should know that they were in the presence of a great man.

It was all magnificently effective, and Selfridge was regarded as one of the most eligible bachelors in Chicago. He was prosperous; neither drank nor smoked; attended church regularly; and was the most devoted of sons to a mother whose photograph always graced his enormous mahogany desk.

In 1903 Selfridge, at the age of forty, sold his interest in Marshall Field's and retired to a life of leisure. It lasted scarcely a year, for business was the only game that he truly loved, and he found it impossible to remain beyond the field of play. In 1904 he purchased the Chicago mercantile firm of Schlesinger and Mayer and changed its name to Gordon Selfridge and Co. But so successful was the new venture that his competitors found it necessary to buy him out quietly in order to protect themselves. And so, for a second time, a now much-enriched Gordon Selfridge retired—temporarily!

In 1906 he arrived in London with $1.5 million to his credit. He and his wife had spent a number of holidays in the British capital, and it did not take long for him to realize that here was an ideal location for the establishment of a new commercial empire. Selfridge, like George Peabody two generations earlier, saw the potential in the English market. There were no department stores run along the American lines, and Selfridge was convinced that in the absence of competition he would, using American training, experience, and psychology, fashion a lucrative market into his own mold.

With boundless enthusiasm he began a search for an appropriate site and, after closely studying traffic and commuter patterns, as well as established mercantile districts, he settled on Oxford Street which, at the time, was far out of the mainstream of general shopping.

Many argued with Selfridge that it was a doomed plan. Not only was the site inappropriate but London had too many shops already. But his critics had never seen the inside of Marshall Field's or Wanamaker's. They could not appreciate that Selfridge intended to erect a department store, not another shop. The whole concept was simply unknown in Britain, and therein lay Selfridge's advantage.

Determined to have the finest premises in London, he engaged the Chicago architect, Daniel Burnham, to design a unique structure for the British metropolis. The Selfridge building was and is a marvel. Its foundations descended seventy feet into London's clay, deeper than any other building; its walls were twenty-seven feet thick at the bottom, and its fireproof floors of concrete rested on three thousand tons of steel girding.

Over ten thousand applications were received for employment in the new store. This in itself was remarkable for, in the main, conditions for staff in retail establishments were very poor. As a rule, employees had to reside on the premises in public dormitories devoid of all privacy. Food was appalling, and there were numerous fines for small offenses. But Selfridge changed all this. He advised his managers, with one of his typical homilies, "Do your best for the staff, and they will do the best for us." Seventeen acres of playing fields were laid out for Selfridge's employees at Wembley, where every sport from cricket, football, and hockey was played along with lawn tennis, bowling, and volleyball. All sorts of societies—social, dramatic, and musical—were set up by the company. And, in order to improve the minds of his people, Selfridge organized staff tours of Europe and America which he delighted in calling "Merchant Adventures" parties.

In March 1909, Selfridge's finally opened its doors to a curious public who flocked to see the only shop in town where one could buy everything from a pin to a gramophone. With their interest piqued by a £36,000 advertising campaign, the curious swept into the store's 130 departments, American barber shops, writing rooms, restaurants, libraries, and roof gardens. Every language group had its interpreter, for customers were expected from throughout the world. Selfridge dressed his windows with great panache, leaving them for all to see even after hours, when other firms pulled down their blinds. Thus the sidewalk sport of window-shopping was inaugurated by the man who vowed, with Marshall Field, that "the customer is always right."

The first of twenty-nine full-page newspaper advertisements commissioned by Gordon Selfridge to announce the opening of his department store. Bernard Partridge, 1861–1945. Newspaper advertisement, 1909. (Richard Kenin)

"The whole art of merchandising," declared Selfridge, "consists of appealing to the imagination. Once the imagination is moved the hand goes naturally to the pocket. But if the first appeal is to the purse, the imagination is apt to revolt and raise barriers against buying. In trade, as in most things, the mind is master."

Here was the sum total of Selfridge's philosophy. Shopping was an exercise in fantasy and, to succeed, one had to cater to the imagination of one's customers. For the new master of Oxford Street, the creation of fantasy became nothing short of an evangelistic crusade: "In my store women can realize some of their dreams. They come here as guests, not customers to be bullied into buying. This is not a shop, it is a social centre. I would rather lose sales than give women visitors here the impression that the store exists only to sell goods. I want them to enjoy the warmth and light, the colours and styles, the feel of fine fabrics. That is the basis of this business. . . ."

Selfridge saw his role as a significant one in the emancipation of women or, more correctly, ladies. "I came along just at a time when they wanted to step out on their own. They came into my store and realized some of their dreams," he wrote.

Within a week of opening, it was clear, from the increasing stream of humanity that flowed into Selfridge's, that the great entrepreneurial gamble had paid off, and that this most American of institutions was rapidly being adopted by the British.

Advertising was the cornerstone of Gordon Selfridge's marketing technique. No other merchant in London took nearly as much space in the daily newspapers as he and, in return, no commercial establishment received quite as much free publicity. "Never quarrel with a newspaper," Selfridge warned one of his subordinates, "no matter how right you feel you are. Remember this: a newspaper can always have the last word."

Selfridge himself wrote a daily column, which appeared in *The Times* and other newspapers under the pen name Callisthenes. The articles, which cost over £60,000 in the course of twenty-six years, contained no overt advertising and were headed with the observation: "This space is occupied every day by an article reflecting the policies, principles, and opinions of this House of Business upon various points of public interest." Thus Selfridge the merchant prince became one of the best-known lay philosophers of capitalism and finance in the kingdom.

Knowing that his department store could not move to Fleet Street, Selfridge was determined to bring Fleet Street into his establishment. Special facilities were provided in the store for journalists who were working in the Oxford Street area. Telephones, writing paper, typewriters, and refreshments—all were laid on in the name of good press relations. Of course it paid off, for whenever a store promotion was being launched, it received full coverage in all the London dailies as if it were an event of national importance.

Journalists as a breed clearly attracted Selfridge; they understood, as he did, how the tastes and opinions of the masses could be conditioned, formed, and directed.

Consequently, it was not surprising to find a large number of prominent newspaper proprietors and editors invited to the daily luncheon parties for which Selfridge became justly famous. One of those who frequently appeared was Ralph Blumenfeld who, as the years passed, became one of Selfridge's boon companions and chief associates in the promotion of Anglo-American friendship.

In 1900 Blumenfeld gave up his linotype business. He was lured, with great ease, to the news editor's desk of the *Daily Mail* by its phenomenally successful proprietor, Alfred Harmsworth, the first Lord Northcliffe, who established one of the great press dynasties of the modern era. After two years with the *Mail,* Blumenfeld, whose services were highly sought after in Fleet Street, accepted an offer from Harmsworth's chief rival, Cyril Arthur Pearson, who was in the process of organizing the *Daily Express.*

Oil on canvas,
circa 1930
30⅛″ × 20″
(Museum of London)

Amongst the Nerves of the World. A 1930 view of the Daily Express *in Fleet Street during the journalistic hegemony of Ralph David Blumenfeld. C. R. W. Nevinson, 1889–1946.*

In 1902 he joined the *Express*, first as foreign editor and then as news editor. Two years later he was promoted to editor-in-chief and, in 1908, was made a director of the company. It was in that capacity that Blumenfeld brought the Canadian millionaire Max Aitken (later Lord Beaverbrook) into journalism, a man whose mark on the style of the British press remains unmistakably evident even today. Blumenfeld remained editor-in-chief of the *Daily Express* for the next thirty years before being elevated to the chairmanship of the board. During that period his power became sufficiently great that, as an acknowledged doyen of the journalistic profession, Blumenfeld always commanded attention in the highest circles of power.

It was RDB who did much, after the Great War, to introduce the tabloid style of journalism, so popular in America, to Britain. Having been brought up at the knee of Commodore Bennett, Blumenfeld well understood the market potential for just a whiff of sensationalism in reporting. And it was he who introduced the banner, or streamer, headline to the front pages of English newspapers. This, in many ways, was the launching pad of popular journalism. "A certain amount of exaggeration is legitimate, even necessary," wrote Blumenfeld, "but exaggeration does not mean falsification. A magnifying glass is not the same thing as a distorting mirror." His papers did not attempt to emulate the sobriety of diction pontifically handed down in a *Times* leader; instead "Brevity and directness, clear forcible statement, boldness in generalisation, staccato rhetoric, exaggeration of emphasis—these are the essential qualities in the style of a good popular leader." It was the beginning of the Americanization of the British press.

Blumenfeld's enthusiasm for the press as a social institution was so great that at times he waxed evangelical in his praises of it. In the depths of the Depression, the world was in the throes of a new birth. Economic systems were collapsing, and the structure of society was being transformed before one's eyes: "On all sides forces are at work destroying and rebuilding. In every department of our life our ideas are being revolutionised and our traditional beliefs questioned. There is much quackery and unwisdom in it all as well as high constructive endeavor; much crude ignorance masquerading as the new enlightenment. Moral and spiritual values, which represent the accumulated wisdom of mankind through the ages, are being ruthlessly discarded in the name of a Modernity which is at present incapable of defining itself in any terms of value at all."

Amid all this apparent chaos, Blumenfeld pronounced the need for a new source of leadership. It could not be found in the churches, which were too disunited themselves and too far removed from secular questions. It could not be found in Parliament, which was devoid of popular leaders, nor in the universities, which seemed incapable of diffusing their vast stores of knowledge for the benefit of the commonweal. There remained only the press to democratize and humanize the popular consciousness: "It is the one great democratic institution whose popularity has increased since the [Great] War. Its potential moral influence is enormous. It is read by everybody, and everybody looks to it for information and authoritative

Photograph, 1926
5″ × 7″
(Sir John
[Blumenfeld] Elliot)

RDB working in the composition room of the Daily Express *during the general strike of 1926. Unidentified photographer.*

opinion. Never in all its history has the press had such an opportunity of leadership. Never was it more necessary that it should use it wisely and conscientiously."

The responsible leadership which RDB arrogated to the press distinctly fell under the banner of the Conservative party. Politically, Blumenfeld was a Tory, as was the paper he directed. RDB knew his constituency and wrote for it assiduously. In the midst of the Great War, he noted in an editorial that war, like politics, made strange bedfellows, and that those of the proletariat who clamored for the abolition of the House of Lords would now feel slighted if the majority of their national leaders were not drawn from the Upper House. Only a completely Anglicized American, conducting a love affair with the popular feudal mythology of masters and their loyal serfs, could write that what made Britain great was

> the peer's son and the labourer's son who, accustomed to fight England's battles, from the first day of England's history, lived up to their traditions, the peer's son as leader, the labourer's son as enthusiastic follower. They think alike, they act alike, the one merely with a little more polish than the other, but in the main they are the true representative English. It is nonsense to say, as it has been said for generations, that the middle classes are the backbone of England. They may be so in trade, but they certainly are not so in war. The middle classes fight just as bravely, just as patriotically as the upper and lower, but their contribution is not so spontaneous.

So highly regarded were his services as a propagandist for the party that one Conservative prime minister offered him the honor of knighthood. But Blumenfeld, who was a naturalized British subject, turned it down, arguing that it was most inappropriate for one who ostensibly spoke objectively to the public to be seen as the beneficiary of honors from any political source. When the politician in question then asked what he could do to reward his friend, RDB replied that he would appreciate election to the Carlton Club, the favorite haunt of Conservative politicians. His wish was facilitated, and Blumenfeld became the first journalist admitted as a member to the sanctum sanctorum of Toryism. It was a great coup, for nowhere else would a member of his profession have access so easily to authoritative information from the highest circles of government. And while RDB exploited his advantage to the fullest, there were those who charged that, in his later years, as Master of the Livery Company of Newspaper Makers and grand old man of British journalism, he was often fed information of dubious veracity, by politicians at the Carlton, which he accepted uncritically as gospel.

But there were many realities which RDB did not ignore. He was one of the first to predict publicly the rise of the United States as the creditor nation of all the world. He saw, sooner than most, that both the sustained affluence of Great Britain and her position as a leading world power could not be maintained indefinitely. Not that he acted the part of journalistic Cassandra to the British people; rather he purveyed a tonic of reason, heavily laced with nostalgia, to make acceptance of the future somewhat more palatable.

Gordon Selfridge, who, like Blumenfeld, always kept a pair of crossed British and American flags on his desk as a symbol of joint allegiance, also saw the political and military ascension of America as inevitable. Prior to the entry of the United States

*Photograph,
May 25, 1915
7'' × 5''
(Sir John
[Blumenfeld] Elliot)*

Blumenfeld (left) *coming out of the Carlton Club with the Ulster leader, Sir Edward Carson. Unidentified photographer.*

into World War I, Selfridge composed numerous articles for the American press urging U.S. action against German submarines as an expression of transatlantic solidarity. When Congress finally did declare war, Selfridge remarked, "All the fine things we have given to the world are safe. We can now confidently plan for the future."

But the future which Selfridge planned bore little resemblance to the nothing-but-business dynamism of his past. In the *Saturday Evening Post* he wrote, "When I begin to cast my mind back over the years, I encounter the curious sensation of having lived two entirely different lives. An American life, begun and ended, and an English life, begun and not yet ended, but whereas my American life was wholly devoted to a material ambition, to win what men call success, my English existence has been a much more placid affair, passed in a much more placid atmosphere, and has for its main inspiration the building up of certain ideals rather than of bank balances." Never was a more disingenuous pen put to paper. Yes, Selfridge had two lives, but the second was not a placid idyll in an English Elysium. And, if he was not concerned with the building up of bank balances, it was because he was far too busy spending money on new diversions.

Gordon Selfridge had always been a natural showman, with a flair for the theatrical. Predictably, he was drawn to individuals of like temperament. There was nothing he enjoyed more than having celebrities into his office to etch their names into one of his plate glass windows as a permanent memento.

But, as he grew older, Selfridge's fascination with theatrical people grew more and more childlike, and this was to be his undoing. Like an enamored stage-door

The nightclub entertainers, Gaby Deslys (right) and the twin Dolly sisters (opposite), who received Selfridge's lavish attentions. (Photographs courtesy Radio Times Hulton Picture Library)

Johnny, Gordon Selfridge became enraptured: first, with the French cabaret star Gaby Deslys, and later, with the American nightclub entertainer Jenny Dolly who, with her twin sister Rosy, had scored a great success in London in the twenties in a revue called *Jigsaw*.

All these ladies had a well-developed appreciation of just what Gordon Selfridge could do for them. And, in a tale that reads like a Busby Berkeley farce coupled with a melodramatic tragedy, they succeeded, over eight years, in acquiring at least £2 million of Selfridge's fortune to purchase the most lavish of entertainments and gifts.

Houses, gems, furs, automobiles—every possible luxury was produced for Selfridge's new flames. But even the Croesus-like wealth of the prodigal septuagenarian had its limits. The financial strain of maintaining not only his paramours, but also his elaborate private establishments at Lansdowne House (where he succeeded William Waldorf Astor as tenant) and Highcliffe Castle in Hampshire, was too much. Selfridge had purchased Hengistbury Head near Bournemouth, with plans to erect a mammoth castle that would rival the legendary Fonthill of William Beckford. It was to be his final romantic mark on England. But, as cash dwindled, it was one of many projects that had to be shelved.

Gordon Selfridge, like Ralph Blumenfeld, was a devoted supporter of the Conservative party, which he saw as the guardian of the free enterprise system which had made him a millionaire. As a testament both of his loyalty to the party and his appreciation of the doctrine of self-interest rightly understood, Selfridge had made it a practice to host a massive Lucullan banquet in the store on the eve of each

The dining room at Lansdowne House, where Gordon Selfridge gave many of his celebrated luncheons. It is now installed at the Metropolitan Museum of Art. (Photograph courtesy the Metropolitan Museum of Art)

general election. Here the elite of the Tory establishment gathered in grand communion to receive the blessing of this great merchant prince's bounty. But even this most vivid expression of conspicuous consumption was to fall by the wayside in the face of economic and political imperatives.

The last of the great election feasts was held in 1929, when the British people, desperate for a credo that would lead the nation out of the depths of depression, turned the reins of power over to the Labour party, led by Ramsay MacDonald. As the election results poured in and it became clear that seat after seat was falling to the Socialists, the mood in Selfridge's was transformed from lighthearted gaiety to a kind of fear bordering on hysteria. The crowd began to drink to great excess and, as the sound of conversation grew louder and louder, shrieks of forced laughter swept infectiously across the ballroom. As the pace of the party increased, the dance bands responded, playing faster and louder, as if in competition with the guests.

One of Selfridge's key managers sensed that things were getting out of hand. Walking over to a friend he remarked, "What's come over these people? Do you notice anything out of the ordinary, or am I dreaming?"

"Labour's going to win, and they can't stand it," he replied. "It might be their last night on earth, the way they're behaving."

"They probably think it is."

The crash of breaking crystal resounded all over the room as guests threw their empty champagne goblets to the floor. By the end of the evening the pile of broken glass was ankle-high, "testifying to toasts of defiance and despair," wrote one observer.

In the distance another, even more ominous, roar could be heard. Selfridge's guests rushed to the windows and looked out over Oxford Street. There they beheld an enormous crowd gathering, not only to celebrate jubilantly the arrival of the new order, but to hurl epithets at Selfridge's guests, the very class they most despised. Across the street, a huge red neon sign bathed the crowd in a crimson glare. The symbolism was all too heavy. It was as if Sergei Eisenstein were about to restage *Ten Days that Shook the World.*

One of Selfridge's guests turned to a group of friends and said, "This is the end. To-night is the end of an age. Our world is going out." In retrospect, it seems a supremely hackneyed, theatrical thing to have said. But, at the time, given the setting and the nature of the gathering, it was an immensely forceful remark that emotionally bespoke the feelings of a great many people.

By 1937, in his eightieth year, Selfridge, still in full command as chairman of a department store empire which had increased manifoldly in size, was facing a crisis. Ten years earlier he had sold control to the company, and now that money was all exhausted. Yet, with each passing month, his indebtedness, due to overspending, grew and now stood at £118,000.

At that point he decided to opt for British citizenship, writing facetiously to Ralph Blumenfeld that he could now truly be called a gentleman. It was a final quixotic turn. Somehow Selfridge took it into his head that, if he revisited America as a British subject to secure new financial support, his social status would be significantly elevated and this would produce success in his negotiations. It was a last poetic dream of an old man who had come not only to believe in, but act out, a Jamesian fantasy that was out of date by fifty years.

When Selfridge returned empty-handed to London, he was almost at the end of his tether, but not quite. The Coronation of George VI was about to take place, and the aged king of Oxford Street passionately believed that this would act as an antidote to the financial poison that threatened to destroy him. Here was a last momentous chance to demonstrate the showmanship on which he had built his reputation. Banging his fist on the table, he declared, "I'm going to get the world into Oxford Street. I said the world. . . . My decorations will stun London. All the world's coming to London for this coronation, and they'll all come to see the store. I expect record sales for months to come." And somehow, out of all this hoopla, Selfridge expected to spend his way back into solvency.

But there was scant method to the madness. It was virtually impossible for enough business to come to the store to raise dividends sufficiently, on Selfridge's shares, to cancel out his monumental indebtedness to the company. Yet there was no one to stop the aged titan. He still held the reins of power, even if not quite as firmly as in the past. Forty thousand pounds was spent on exterior decorations for the store. Ralph Blumenfeld confirmed that London had never seen anything like it; the Ottoman sultans would have marveled at such extravagance.

Business did pick up, but so, too, did Selfridge's personal expenditure. He gave up Lansdowne House in Berkeley Square as a mark of economy, but exchanged it for an almost equally expensive mansion in Carlton House Terrace overlooking St. James's Park, an area perennially popular with wealthy Americans. There he continued to entertain on a lavish scale; such was his method of maintaining public confidence.

But the charade could not be maintained indefinitely. When Britain slid fitfully into war with the Axis alliance, public spending power was slashed as wage-earners and their salaries disappeared into the armed forces. Like all commercial establishments, Selfridge's had to regear, and a financial millstone such as its venerable founder could no longer be tolerated.

In the early part of 1940, an ultimatum was presented by the board to Gordon Selfridge. Either he had to repay the £118,000 owed to the company immediately, or else resign effective control of the organization and accept the honorary title of president with a nominal salary of £2000 per annum.

There was no choice. Selfridge had to go. First, he had an office in the building, but that was soon taken. The old man moved across the street to quarters provided by the company, but he could do nothing but daily survey the magnificent object of his creative genius, and that simply was not enough.

From Carlton House Terrace he removed to a flat on Park Lane but, as finances became tight, he was forced to take a room in the Putney home of his daughter, Princess Wiasemsky. Gone was the chauffeur-driven limousine which, in former days, had carried him in style into London's West End. Now there was no option but to queue for buses like so many of his former employees. Selfridge could no longer afford boxes at the theater stocked with iced bottles of champagne. Instead he spent hours in the darkened recesses of cinemas, frequently in the cheapest seats, a lonely, isolated, and generally unrecognized figure stripped of the polished top hat, frock coat, and striped trousers which had been his hallmarks.

Finally in 1947, in his ninetieth year, Gordon Selfridge died, an all-but-forgotten figure. But in death there was a brief flash of notoriety. All of the major London newspapers, together with *The New York Times,* noted his passing with lengthy obituaries. The foibles of the man could not diminish the estimability of his achievement.

At his country home in Essex, the aged Ralph Blumenfeld, now retired from Fleet Street, read of his compatriot's demise. RDB was one of the last American-

Edwardians to survive. There were not many who could intimately recall with him the splendor of that day in 1909, when thousands flowed into Oxford Street to see the inauguration of American mercantilism in England, as Gordon Selfridge threw open the doors of his great public palace.

Blumenfeld had not been well for some years, and his own death was not far distant. A few weeks before the end, he asked his son to drive him to the nearby American Air Force base at Stanstead. He had no business to conduct but merely wanted to see the American flag flying at the entrance to the installation. The two men sat silently in their car watching the flag for a few moments. There was nothing to say; it was merely a last nostalgic remembrance.

Selfridge's store decorated for the coronation of King George VI.   It was the aging tycoon's last gasp of Edwardian extravagance. (Photograph courtesy Selfridge's Ltd. of London)

10

"Make it New!":
The Pound–Eliot Axis

What did twenty-three infantile years in America signify? "I dunno," wrote Ezra Pound, "I left as soon as motion was autarchic." Pound, a prophet who humorously declined comparison with Ezra the Mormon, "however charming and sympathetic or fictitious he may have been," preached poetic jeremiads to his people and proclaimed artistic alienation to a generation for whom the word was just beginning to have meaning.

His poems were unpublished, while much that was trash was readily available. His position as teacher in a small college terminated due to an alleged sexual indiscretion. In America he remained unrecognized, stigmatized by a poverty that was not "decent and honorable" as it was for artists in Europe. The path seemed clear: "The only way I could educate the educatable minority in the United States was to come to London . . . to the metropolis, to the capital of the U.S. so far as art and letters and thought were concerned." The shadow of Henry James had cast long, and Ezra Pound, still a colonial by his own reckoning, fled the "immensity" of a country "almost a continent and hardly yet a nation"; an estimable action "as long as the American *vie intellectuelle* sits patiently under the great British bum, carefully collecting and cataloguing the droppings." For Pound, "Hardly a week goes by but I meet or hear someone who goes into voluntary exile—some reporter who throws up a steady job to come to Europe and breathe; some professor from a freshwater college who comes away on scant savings. Our artists are all over Europe. We do not come away strictly for pleasure. And, we who are constantly railed at as 'expatriates,' do not hear this with unconcern. We will not put up with it for ever." Hardly a manifesto—more a clarion call, an unapologetic declaration of cultural independence, an unrepentant separation from " 'the people,' undependable, irrational, a quicksand upon which nothing can build, and which engulfs everything that settles into it; docile, apathetic, deenergized, or rather, unacquainted with energy, simply the Quicksand." Whistler had understood this better than most, and it was his banner that Pound sought to resurrect. "There is no misanthropy in a thorough contempt for the mob. There is no respect for mankind save in respect for detached individuals." Henry James, too, had complained of America as the land of the many where the few "find less and less place," where "the individual has quite ceased to be recognized." Pound heartily agreed, for, as his friend William Carlos Williams saw it, he was one of a well-recognized group of distinguished Americans who, by the very circumstances of their environment, could not "take the democratic virus and stand up under it." How comely and soothing a balm England must have seemed to such a temperament.

Pound, like Whistler, made no secret of his calling. He looked as much as acted the part of the poet. An exercise in high theater, perhaps; but few forgot the tall figure with a leonine shock of blond hair and a pointed, reddish blond beard of vaguely satanic form, rimless pince-nez perched on the bridge of the nose, and a single turquoise earring worn, as a jest, with great effect. His wardrobe was equally startling. Various observers recalled costumes of outlandish excess—trousers of

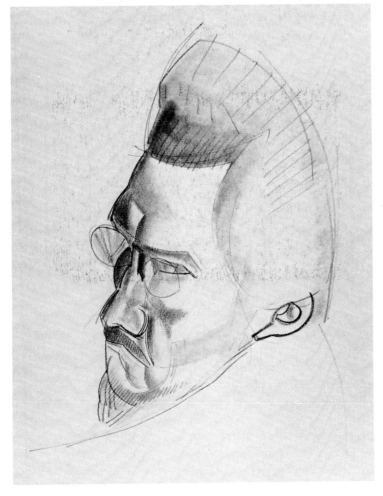

Wash and lithographic pencil, 1938 14" × 10" (Santa Barbara Museum of Art; Gift of Wright S. Ludington)

Ezra Pound, 1885–1972. Wyndham Lewis, 1884–1957.

green billiard cloth; pink coats worn with blue shirts, and ties hand-painted by a Japanese friend; enormous cloaks of clerical cut coupled with an immense sombrero and a walking stick of polished Malacca. Clearly, symbolic costume was as important as poetic substance to Pound in the fashioning of artistic character.

He arrived in London in 1906 as a brief visitor, and returned two years later to take up residence, with £3 in his pocket and a few copies of *A Lume Spento* packed with his clothing. It was an appropriate time for the inauguration of new literary movements. Since the demise of Oscar Wilde in 1900, the new literature of the aesthetes was on the wane. George Meredith's pen was silent and Swinburne's poetic voice barely audible. Conrad and James were still powers, though less visible than in earlier years. George Moore and Maurice Hewlett, George Bernard Shaw and Arthur Symons—these were the arbiters of literary excellence. William Butler Yeats and Ford Madox Ford—here were new voices that could not be ignored, most particularly in the ears of Ezra Pound.

To survive financially, he approached the Regent Street Polytechnic, an institution whose endowment had only recently been enriched to provide cultural as well as utilitarian courses. One of the part-time faculty had unexpectedly died and, with this vacancy in mind, Pound presented his credentials. His father in Philadelphia reported a conversation that bears more than a trace of authenticity: " 'Do you want to register as a student?' Ezra was asked. 'No, I want to register as a teacher. I want to give a course on the Romance Literature of Southern Europe.' 'But we don't want a course on the Romance Literature of Southern Europe,' he was told; 'besides, who are you?' 'Let me give the course,' said Ezra, 'and you'll see.' "

His application was accepted by the governors, and, during the winter of 1908–09, he lectured on "Developments of Literature in Southern Europe" and, a year later, on "Medieval Literature"—lectures which subsequently appeared in print as the first of his prose works, *The Spirit of Romance*. There was an audience for such information, an audience outside universities who knew Latin as any other second language and readily purchased Dante primers (price, one shilling). Such values had not yet been superseded by conflicting demands of introspection and political relevancy. The liberal arts were still widely perceived as liberal. And among those who gathered in the Polytechnic's Marlborough Room to hear the "sometime Fellow in the University of Pennsylvania" was one Dorothy Shakespear, a designer in watercolors, daughter of a prosperous household, whose subsequent marriage to Pound provided a modicum of much-needed financial security.

Pound's anonymity upon arrival in London was short-lived. He deposited copies of *A Lume Spento* in the book shops of Elkin Mathews and John Lane—"two peaks of Parnassus" in the progressive literary world—and quickly he was noticed. A reviewer in the *Evening Standard* proclaimed a discovery. Here was a new voice sporting, "wild haunting stuff, absolutely poetic, original, imaginative, passionate and spiritual. Coming after the trite and decorous verse of most of our decorous poets, this poet seems like a minstrel of Provence at a suburban musical evening. . . . The unseizable magic of poetry is in this queer paper volume, and words are no good in describing it."

Pound was introduced to the Poets' Club which met monthly in St. James's Street. He pronounced it a bore. He was taken to the Monday evening salons which William Butler Yeats held in an opaquely lit room near Euston Station. *Personae* was published and, in the months that followed, most critics noticed it favorably.

With his star in the ascendant, Pound crooned, "London, deah old London is the place for poesy." Even *Punch,* who never hurled brickbats at the unknown, was forced to acknowledge "the palpitating works of the new Montana (USA) poet, Mr. Ezekiel Ton, who is the most remarkable thing in poetry since Robert Browning." *Punch* declared in another issue,

The bays that formerly old Dante crowned;
Are worn today by Ezra Loomis Pound.

At 84 Holland Park Avenue was a fishmonger's and poulterer's shop, above which was situated a maisonette occupied by Ford Madox Ford, the last Pre-Raphaelite, who described himself as "an Englishman a little mad about Good Letters." Ford was one of the founders and now the nominal editor of *The English Review.* He was, in Hugh Kenner's words, "a fixer of nuances, and a man conversant with the troubadours"—the very sort of sponsor Pound required.

Ford introduced Pound into one of London's most distinguished literary circles. *The English Review* had, in its first six issues, published not only Thomas Hardy and Henry James but Walter de la Mare, John Galsworthy, H. G. Wells, and William Butler Yeats. And when, in June 1919, Pound's publication of *Sestina: Alta Forte,* a poem to the stirring up of war, signaled his debut in English magazines, it appeared with works of Joseph Conrad and Hilaire Belloc.

Other periodicals, even the immensely stuffy *Fortnightly Review,* accepted *and paid* for a poem by the new American bard. R. B. Cunninghame-Graham, already an intellectual mandarin, noted in a letter to the *Saturday Review*: "I observe with pleasure that our best writers—as Conrad, Hudson, Galsworthy, George Moore, Henry James, and Ezra Pound—are devoting themselves more and more to short pieces, and in them doing some of their finest work."

The world of *The English Review* was of great importance to Pound. But, for the stimulation of more exotic arcana, he placed himself in the hands of the poet and philosopher T. E. Hulme, who carried him into the progressive circle of A. R. Orage, the Guild Socialist editor of *The New Age.* It was Orage who agreed to publish, on a weekly basis, translations by Pound of Provençal, Tuscan, and Anglo-Saxon poetry with appropriate prosaic annotation. In the pages of *The New Age,* Pound discovered a whole new series of literary lights, including Wyndham Lewis, Rupert Brooke, Middleton Murray, and Katherine Mansfield. Here was a microcosmic world wherein one could cry "Make It New," and be understood. And, when Pound returned from America after a brief visit in 1910, it was to the pages of Orage's journal that he consigned a series of essays, entitled *Patria Mia* (revised the following years as *America: Chances and Remedies*), which called for a poetic renaissance in America, a rebirth predicated on "an indiscriminate enthusiasm" and "a propaganda" for new poets and their poetry. It was a highly impressionistic dogma, occasionally brilliant but lacking in intellectual discipline. The author was passionately dedicated to change, but was not yet sure how his self-conceived renaissance should manifest itself.

But his zeal, his hunger to promote all kinds of activities for the arts—to become a general committee of one—could be sympathetically appreciated. In emulation of Yeats and Hulme, Pound began to hold regular Tuesday evenings "at home" in his room at 10 Church Walk, near the Kensington Public Library—the very house in which, forty years later, Pound's friend T. S. Eliot would celebrate his second marriage.

There Pound waited to receive new poets and discuss their projects, a self-appointed mentor whose charisma was undeniable. But it was not merely his enthusiastic personality that drew poets to his door. Pound had something to offer. In 1912 Harriet Monroe, the Chicago-based founder of *Poetry,* the only American journal to open its pages to verse that was radically new, asked Pound to act as the journal's foreign correspondent, reporting on new trends. Ezra redefined the post as foreign editor and took it upon himself, first to gather in the best of the new poetry, and then to coerce Miss Monroe into printing it.

Photograph, from original negative, circa 1925 10" × 8" (Mrs. John Schaffner)

Hilda Doolittle. Man Ray, 1890–1976.

Among the first whose works were sent to Chicago were Richard Aldington and the woman whom he was soon to marry, Hilda Doolittle—H. D.—who had been Ezra Pound's first adolescent love.

Pound first met Hilda, in 1901, at a friend's Halloween party. She was fifteen, he a year older. They lived close to one another and shared a common appreciation of literature. H. D. recalled, "Ezra Pound was very kind and used to bring me (literally) armfuls of books to read. Among others, there were some rather old de luxe volumes of Renaissance Latin poets. I was happy with those because the Latin was easy yet held the authentic (though diluted) flavor of the overworked and sometimes slavishly copied Latin and Greek originals." Pound wrote poems for her. Eventually they were tied up together in a sheaf that was simply called "Hilda's Book."

In 1905 William Carlos Williams was taken by Pound to meet the tall blond girl of whom he was so enamored. Williams remembered,

There was about her that which is found in wild animals at times, a breathless impatience, almost a silly unwillingness to come to the point. She had a young girl's giggle and shrug which somehow in one so tall and angular seemed a little absurd. She fascinated me, not for her beauty, which was unquestioned if bizarre to my sense, but for a provocative indifference to rule and order which I liked. She dressed indifferently, almost sloppily and looked to a young man, not inviting—she had nothing of that—but irritating, with a smile. Ezra was wonderfully in love with her and I thought exaggerated her beauty ridiculously. To me she was just a good guy and I enjoyed, uncomfortably, being with her.

Hilda entered Bryn Mawr in 1904. Marianne Moore was one of her classmates. But, with fragile health, she was forced in her second year to withdraw. The next five years were spent with her family, trying seriously to attempt the craft of *vers libre*.

In 1911 she sailed for Europe, first to Italy and then on to England. Pound sent his friend, the novelist Brigit Patmore, to meet her, and a reunion was effected. Pound, Mrs. Patmore, Hilda, and the nineteen-year-old Aldington met to read poems and take tea almost every afternoon, either at the Grosvenor Gallery in Regent Street or at a small tea shop in Museum Street. It was at one of these meetings that Pound read and corrected a poem of Hilda's, entitled "Hermes of the Ways," and, when he was finished, he signed it "H. D. Imagist"—a word he had used once before in his own *Ripostes*.

Richard Aldington had no exact memory of what was said at that bunshop meeting. But he did recall, in his autobiography, that "H. D. looked very much pleased by the praise Ezra generously gave her poems. I didn't like his insistence that the poems should be signed 'H. D. Imagist,' because it sounded a little ridiculous. And I think H. D. disliked it too. But Ezra was a bit of a czar in a small but irritating way, and he had the bulge on us, because it was only through him that we could get our poems into Harriet Monroe's *Poetry* and nobody else at that time would look at them."

Pound sent three of H. D.'s poems to Harriet Monroe with an enthusiastic cover note, telling her that he had been lucky enough to secure some *"modern* stuff by an American, I say modern for it is in the laconic speech of the Imagistes, even if the subject is classic." Miss Monroe, of course, had no idea who the "Imagistes" were, since they existed, for the moment, solely in the mind of her foreign editor. But Pound assured her that this was the sort of poetry which cut full force into *vers libre* with an authentic ring of classicality. It was American poetry that he could show unashamedly in either London or Paris without fear of ridicule. There was "no excessive use of adjectives, no metaphors that won't permit examination. It's straight talk, straight as the Greek!"

H. D. credited Pound with having "discovered" her. Around her anonymous person, he loosely fashioned a movement which, over the next five years, repudiated the irrelevant extrapoetic values and sloppy technique so common to much of nineteenth-century verse.

In January 1913, H. D.'s imagist offerings appeared in the pages of *Poetry* and created just the sort of stir Pound had anticipated. The author was cryptically described in a footnote as "an American lady resident abroad, whose identity is unknown to the editor."

Though the imagist movement would come to mean little more than a way to describe short *vers libre* in English, from this moment H. D.'s name was irrevocably

Photograph, January 18, 1914 5½'' × 7½'' (Humanities Research Center, University of Texas at Austin)

Yeats, Pound, and Aldington photographed at a house party given in 1914 in honor of Wilfred Scawen Blunt (center). *Yeats stands at Blunt's right, and Pound and Aldington to his left. Unidentified photographer.*

tied to it, even though her own career survived the movement by over four decades. But, with his flair for attracting attention, Pound had convinced serious readers of poetry in America that a new movement was now under way in England.

F. S. Flint, the literary taxonomist of French symbolist poetry who, when no one else could, managed to find distinctions between the various "isms"—*Néo-Mallarméisme, Néo-Paganisme, Unanimisme, Paroxysme, Impulsionisme, Futurisme*—then in vogue, added credit to the illusion of a new poetic movement by publishing, at the editor's request in the March issue of *Poetry,* a note on the imagists supplemented "with further exemplification by Mr. Pound."

Finding nothing about imagism in print, Flint sought out an *Imagiste* (Pound) to discover just what the movement was all about. He was told that while the *Imagistes* were contemporaries of the postimpressionists and futurists (so many tiny groups all competing for center stage!), still they had nothing in common with these schools of thought. There was no public manifesto of imagism, no revolutionary creed; only a desire to create, in the best traditions of Sappho, Catullus, and Villon, poetry that conformed to three simple rules: (1) To directly treat the "thing" whether subjective or objective; (2) to use absolutely no word that does not contribute to the presentation; and (3) as regarding rhythm: to compose in the sequence of the musical phrase, "not in sequence of a metronome." Pound declared, through Flint, that no one else was following this course. And, like Whistler, he was determined to bring his art back to the pure uncompromised beauty of basic structure and idea. It was a return of precise diction to poetry that was perhaps more profound than the discoveries of

Photograph, 1916
6⅛″ × 4⅝″
(The Harriet Monroe
Modern Poetry
Collection, University
of Chicago Library)

Amy Lowell. Moffett, dates unknown.

Coleridge and Wordsworth because, by the advent of Pound's era, language, like biology, was much more completely understood. In a very real sense, what Pound and his circle were attempting to create was as romantically inspired as anything produced by poets of the previous century. Yet the imagist penchant for technical hygiene was such that it could not long exist in pristine isolation.

In Brookline, Massachusetts, a stout lady of substance, "America's only hippo-poetess," said Pound, sat reading H. D.'s imagist verse as she puffed slowly on a cigar. Suddenly, with Archimedean enthusiasm, she exclaimed, "Why, I too am an *Imagiste.*" And with that, Amy Lowell hastened to London, a generously endowed Daisy Miller encumbered with numerous portmanteaux and a letter of introduction, or perhaps more correctly annunciation, to Ezra Pound from Harriet Monroe. It was a scenario straight from the pages of Feydeau or Molière.

She came first in 1913, like a "great blue wave," said Hugh Kenner. And returned the following year to appropriate a movement into which she had not been fully accepted. (Pound's anthology, *Des Imagistes,* contains only one of her poems.)

With her suite at the Berkeley, her maroon limousine with chauffeur in matching attire, and her desire to become a participating patroness backed by an appreciable fortune, Amy Lowell had little difficulty in luring Aldington, H. D., John Gould Fletcher who never liked Pound, F. S. Flint, and, more surprisingly, D. H. Lawrence, who was prepared to don the mantle of imagism, into her camp.

She preached democracy in the arts and, as Orwell would have put it, was able to demonstrate that in such a system some, namely, herself, were still more equal than others. Nevertheless, Lowell could deliver the poetic goods, and, under her editor-ship, Houghton Mifflin published three anthologies of imagist poetry during World War I.

Pound separated himself from the movement completely, renaming it *Amygisme.* It was not merely a point of principle. He was also angry with Miss Lowell for not agreeing to his proposal that she fund the journal *Mercure de France* with himself as salaried editor. As she explained to Harriet Monroe, "Like many people of no income Ezra does not know the difference between thousands and millions, and thinks that anyone who knows where to look for next week's dinners, is a mil-lionaire." For Pound, with an annual earned income of around £40, this was very much the case. It was all a matter of perspective.

From the poetry of imagism, of energy and effort, Pound glided on to the motifs of the Orient. In 1915 he published *Cathay;* in 1916 *Certain Noble Plays of Japan;* and in 1917 *Noh or Accomplishment.* Here was a new sense of energized pattern, a language that was as much an exorcism of dead ghosts and unrealized dreams as it was a new exploration. It presaged a harmony, a Whistlerian arrangement that whispered of nascent ambitions. As *Cathay* went to press, Pound wrote to a friend, "I am also at work on a chryselephantine poem of immeasurable length which will occupy me for the next four decades." It was a prophetic enunciation that began to take public substance two years later, when, in volume X of *Poetry,* the first three *Cantos of Ezra Pound* were published.

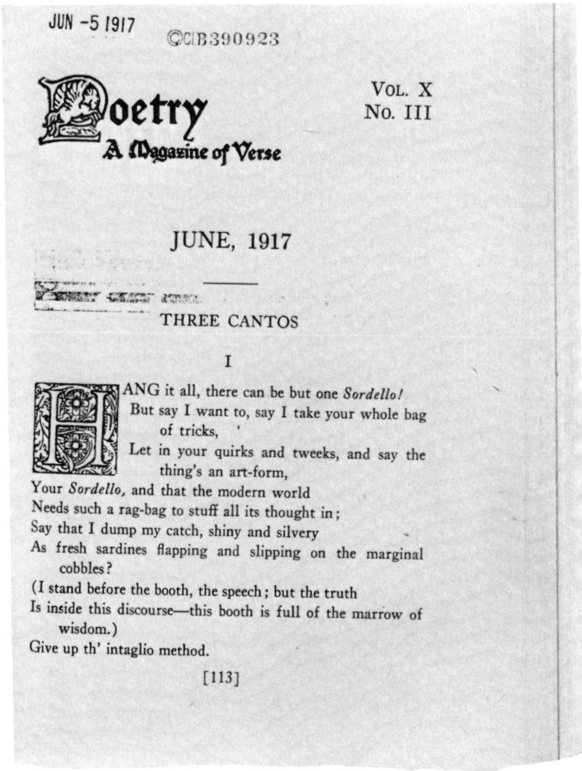

JUN -5 1917 ©CIB390923

Poetry
A Magazine of Verse

VOL. X
No. III

JUNE, 1917

THREE CANTOS

I

HANG it all, there can be but one *Sordello!*
But say I want to, say I take your whole bag
    of tricks,
Let in your quirks and tweeks, and say the
    thing's an art-form,
Your *Sordello*, and that the modern world
Needs such a rag-bag to stuff all its thought in;
Say that I dump my catch, shiny and silvery
As fresh sardines flapping and slipping on the marginal
    cobbles?
(I stand before the booth, the speech; but the truth
Is inside this discourse—this booth is full of the marrow of
    wisdom.)
Give up th' intaglio method.

[113]

Poetry, A Magazine of Verse. *In this, the first Canto of Ezra Pound was published. Vol. X, No. III, June 1917. (Library of Congress)*

The Great War altered perspective. As Henry James lay dying and John Singer Sargent continued to paint in the Tyrol, Richard Aldington moved back and forth from the front, while H. D. sat in their apricot-colored room lined with dark blue curtains and witnessed the passion of her marriage slowly ebb away. By 1919 it was finished, and the two separated: he destined for prominence as novelist, essayist, and translator; she for distinction, though not great fame, as an eternal expatriate producing numerous collections of verse.

Pound remained busy, not only with the *Cantos* and his oriental preoccupations, but with the promotion of those whose work he considered essential to society's notice. Paramount among this group was James Joyce. It was William Butler Yeats who first spoke to Pound, in December 1913, of the writings of the then totally unknown Irish author living in exile in Trieste. Yeats sent Pound a copy of Joyce's poem "I Hear an Army Marching," and Pound immediately asked for permission to anthologize it in *Des Imagistes.* Permission was received the following month, and thereafter Pound devoted considerable energy to promoting Joyce's cause in the literary marketplace. He printed a long letter from Joyce in *The Egoist,* concerning the author's difficulty in securing publication for *Dubliners,* and subsequently persuaded that journal's editor, Harriet Shaw Weaver, to serialize *A Portrait of the Artist as a Young Man.*

When Joyce moved to Zurich during the war, he wrote to Pound, detailing his financial straits. The result was a grant from the Royal Literary Fund. Joyce thought Yeats responsible, and wrote to thank him, but was informed, "You need not thank me, for it was really Ezra Pound who thought of your need. I acted at his suggestion." The grant, though not immense, did inject a modicum of security into Joyce's life and allowed him to finish the Bloom episodes of *Ulysses.*

Pound continued indefatigably to promote the work of the man he identified as "by far the most significant writer of our decade." He took it upon himself to act as Joyce's unofficial literary agent, wrote letters to journals praising his work, and even offered pieces of domestic advice on how to live cheaply and still care for one's health, for by this time the Irishman's eye trouble was beginning to manifest itself seriously. Years later Joyce freely acknowledged that, had it not been for Ezra Pound, many of his most important works might never have reached the public eye. It was not an atypical example of Pound's enthusiastic magnanimity.

Collotype, Kensington, October 22, 1913; plate from Coburn's More Men of Mark, *1922 6½″ × 5¼″ (National Portrait Gallery, Smithsonian Institution)*

Ezra Pound. This photograph became the frontispiece to Lustra. *Alvin Langdon Coburn, 1882–1966.*

In 1916 Pound published a collection of verse entitled *Lustra*. And, for a frontispiece to the volume, he used a photograph that had been taken several months earlier by the youthful American photographer, Alvin Langdon Coburn. At the time of that sitting, Pound was recovering from a bout with jaundice and thus posed in his dressing gown. His future father-in-law, H. H. Shakespear, thought that the photograph depicted "a sinister but very brilliant Italian," while his landlady, Mrs. Langley, told him with acute embarrassment, "I hope you won't be offended sir it *is* rather like the good man of Nazareth, isn't it sir?"

It was altogether fitting that Pound's visage should reach the public through the hands of a compatriot barely three years his junior, one whose impact on London at the time was arguably greater than Pound's own.

Success had come easily to Alvin Langdon Coburn. The precocious son of a prosperous New England manufacturer, he began to experiment with photography at a very early age—between the years of eight and nine. At the age of sixteen he sat at the feet of his cousin, the photographer F. Holland Day, and it was Day who first took him to London to exhibit in "The New School of American Pictorial Photography," a show which opened at the Royal Photographic Society in October 1900.

Photogravure, 1905; reproduced from Alvin Langdon Coburn: Photographer, *1966*

Alvin Langdon Coburn, 1882–1966. Self-portrait.

Here Coburn was in his milieu. In London, and later in Paris, he became intimate with many of the great photographers then in practice: Frederick H. Evans, Frank Eugene, Edward J. Steichen, and Robert Demachy. Existence was all a celebration, "for we were young and carefree and life was richly endowed."

Back in New York, the evanescent, almost mystical, quality of Coburn's prints attracted the attention of Alfred Stieglitz who, in 1902, brought him into the membership of the Photo-Secession movement. The following year The Linked Ring, an avant-garde competitor of the Royal Photographic Society, also offered him membership. Thus, at the age of twenty-one, Alvin Langdon Coburn achieved international recognition as a leading practitioner of the photographic art.

In 1906, having returned to England more or less permanently, Coburn was accorded the honor of a one-man exhibition at the Royal Photographic Society. His greatest fan was George Bernard Shaw, himself a photographer of some accomplishment. "You will need someone to beat the big drum for you," Shaw declared, and offered to write a preface to the exhibition catalogue, which contained his oft-quoted simile, "The photographer is like a cod, which produces a million eggs in order that one may reach maturity."

Shaw was a great asset to Coburn's career. Through his good offices, sittings were arranged with the most eminent writers, musicians, and actors of the day. And, in 1906, when Coburn accompanied Shaw and his wife to Paris for the unveiling of Rodin's *The Thinker* outside the Pantheon, he was given entrée to the great sculptor, and took what are perhaps the most telling photographs extant of Rodin, cast in flowing beard and black skullcap, reminiscent of an ancient patriarch or sage. Yet the more surprising part of the journey occurred the morning after the unveiling, when Shaw suggested to the young photographer that, after his bath, Coburn should photograph him in the nude in the pose of *Le Penseur.* Was it not, Shaw suggested, correct to photograph him in his true role in life as the thinker? Not surprisingly,

Alfred Stieglitz.
Alvin Langdon Coburn, 1882–1966. Photogravure, 1908,
plate from Camera Work, *No. VI. 4¼'' diameter.*
(National Portrait Gallery, Smithsonian Institution)

when the anonymous photograph was shown at the London Salon of Photography, it caused considerable comment in the press.

Yeats wrote that "Coburn, who understands photography, is celebrated in our world." He was commissioned by Scribner's, which was bringing out a collected edition of Henry James's novels, to do a series of photographs which would act as compelling frontispieces to James's prose. He worked closely with the Master, plotting out the site of each fictional venue. A little gateway and house in London's St. John's Wood illustrated the second volume of *The Tragic Muse*; Lamb House, James's retreat at Rye, was given life as Mr. Longdon's of *The Awkward Age*; and, perhaps most triumphantly, Portland Place on a misty morning, with a hansom pulling off into the distance, evoked sentiments evident in *The Golden Bowl*. James insisted that photographs were " 'all right' in the so analytic modern critical phrase, through their discreetly disavowing emulation." But Coburn's images were not to compete with his text. They were to remain "always confessing themselves, mere optical symbols or echoes, expressions of no particular thing in the text, but only of the type or idea of this or that thing. They were to remain at the most small pictures of our 'set' stage with the actors left out." The Master could not brook competition from such a seductive medium.

In 1909 Coburn moved to Thameside, an old house on the river near Hammersmith Bridge. There, in his studio, with its fifteen-foot window, he commanded a magnificent view of the Thames, much as Whistler had done from Lindsey Row. Coburn was enamored with the legend of Whistler. He took to wearing a top hat, in emulation, and set up two printing presses in his house as an adjunct to his darkroom and studio.

There, in 1909, he printed by hand the twenty plates for *London,* his first illustrated book, with an introduction by Hilaire Belloc. It was an emotive testament of his love affair with the British metropolis, and was reminiscent of many of the

Auguste Rodin.
Alvin Langdon Coburn, 1882–1966. Photogravure, 1906·
plate from Coburn's Men of Mark, *1913. 14¼″× 11¼″.*
(International Museum of Photography)

nocturnes in black and white that Whistler had created a generation earlier—nocturnes that only a stranger who took nothing visually for granted could have captured.

It was this aspect of Coburn's creative genius that attracted the attention of Ezra Pound. In an article entitled "The Future of Pictorial Photography," Coburn asked,

> Why should not the camera also throw off the shackles of conventional representation and attempt something fresh and untried? Why should not its subtle rapidity be realized to study movement? Why not repeated successive exposures of an object in motion or on the same plate? Why should not perspective be studied from angles hitherto neglected or unobserved? Why, I ask you earnestly, need we go on making commonplace little exposures of subjects that may be sorted into groups of landscapes, portraits and figure studies? Think of the joy of doing something which it would be impossible to classify.

To do something that would be impossible to classify—to create a movement unique unto itself—that idea had already lodged in the brains of Ezra Pound,

George Bernard Shaw as Le Penseur, after Rodin's statue. Alvin Langdon Coburn, 1882–1966. Photogravure, 1906. 11½″ × 9″. (International Museum of Photography)

Wyndham Lewis, and the sculptor Henri Gaudier-Brzeska. These three who, in June 1914, thrust onto the consciousness of London an incantation of "patterned energy" which Pound called "a radiant node or cluster . . . what I can, and must perforce, call a VORTEX, from which, and through which, and into which, ideas are constantly rushing." *Blast #1—The End of the Christian Era* was the organ of the vorticist movement wherein the propaganda of the imagists was blended with a new sieve. Sculptors, painters, poets, and musicians together stood on the brink of the vorticist renaissance. Pound and Lewis held that "every concept, every emotion presents itself to the void consciousness in some primary form. It belongs to the art of this form. If sound, to music; if formed words, to literature; the image to poetry; form, to design; colour in position, to painting; form or design in three planes, to sculpture; movement to the dance or to the rhythm of music or verse."

Imagism was created to launch H. D. and Aldington. Vorticism was a union by Pound with Gaudier-Brzeska and Lewis—his own kin. Yet Pound rejected the notion that he was head of the movement: "The pleasure of Vorticism was to find one-self at last *inter pares*." And if Lewis supplied the volcanic force, and Gaudier-Brzeska the animal energy, "perhaps I had contributed a certain Confucian calm and reserve."

Portland Place. This was used as a frontispiece for Henry James's The Golden Bowl. *Alvin Langdon Coburn, 1882–1966. Photogravure, 1906. (International Museum of Photography)*

The Houses of Parliament. Alvin Langdon Coburn, 1882–1966. Photogravure, circa 1904–06; plate from Coburn's London, *1909. (International Museum of Photography)*

The vorticists descended from two principles. The first, Walter Pater's "All arts approach the conditions of music." The second, James McNeill Whistler's "We are interested in painting because it is an arrangement of lines and colours." They were against respectability and tradition, bereft of substance, and damned those who stood as idols undeserving of praise. Lewis made it clear that by vorticism he meant the same instincts that motivated the cave painter of the Dordogne, the funereal decorators of ancient Egypt, the masters of natural form of Assyria whose genius had been compromised in the decadence of Greece: "(a) ACTIVITY as opposed to the tasteful PASSIVITY of Picasso; (b) SIGNIFICANCE as opposed to the dull or anecdotal character to which the Naturalist is condemned; (c) ESSENTIAL MOVEMENT and ACTIVITY (such as the energy of a mind). . . ."

Activity! Activity! Activity! What did it mean? Were the vorticists merely English cubists, or futurists desperately attempting to place a nationalist label self-protectively on their work? No, was the loud response. The French cubists were tastefully passive and the Italian futurists hysterical and fussy. Vorticism was *le mot juste*: it was "the power of tradition, of centuries of race consciousness, of agreement, of association." It was everything that artists knew instinctively and did not have to invent. It was at once national (read "English") and personal. So personal, indeed, that few appreciated its ingenious and subtle distinctions, drawn up as shields against the continental avant-garde of abstraction.

Alvin Langdon Coburn was, however, an exception. He was philosophically attracted to the propaganda of the vorticists, and pondered how his art could be adapted to their purpose. The result was his invention, in 1916, of the vortoscope, a camera designed to compose abstract pictures by using three mirrors fastened together in the form of a triangle resembling a kaleidoscope.

The mirrors acted as a prism, splitting the image formed by the lens into segments, all rushing toward a center of energy—a photographic vortex. Coburn christened his creations "vortographs"—one of the most famous of which portrayed the creator of the movement, Ezra Pound.

When an exhibition of Coburn's vortographs was held, Pound obliged with an introduction to the catalogue. He told his readers, echoing Whistler, that "the Vorticist principle is that a painting is an expression by means of an arrangement of

Alvin Langdon Coburn pulling the plates for his book. Self-portrait. Photogravure, 1908. 9″ × 11³/₁₆″. (International Museum of Photography)

First page from the Blast *manifesto, by Wyndham Lewis and Ezra Pound. The credo of the vorticist movement. June 20, 1914. (Library of Congress)*

form and color in the same way that a piece of music is an expression by means of an arrangement of sound." Here was a movement that had reawakened in occidental artists a sense of form long dead. Just as some people were tone-deaf and color-blind, so too were others form-blind: "Some ears cannot recognize the correct pitch of a note, and some eyes get no pleasure from a beautiful or expressive arrangement of form." This form blindness the movement sought to correct.

Pound thought that vortography stood below the other vorticist arts, because it was an art of the eye, not of the eye and hand together. It was superior to photography, because the artist combined his forms at will. "He selects just what forms, lights, masses, he desires, he arranges them *at will* on his screen. He can make summer of London October." In essence, Pound was arguing that the eye of man was drawn to certain forms, regardless of whether they combined to form a replica of known objects. It liked them for their plainness or complexity; for their arrangement and variety. And it was the task of the vorticist practitioner to train and harness these natural instincts so as to broaden effectively the parameters of man's visual experience.

Alvin Langdon Coburn did not have a sustained interest in vorticism. Indeed, for a long period, serious professional photography all but disappeared in his life. He found succor instead in the mountains of North Wales, to which he retired for thirty years, beginning in 1918: "I became a Freemason, and with keen zest investigated

Ezra Pound. Alvin Langdon Coburn, 1882–1966. Vortograph, 1916. 8¼″ × 6¼″ (International Museum of Photography)

the hidden mysteries of nature and science." There he found an inner world of profound beauty and spiritual satisfaction. Coburn became an acolyte to the philosophy of Zen: "I had lost nothing of my devotion to photography, it had just been changed, lifted up and oriented into another and more spiritual channel. . . . Photography teaches its devotees how to look intelligently and appreciatively at the world, but religious mysticism introduces the soul to God." For Coburn, all art belonged to the same great reality. But earthly beauty was at the bottom rung of a ladder which, in perfect symmetry and order, ascended to "Divine Reality," the crowning glory of creation.

It was a serenely quiet world—contented, fulfilled, enriched. Perfect for Alvin Langdon Coburn; comprehensible but as yet unappealing for Ezra Pound.

The vorticists were nothing if not enthusiastic. Wyndham Lewis, a unique phenomenon, hurled provocative missiles at the Enemy:

> *Our Vortex is fed up with your dispersals reasonable chicken men*
> *Our Vortex is proud of its polished sides*
> *Our Vortex will not hear of anything but its disastrous polished dance*
> *Our Vortex desires the immobile rhythm of its swiftness*
> *Our Vortex rushes out like an angry dog at your Impressionist fuss*
> *Our Vortex is white and abstract with its red hot swiftness*

Wyndham Lewis.   In the background is one
of Lewis's lost vorticist canvases. Alvin
Langdon Coburn, 1882–1966.

They plotted the structure of the movement over dinners at the restaurant La Tour Eiffel, near Tottenham Court Road, and on occasion adjourned to the Cabaret Theatre Club off Regent Street. The Cabaret, known also as the Cave of the Golden Calf, was one of London's first nightclubs and one of the very few, said Pound, which admitted impoverished artists. It was owned by Freda Strindberg, the playwright's second wife, who commissioned Wyndham Lewis and Pound's compatriot, Jacob Epstein, to fill its walls and pillars with elaborate decorations in violent colors. Some time later the police raided the establishment, and Mme. Strindberg, together with her avant-garde decorations, disappeared from sight.

Epstein, who had arrived in London a few years before Pound, was one of the subjects of the poet's first piece of art criticism, which appeared in *The Egoist* in February 1914. In the article, entitled "The New Sculpture," Pound declared that the state of war that existed between the artist and the world was a conflict where truce was impossible. The old elite must be slaughtered so that the new aristocracy of achievement might take their rightful place: "The artist has been at peace with his oppressors long enough. He has dabbled in democracy and he is now done with that folly. We turn back, we artists, to the powers of the air, to the djinns who were our allies aforetime, to the spirits of our ancestors. The aristocracy of entail and of title is decayed, the aristocracy of commerce is decaying, the aristocracy of the arts is ready again for its service . . . and we who are the heirs of the witch-doctor and the voodoo, we artists who have been so long the despised are about to take over control."

Left: *Jacob Epstein, 1880–1959. Alvin Langdon Coburn, 1882–1966. Collotype print, London, January 24, 1914; plate from Coburn's* More Men of Mark, *1922. 6¾'' × 5¼''. (National Portrait Gallery, Smithsonian Institution).* Right: *Jacob Epstein. Self-portrait. Bronze, 1912. 19¼'' height. (National Portrait Gallery, London)*

It was Pound's penchant for messianic pronouncement that attracted Epstein. The corruptions of the proto-fascist and the anti-Semite were not yet manifest in his personality, though the large-boned New York Jew who spoke English with a broad Lower East Side inflection thought he detected, even at that time, something unsettling in Pound which bore the mark of instability.

A child of Polish immigrants in flight from the pogroms of Eastern Europe, Jacob Epstein was raised amid the teeming humanity of New York's Hester Street, where he recalled that "swarms of Russians, Poles, Italians, Greeks and Chinese lived as much in the streets as in the crowded tenements, and the sights, sounds, and smells had the vividness and sharp impact of an oriental city."

A natural draftsman, Epstein gravitated to the Art Students League where he studied drawing with James Carroll Beckwith. But his passions were eventually devoted to the three-dimensional, and, in time, it was the modeling class of George Grey Barnard that claimed his exclusive attention. Yet native American sculptors did not give Epstein much inspiration, and at the time no one thought of Mexican or Pre-Columbian Indian work. He recalled, "I met Tom Eakins, but as a sculptor he impressed me as being too dry and scientific, and I looked forward to the day when I would be able to see the Ancients and Rodin. I longed to see the originals of Michelangelo and Donatello, and Europe meant the Louvre and Florence."

In 1902, with money saved from the sale of various drawings, some for publication, Epstein booked passage for France. "I can recall with unthinking heedlessness of youth, climbing the gangway to the vessel that was to take me away from America for a period of twenty-five years," he later wrote. "When I reached the top of the gangway, my mother ran after me and embraced me for the last time. One night, in March, 1913, in Paris, I dreamed of my mother, and immediately received news of her early death."

After three years of study in Paris, the deliquescent charm of *la belle époque* wore thin on Epstein, and he elected, in 1905, to cross the channel to England, carrying in his hands and his head what were to be the seeds of the new British sculpture. He was quickly adopted by several members of the New English Art Club—Augustus John, Francis Dodd, Ambrose McEvoy, and Muirhead Bone—who saw in his hands a remarkable future. Both John and Dodd drew portraits of Epstein, while he in turn sculpted busts of Bone, John, his younger son Romilly, and the wives of McEvoy and Dodd.

Although still in his own mind a student, Epstein had already become an acknowledged master. As his biographer, Richard Buckle, has written, "There was no one living—in London at least—against whom the young knight-errant of sculpture, who slept in a slum on newspaper, would deign to match himself: when he felt the need to break a lance, as it were, to measure his wrath or suffer humiliation in the interest of self-improvement, he had to turn to the greats of the past."

In 1907 a series of momentous events occurred. Epstein became a British subject and married the energetic Scotswoman, Margaret Dunlap, who already had asserted her position as one of the driving forces in his life. He won important recognition when Queen Alexandra purchased his bronze *Head of an Infant*. And that spring, on Muirhead Bone's recommendation, Epstein was commissioned to decorate the new building of the British Medical Association which overlooked the Strand on the corner of Agar Street.

Epstein thought he was wealthy. The future looked bright, and, for the first time, he could afford to pay for models. It was now even possible to arrange an escape from the slums of St. Pancras to the quiet salubrity of a studio on Whistler's Cheyne Walk.

The scale of the Strand statues was unlike anything London had previously seen: eighteen larger-than-life-size figures representing "man and woman, in their various stages from birth to old age—a primitive, but in no way a bizarre programme," wrote Epstein. The statues, although entirely devoid of academic sentimentality, showed little break with the traditions of European sculpture. What made them unique was the sculptor's refusal to create something that was merely decorative: "The figures had some fundamentally human meaning instead of being merely adjunct to an architect's mouldings and cornices."

It was a magnificent scheme, all the more remarkable when carried out by a youth who, only eight years earlier, had first placed his hands round a chisel. But from the moment the first statue was unveiled, a hue and cry was raised by a public critically unprepared for what it saw. "All was quiet," recalled Epstein, "until after the scaffolding was removed from the first four figures, then a storm of vituperation burst out [in June 1908] in the *Evening Standard* and *St. James's Gazette* that was totally unexpected and unprecedented in its fury." One anonymous critic wrote, "They represent a development in art to which the British public are not accustomed. . . . They are a form of statuary which no careful father would wish his daughter or no discriminating young man his fiancée, to see." Thus began a fury of hostile abuse which, in years to follow, erupted each time Epstein exhibited a new monumental piece of work.

After much debate the Strand statues were allowed to remain. But the controversy surrounding their erection did leave an embittering mark on the sculptor's personality and contributed mightily in developing the defensiveness that became so manifest a part of his character.

Yet, however unfortunate Epstein's experience with the Strand statues, there were those who considered them a masterpiece. One of these was Robert Ross, the literary executor of Oscar Wilde, who, shortly after the completion of the statues, commissioned Epstein to carve a monumental tomb for Oscar Wilde's gravesite at Père-Lachaise in Paris.

When his design for the tomb was formalized on paper, Epstein visited the Hopton Wood stone quarries in Derbyshire, where "I saw an immense block which had just been quarried preparatory to cutting it up into thin slabs for wall-facings. I bought this monolith, weighing twenty tons on the spot, and had it transported to my London studio."

He began work immediately and continued for nine months, creating a piece which combined simplicity with ornate decoration in the formulation of what he called "a flying demon-angel," strongly reminiscent of the great Assyrian winged bulls from Khorsabad in the British Museum. The angel's headdress was decorated with representations of the seven deadly sins. Epstein was not one to mince symbols, for this was no memorial to a seraph of humankind, but rather to a fallen creature, victim of its own and society's flaws.

Prior to shipping the tomb to France for installation, Epstein opened his studio for a public viewing, and this time the press comment was favorable. Unhappily, it was not to be the same in France. When Epstein arrived at the Paris cemetery to finish the head, he found the tomb covered with a tarpaulin under the guard of a gendarme. The sculpture had been banned by the authorities. There was an uproar from French artists and men of letters when a bronze plaque was placed over the angel's genitals; subsequently it was stolen in a night raid by persons unnamed. But, again, the tarpaulin was restored and remained in place until the outbreak of the Great War. Controversy had again marred the sense of occasion which Epstein had hoped to create.

While working on the Oscar Wilde tomb, Epstein met the poet T. E. Hulme, who became a close friend and early patron. And it was through Hulme that Pound, Lewis, and Gaudier-Brzeska came into Epstein's life. One morning, said Pound, Gaudier-Brzeska, at the age of eighteen, wandered into Epstein's studio to view the

Wilde memorial. "UMMHH! Do . . . you cut . . . direct . . . in the stone?"asked Epstein in his broad New York accent.

"Most certainly!" said Gaudier-Brzeska, who had never yet done anything of the sort.

"That's right," said Epstein, "I will come around to your place on Sunday." So Gaudier-Brzeska at once went out, got three small stone blocks, and by working more or less night and day had something ready by Sunday.

Epstein contributed a few drawings for the first issue of *Blast.* In March 1915, when the vorticists mounted an exhibition at the Dore Gallery in Bond Street, he showed a sculpture entitled *Rock Drill,* to which he was tempted to attach an actual live pneumatic drill. But it was suggested that this would be futurist rather than vorticist, and so the idea was abandoned. Pound commemorated the name in *Section: Rock Drill 85–95.* He believed that Epstein was a great sculptor. He wrote to his mother, "I wish he would wash, but I believe Michel Angelo *never* did, so I suppose it is part of the tradition."

The vorticists valued objects that were dynamic, and drew their significance from clear, essential characteristics that cut to the elemental bone of visual sensation. "Hard," "geometrical," "clear"—these were the sort of words they frequently employed to describe quality of form. *Rock Drill,* the streamlined machine with its visor face, long beak, and piston arm, was quintessentially vorticist. So, too, were Epstein's various *Marble Doves* copulating, the third example of which is arguably the masterpiece of the sculptor's vorticist period. Soon after their completion, Epstein and Lewis began a feud over issues that remain clouded. Pound was looking for a

*Bronze, 1913
27¾'' height
(The Tate Gallery,
London)*

Rock Drill. Epstein's first great vorticist sculpture. Jacob Epstein, 1880–1959.

reconciliation but, when it failed to materialize, chose to remain close to Lewis who was a far more intimate friend.

The quarrel marked the end of Epstein's interest in the principles of vorticist sculpture and, by 1920, at the age of forty, Epstein put vorticism and total abstraction behind. Ahead lay the numerous portraits in bronze for which he became so famous. The great and near-great of English society were drawn to Epstein's studio for memorialization, and it was through this medium that he achieved both popular recognition and financial security.

But, for his other work, the monumental religious sculpture that he so highly prized, there was scant approval. Indeed, until expressionism became fashionable after World War II, it was only the strident youngsters of the *Blast* generation and those that followed them who hailed Epstein as a true master.

Yet it was Rodin, not Brancusi, with whom Epstein was in spiritual communion. In works like *Christ, Genesis, Adam, Ecce Homo, Jacob and the Angel,* and *Consummatum est,* he declared an interest not merely in the relationship between one geometric form and another, but with the great constants of existence: with Good and Evil, Love and Hate, God and Resurrection. The emotions that Epstein sought to capture were those that confronted all mankind. And no doubt much of his notoriety, adverse though it was, arose from his willingness to deal with ideas that easily fell within the public's grasp and thus were open to popular judgment. Perhaps it was this clash between a subject which was familiar and an idiom which was not (except to those acquainted with the British Museum's ethnographic collections) that led to the indictment that Epstein had barbarized themes closest to the hearts of the average Englishman.

Nevertheless, however predictable, the end result was disappointing. The Bloomsbury group, which dominated the left wing of the English art world, spurned him, as did the Royal Academy. Museums scorned him; the Tate Gallery would not even accept a certain piece as a gift. The fascists and anti-Semites had a heyday whenever a new monumental piece by Epstein was exhibited. They defaced his outdoor sculpture with swastikas, and it was only the owner of a Blackpool amusement park who expressed interest in housing Epstein's large works, as objects of public curiosity and derision. Not until well after World War II, when he was finally acknowledged as the grand old man of British sculpture, did Epstein gain public acceptance of his large religious pieces. But by then he had suffered too many attacks not to evince great bitterness, much like Whistler, against a society that refused to acknowledge an important element of his genius.

Relations between Epstein and America remained ambivalent. He thought that "the greatest mistake that American artists can make in the future will be to look to Europe for direct inspiration." He considered his own art international rather than national, and urged his compatriots to establish roots in their own native soil, which was bound to produce works "worth more than all the Romanesque or Buddhist imitations. Each country must have its own genuine primitives." Epstein considered himself one of the last Americans for whom it was necessary to practice art abroad. After all, the United States was coming of age.

When Epstein died, Henry Moore said of him, "He took the brickbats, he took the insults, he faced the howls of derision with which artists since Rembrandt have learned to become familiar. And as far as sculpture in this century is concerned, he took them first . . . he was scarcely an innovator let alone a revolutionary . . ." and yet the great English vortex had labeled him as such, and from that time there was apparently no escape. Epstein was an expatriate who found a *patria* in England, but it was not until the last years of his life that an aura of venerability softened the distress of his artistic exile.

There was one other American who glided round Pound's vortex, more an outsider than a participant, yet always conscious of his role. Thomas Stearns Eliot—T. S. E.—Ezra Pound's "Parson Possum." A man carrying the Augustan traditions of a neutral tongue, neither English nor American, on his lips. A poet with a sense of responsibility that equated reason and order with the structure of language itself.

From St. Louis to Harvard: a not impossible transition for a descendant of a judge at the Salem witch trials. Into the classes, first of Irving Babbitt, denouncing romanticism in favor of logic and continuity. And second, of William James, preaching quality of critical thought.

From Harvard to Europe, on a Sheldon Traveling Fellowship, to finish a dissertation on the philosophy of F. H. Bradley. But it was June 1914. An Austrian archduke died at Sarajevo, and the blast of war trumpets echoed all the way to Marburg where sat ensconced the young American scholar who had intended to spend a few months listening to lectures on the relationship of man and spirit. Such speculations were now impossible as the martial leviathan rose to do the bidding of the Imperial High Command. There was no choice but to continue on to Oxford for the year's residence which had been planned at Merton College. The doctorate, however, was never completed. Far more important claims were being made on Eliot's consciousness.

And so it was, recalled Pound, that

Mr. Eliot came to London with all the disadvantages of a . . . symmetrical education . . . and dutifully joined the Aristotelian Society . . . and he took me to a meeting. And a man with a beard down to here . . . spoke for twenty minutes on a point in Aristotle; and another with a beard down to here rose up and refuted him. . . . And I wanted air. So we were on the portico when old G. R. S. Mead came up, and catching sight of me said, "I didn't expect to see you here"; whereat Eliot with perfect decorum and suavity said,

"Oh, he's not here as a phil-os-opher;
He's here as an an-thro-pologist."

How well was the species understood.

It was through Conrad Aiken that Eliot had first met Pound in September 1914. Ezra's verse was not unknown to T. S. E. He had read *Personae and Exultations* the year before at Harvard, but dismissed them in his mind as "rather fancy, old-fashioned romantic . . . cloak and dagger . . . stuff." Yet, archaeological though they were in his opinion, Eliot, whose knowledge of the current literary scene was a complete blank, did regard Pound's work as "the only interesting poems by a contemporary" he had found. Such was the fate of one whose undergraduate curriculum was confined to the English poets of the nineties, who were now dead: "That was as near as we could get to any living tradition," said Eliot.

It was left to Pound, who, in his small Kensington flat, seemed to Eliot "always to be only a temporary squatter" (so great was his resistance against growing into any environment), to direct his new friend to the best of contemporary verse.

Among the poems that Eliot had written while at Harvard was "The Love Song of J. Alfred Prufrock." Aiken had unsuccessfully attempted to place it with a publisher in London, but, when Pound read it, he was determined that it should appear in print. It was the best poem by an American that he had seen: "PRAY GOD IT BE NOT A SINGLE AND UNIQUE SUCCESS," he wrote Harriet Monroe, "he is the only American I know of who has made what I can call adequate preparation for writing. He has actually trained himself and modernized himself *on his own*. The rest of the *promising young* have done one or the other but never both (most of the swine have done neither). It is such a comfort to meet a man and not have to tell him to wash his face, wipe his feet, and remember the date [1914] on the calendar."

After much haranguing from Pound, Miss Monroe finally consented to include "Prufrock," and it appeared in the June 1915 issue of *Poetry*. Two years later, again through Pound's urging, the Egoist Press brought out Eliot's first volume, *Prufrock and Other Observations*. Had it not been for Pound, his poems might have been years in reaching the eyes of the public.

Pound did not create poets, but he did provide the situation in which English and American poets joined to create a modern movement in the art. He brought his compatriots out of isolation into the mainstream of progressive writing, and, although occasionally evincing an impatient arrogance with his protégés, of whom he expected so much, there was no kinder and more thoughtful mentor than he. Eliot likened Pound's passion to teach to that of Irving Babbitt: it was not a comparison either individual would have appreciated. Thirty-four years after the publication of "Prufrock," when Pound languished in disgrace as a traitor to his country, Eliot could still write with an emotion that remained uncooled,

I think of a friend who, in the early days, was as much concerned with the encouragement and improvement of the work of unknown writers in whom he discerned talent, as with his own creative work; who formulated, for a generation of poets, the principles of good writing most needful for their time, who tried to bring these writers together for their reciprocal benefit; who, in the face of many obstacles saw that their writings were published; saw that they were reviewed somewhere by critics who could appreciate them; organized or supported little magazines in which their work could appear—and incidentally, liked to give a good dinner to those who he thought could not afford it, and sometimes even supplied the more needy with articles of clothing out of his own meagre store. To him, several other authors since famous, have owed a great deal.

While Pound rushed about—"I seem to be a universal committee for all the arts," he told his New York patron, John Quinn—Eliot quietly slipped, in June 1915, into what was to prove a disastrous marriage. Her name was Vivienne Haigh-Wood, the daughter of a painter and etcher of limited private means. Issuing from a world of culture and elegance, Vivienne was handsome, witty, and graceful. But there were moments, frightening moments, of intense melancholia that whispered of great emotional instability. They were warnings that went unheeded.

For several months, the Eliots lived with Vivienne's parents in Hampstead. But then an offer came from Bertrand Russell, who had taught Tom at Harvard, to share his flat which had an extra bedroom. It was once said of Russell that he "had a first-rate mind, humane aspirations and the sexual morals of an alley cat." Only the very jaded or the incredibly naïve would have accepted his offer without question, and, needless to say, the young Eliots were far from sophisticated.

Russell, already separated for several years from his American wife, Alys, who had proved barren, had launched into a passionate affair with the fabulous Lady Ottoline Morrell, half-sister of the sixth Duke of Portland, who kept court amid the Elizabethan splendors of Garsington Manor near Oxford. There Leonard and Virginia Woolf, Lytton Strachey, Aldous and Maria Huxley, Katherine Mansfield, Vanessa and Clive Bell, Middleton Murry, and Duncan Grant, along with numerous others, gathered for well-fed literary weekends. And it was into this circle that the Eliots were introduced.

Russell visited Garsington frequently, but, as passions cooled, he found Lady Ottoline "comparatively indifferent." Not until the following summer of 1916 did he become enamored of Lady Constance Malleson, and it was during this romantic hiatus that he asked the Eliots to become his houseguests. There were all the makings of a *ménage à trois*.

Prior to their first meeting, Russell fully expected Vivienne to be terrible, so mysterious had Tom been about the circumstances of the marriage. But he was pleasantly surprised: "She is light, a little vulgar, adventurous, full of life, an artist, I think he said, but I should have thought her an actress." He found Tom "exquisite and listless." Vivienne indicated that she had married him in order to stimulate him but was finding it impossible. Obviously, he married in order to be stimulated, thought Russell.

But however interested he was, Russell had reservations that restrained him from embarking on a full-blown affair. Vivienne suffered terribly from acute migraine. Her nerves, people said, were too close to the surface. And, with an intense sensitivity to noise, she frequently required doses of drugs to alleviate the pain. In Russell's eyes, "She is a person who lives on the knife edge, and will end as a criminal or a saint; I don't know which yet. She has a perfect capacity for both."

Tom was not unaware of Vivienne's unstable condition, and for the next sixteen years the problems of merely existing with her, together with earning a living, were insoluble preoccupations. He began to teach school, first at High Wycombe Grammar School (at £140 per annum with dinner), and later at the Highgate Junior School, near Hampstead (at a £20 increase in salary plus dinner and tea). The work was hardly stimulating, and Eliot was forced to supplement his income by writing occasional literary reviews and giving evening lectures to working people.

In March 1917, at the age of twenty-eight, he chucked teaching to take a post in the colonial and foreign department of Lloyds Bank. Vivienne's family had secured him the position under the false pretense of his being a linguist. The salary was somewhat smaller (and there was no food), but Eliot hoped for more time to devote to his writing, *and* the bank had been so good as to hold out the hope that one day he might aspire to a branch managership! He was to remain there until 1925—at least in the bank there was a modicum of financial security and a predictable number of hours away from Vivienne, which had become a necessity.

Pound, meanwhile, was busy promoting Eliot. He persuaded Elkin Mathews to publish five hundred paperbound copies of *Prufrock* at a shilling a copy. Clearly it did more for Eliot's reputation than for his bank account. When Eliot, as a patriotic gesture, attempted to secure a commission in the U.S. navy, it was Pound, under the letterhead of *The Dial,* his latest magazine, who wrote a letter of recommendation. And when Richard Aldington went off to the front, Pound successfully moved Eliot into his place as assistant editor of *The Egoist* (salary £52 per annum). There, for the next two years (H. D. in turn succeeded Eliot in 1919), Eliot actively engaged in the literary marketplace and had ample opportunity to indulge his well-developed, but not always appreciated, sense of humor. When it was decided to print readers' views on material in *The Egoist,* T. S. E. started the ball rolling by writing pseudonymous letters to the editor. He became Charles Augustus Conybeare of the Carlton Club, Liverpool, and the Reverend Charles James Grimble of the Vicarage, Leays. Soon was added J. A. D. Spence, a master at Thridlingston Grammar School, who wrote surprisingly like Muriel A. Schwarz of Alexandra Gardens, Hampstead, and Helen B. Trundlett of Batton, Kent.

One character after another, each a playful shadow of himself. Disguise after disguise—a playwright in the making perhaps—one that, in later years, would send a cadaverous ear to his publisher as a bizarre jest. "The critics say I am learned and cold, the truth is I am neither," he once remarked. But Eliot was a great joker. It was a principal form of escape. "I no longer pretend I am pretending," he told Pound years later. But some thought that this was his most insidious pretense of all. Pound, however, cared little, for he saw the depth of inventive talent that lay within the superstructure of the oh-so-carefully constructed shell of respectability.

When Alfred Knopf decided to publish a brochure on Pound's work to accompany the first edition of *Lustra,* thus introducing him to the American people, the poet insisted that Eliot compose the text, albeit anonymously. As he later told H. L. Mencken, Eliot was "the only person one could trust not to talk about the Rocky Mountains, the bold unfettered West, the Kawsmos etc."

Two poetic voices of radically different temperament. The one (Pound) moving away from symbolism. The other (Eliot) working deeper into it. Each carrying his private Dantean vision to its logical conclusion, yet at the same time relying heavily on the criticism of the other to legitimize what had been created. Thus was laid the foundation of a literary revolution in the twentieth century.

In 1919–20 Pound composed *Hugh Selwyn Mauberly,* a series of poems in which he attempted to summarize his conception of the European experience and scene— to "condense the James novel," he said. He wrote of "old lies and new infamy," of "usury age-old and age-thick." It was an elegiac paean to the great vortex and was, in truth, Pound's poetic farewell to England.

One by one the journals which had been the outlet of Pound's vision were closed to him. *The Quarterly Review, The Athenaeum,* even *Poetry*—"cat-piss and porcupines!!" he had written to Harriet Monroe; she did not appreciate his tone and found it impossible to deal with the tactless and uncontrollable Ezra. Eliot wrote with concern to John Quinn, in January 1920: "The fact is that there is now no organ of any importance in which Pound . . . can express himself, and he is becoming forgotten. It is not enough for him simply to publish a volume of verse once a year—or no matter how often—for it will simply not be reviewed, and will be killed by silence. . . . I know that Pound's lack of tact has done him great harm. But I am worried as to what is to become of him." In 1920 Pound's thinking was in a state of dynamic flux. His thoughts were filled not only with continuing the cause in favor of individual genius, "the favoured of the Gods," but also with a passion for a new politico-economic theory which bore the name Social Credit.

Two years earlier, in the office of *The New Age,* Pound had encountered Maj. C. H. Douglas, a Scots engineer who, along with Orage, the editor of the journal, had devised a scheme whereby modern industry and private property could be protected and allowed to expand without the attendant risks of inflation, government debt, or any form of authoritarian collectivism. Under Douglas's influence Pound began to consider whether the root cause of individual poverty lay in what was called "false credit." This was a perversion of natural law, whereby the "real credit" of a nation, the work of its people, was subverted by those who could manipulate the money market and thus use "financial credit" for their own selfish ends.

Who were the enemy? Why, the Jews, of course. The Rothschilds, the Warburgs, the de Wendels, the Comité des Forges. They who were "bent on the acquisition of world-empire," who sought to frustrate the national will as expressed in individual genius: they were the root cause of society's many ills.

Thus Ezra Pound, himself fast becoming a literary pariah, found an explanation for his rejection by the establishment—he discovered and embraced anti-Semitism. The question for Pound still remained, What to do? Major Douglas had instilled in him a desire to be at the center of contemporary activity, and London was no longer that place. In 1921 Pound wrote, "Ten years ago I should have advised, and did advise, other American writers to come to England for the sake of their work; at the present moment there is no *literary* reason for my not leaving the country."

He briefly considered returning to America to take up the study of medicine, but had to admit that the financial demands of such a course were beyond him. Finally, he decided that Paris was the only lively spot on the map of Europe where he might live with contentment, and by Christmas of 1920 Ezra and Dorothy Pound were ensconced in a flat at 70 bis rue Notre-Dame des Champs. Three weeks later, as a final exorcistic gesture to England, Pound published, in *The New Age* (January 15, 1921), "Axiomata," his "intellectual will and testament," in which he outlined his reasons for leaving Britain, chief among them being, as he told a reporter for the

Oil on canvas, 1938 53″ × 34″ (Durban Art Gallery, South Africa)

Thomas Stearns Eliot, 1888–1965. Wyndham Lewis, 1884–1957.

Paris edition of the *New York Herald,* that "the decay of the British Empire is too depressing a spectacle to witness at close range. . . . Having a number of pleasant memories of England in the last ten years, he finds that he can retain them more easily by being away now."

One of the memories of which Pound was most proud was his effort to bring the poetry of T. S. Eliot to the attention of the public. It was an achievement that Pound was determined should not have been in vain. He was genuinely concerned that, if Tom continued to waste away in the bowels of Lloyds Bank, much of his greatest work would simply never be written.

From his Parisian perch, in 1922, Ezra decided that the answer lay in the creation of a fund, supported by thirty guarantors who would each contribute £10 per year for Eliot's maintenance, so that he might leave the bank and devote all his energies to writing. It was a revival of a plan he had first proposed to John Quinn in 1920. Pound wrote to everyone who might be able to help: Quinn, H. L. Mencken, William Carlos Williams, Natalie Barney, Robert McAlmon, and many others were solicited on Eliot's behalf. Pound wrote an article for *The New Age* on "Credit and the Fine Arts . . . A Practical Application" and printed a broadside, theoretically for private circulation, which outlined the project which Pound's friend, May Sinclair, had christened "Bel Esprit."

Not surprisingly, Eliot soon learned what was afoot, and wrote to Richard Aldington, expressing his reservations: "I think you will agree . . . that the method proposed by Ezra is rather bordering on the precarious and slightly undignified charity. At the bank I am at least independent of the people whom I know and a doubtful income, which I should be obliged to attempt to double by literary work, would not be the slightest advantage from anyone's point of view."

Eventually, after some unfortunate publicity, Eliot was forced to declare publicly that the " 'Bel Esprit' is not in existence with my consent or approval." His cautious pride could brook no compromise, however much he appreciated Pound's beau geste. It was simply too risky a venture which might easily founder after the first year.

One can appreciate Pound's sense of acute concern for his friend's well-being. Richard Aldington reported that "Eliot was going to pieces and for gawd's sake could . . . [he] do something, anything." Eliot's marriage was a nightmare of increasing emotional and financial strains. Reviewing, "one of the most corrupting, degrading, and badly paid means of livelihood that a writing man can play," provided scant relief. And, finally, the pressures of overwork and perennial depression took their toll. Eliot suffered a breakdown and was ordered by his doctor to undergo three months' convalescence. He went first to Margate, and from there to a sanitorium in Switzerland, and it was during this most difficult of periods that he composed the series of poems which bear the title *The Waste Land.*

Drawing his theme ultimately from the *Purgatorio* of Dante, Eliot, in stanza after stanza, gazed into the essential reality of human existence based on the constants of pain and suffering. In language that was at once fierce and horrifying, yet at the same time listlessly calm, the poet declared in a thousand lines the all-pervasive impact of cynical disillusionment on the romantic mind. The world had changed too quickly, and a riot of "enthusiasms" had shaken the foundations of order, raising demons of unanswerable questions that should never have been asked. "Give, Sympathize, Control"—this was the ethic of the *Bhagavad Gita.* In years to come, Eliot would assert that here was the true command which ordered the subtle allusory enigmas of *The Waste Land.* Whatever his source, the poem is, in every sense, a literary promontory which marks the poetic life of this century.

On his way back to England, Eliot stopped in Paris to show his manuscript to Pound, who saw at once the greatness inherent in the work. But it was far too long and chaotic, declared Ezra, who, in his most important literary collaboration, set to work weeding out whole sections and passages which he regarded as second-rate. Eliot hardly demurred. He thought Pound "a marvelous critic because he didn't try to turn you into an imitation of himself. He tried to see what you were trying to do." The end result was a poem stripped of several of the more earthy of Eliot's experiments which Pound disliked, labeling them "music hall techniques." Nevertheless, what emerged was, to its creator, eminently satisfactory. And Pound, as an ample testament of his enthusiasm for the work, not only secured an American publisher for Eliot but convinced the editors of *The Dial,* for whom he was the Paris correspondent, that *The Waste Land* should receive a prize of $2,000, which to Eliot was a God-sent fortune. His only regret "(which may seem in the circumstances either ungracious or hypocritical) is that this award should come to me before it has been given to Pound. I feel that he deserves the recognition [which was forthcoming five years later] much more than I do, certainly 'for his services to Letters' and I feel I ought to have been made to wait until after he had received this public testimony."

The Waste Land was presented to the English public in the first issue of *The Criterion,* the superb intellectual journal, founded in 1922 by Lady Rothermere and Richard Cobden-Sanderson, with Eliot as its first editor. Three years later, when Lady Rothermere made it clear that she no longer wished to financially support the journal alone, the publishing house of Faber & Gwyer (later reconstituted as Faber & Faber) agreed to assume a portion of the burden. Eliot was to remain as editor, resigning his position at the bank to join Faber & Gwyer as a director of the newly incorporated company. This new, and much more congenial, employment was to remain the substantial source of Eliot's income for the balance of his life.

Not surprisingly, Faber & Gwyer subsequently became one of Pound's English publishers, though they always refused to release what Eliot referred to as Ezra's "harmful" books. Eliot once observed, "It is harder to help Pound than anyone else. Apart from the fact that he is very sensitive and proud and that I have to keep an attitude of discipleship to him (as indeed I ought) every time I print anything of his it nearly sinks the paper. And he offers more than I want, thinking that he is helping. I am willing to sink the ship for things like the Cantos, which are great stuff whether anyone likes them or not, but it goes against the grain to do it for his articles."

Pound, on the other hand, believed that "Eliot has paid the penalty for success. Given the amount of that success, the low degree of penalty paid is proof of his solid capacity."

In the years that followed, the always elegant Mr. Eliot survived with dignified grace, according to the ever-ascetic regimen which his intellect demanded. His marriage to Vivienne, hopeless almost from the outset, became impossible, and a Deed of Separation was unavoidable. For the remainder of her tragic existence, she never quite disappeared from T. S. E.'s life. There were visits to his office in Russell Square with attempts to waylay him on the stairs. Stories survive of Vivienne attending his public lectures, wearing a placard declaring, "I am the wife he abandoned." It was the most wrenchingly difficult of emotional experiences, and, for support, Eliot enwrapped himself even more closely in the mysteries of high-church Anglicanism which had become the guiding testament of his existence.

For a period of some years in the 1930s, he took up residence in the clergy house of St. Stephen's, Gloucester Road, where, for a quarter-century, until 1959, he held the post of Vicar's Warden, the highest lay position in the parish. So pious was Eliot's devotion to mother Church that his very presence at Communion was an uplifting ritual for those who were present. One of the curates of St. Stephen's remarked, "It was a spiritual experience to administer the Bread and the Wine to so devout a worshipper. At such a sacred moment the officiating priest could not but be aware that he was in the presence of a sublime spiritual reality."

The Church became a retreat, a source of protective strength for Eliot, where the mysteries of ancient ritual filled the comparative void of pedestrian secular existence. And, as his faith intensified, Eliot was drawn ever more deeply to an appreciation and enthusiasm for religious poetry and poetic drama. Thus it was, while living at St. Stephen's, that Eliot, at the invitation of Bishop George Bell, composed *Murder in the Cathedral* for the Canterbury Festival of 1935. It was to be the most popular of his works, up to that time, earning recognition not only on the professional stage, but in cinemas all over the world.

Pound found it hard to accept Eliot's piety as anything but a corruption of intellect. As late as 1957 he was still able to strike with caustic precision, chiding,

> *In any case, let us lament the psychosis;*
> *Of all those who abandon the Muses for Moses.*

But Eliot was not to be deterred. The *Bhagavad Gita,* the *Divina Commedia,* his close companions of a lifetime, now shared fidelity with the Anglican liturgy of the seventeenth century, as Eliot sought to explore and establish communion with the Church of his ancestors of which he now, too, was possessed.

From the counties of Somerset, Gloucester, and Huntingdon, from the shores of New England, he drew inspiration and emotional support. The result was a cycle of meditative poems, immensely complex in their metaphysics yet constant in one thought: in the end man had no choice but to sacrifice himself and to endure. "Burnt Norton," "East Coker," "The Dry Salvages," "Little Gidding"—the pinnacle of Eliot's poetic achievement brought together as the *Four Quartets.*

Richard Aldington once observed that Ezra Pound had started in a time of peace and prosperity, intent on becoming a kind of literary dictator in London. But through his own conceit, bad manners, and folly, he destroyed whatever chances he may have had, despite the quality of his verse. Eliot, on the other hand, began amid the confusion and chaos of war, emerging in postwar England with handicaps of numerous description. "Yet," as Aldington stated, "by merit, tact, prudence, and pertinacity he succeeded in doing what no other American has ever done—imposing his personality, taste, and even many of his opinions on literary England."

Like John Donne, whom he so admired, Eliot urged people to look at his poems, not at his person. But was such a separation ever really possible? For just as Eliot left his mark on England, so, too, had England created not only what the public read but what it saw.

> *How unpleasant to meet Mr. Eliot!*
> *With his features of clerical cut,*
> *And his brow so grim*
> *And his mouth so prim*
> *And his conversation, so nicely*
> *Restricted to What Precisely*
> *And If and Perhaps and But. . . .*

A humorous self-portrait no doubt, but it does cut close to the bone of the matter. For during all of his active life, Eliot held high the banner of tradition.

At the Sorbonne, in 1910–11, he was exposed to the *Action Française* philosophy of Charles Maurras, who preached that politics, religion, and aesthetics—life itself—were all inextricably tied to a credo based on order, authority, hierarchy, and, most important, tradition. In England, Pound had brought him under the influence of T. E. Hulme, whose watchword was that man was essentially evil and could only overcome this fatal flaw by discipline—ethical and political. In short, institutions were necessary. That was why Britain, authoritarian and traditional, was so attractive. Eliot could play the Englishman, and Pound, with his folksy Uncle Remus accent, could be surrealistically American (Ben Hecht once described him as "the exquisite Showman minus the show"). Yet both envisaged the same organization for society. In years to come, Pound would rush headlong into the political embrace of fascism, while Eliot, with more refinement, found equal satisfaction in the omnipresence of the Church. But the authoritarian goals for both were the same.

It was only in the *Four Quartets* that Eliot began to see, with great exorcistic pain, how mixed his motives truly had been. What he had once in confusion defined as virtues now became errors and sins, and there was no avoiding the conclusion that, faced with the holocaust of World War II, he was absolutely helpless to prevent the destruction of the traditional European values, which he held so dear as to make them an inextricable part of himself.

Boston and East Coker—they were no longer very far apart. For Eliot, as for Henry James, there had ceased to be a Europe and an America which required differentiation. There was only the modern world, come together culturally in god-lessness.

As early as 1927, Eliot declared that he was "classicist in literature, royalist in politics, and anglo-catholic in religion." But this was no credo declaring loyalty to England and things English. If anything, it was a manifesto of cultural alienation, a protest against the increasing inroads that secular, democratic, and manifestly atraditional America had made on Eliot's anglicized consciousness. Like so many Americans before him, Eliot, dissatisfied and unwilling to deal with the world as it was, firmly established his credentials as a citizen of another age, in his case the seventeenth century.

The life of art, which celebrated the freedom to cultivate individuality, was a thing of the past, though many continued to pay lip service to it. Social and economic reform—these were the signposts of the future for everyone. Edmund Wilson urged "American writers to try to make some sense of their world—for their world is now everybody's world." Harold Stearns, an exile returned, disillusioned with the "suicidal nationalism" and "murderous class warfare" which he found in Europe, went so far as to declare that "romance has fled Europe in despair and has found a new home in America." For him, there was no longer a justification for expatriation.

Eliot and Pound remained abroad, each a champion of authority—clerical for the one, secular for the other.

By the end of World War II, Eliot donned the mantle of a supreme master whose authority was unimpeachable. Cambridge and Oxford bestowed honorary fellowships upon him. Learned societies elevated him to their presidency. Official recognition—national and international—was his. The Order of Merit, the Dante Gold Medal, even the Medal of Freedom from an America which still claimed him as her own. He had become, in every sense of the word, an acknowledged arbiter of excellence. And, when he died and his ashes were scattered, a memorial table was affixed in Westminster Abbey where England honors her heroes. (Henry James would have to wait the celebration of the American bicentennial before a like honor was conferred upon his memory.)

On a winter's day in February 1965, the day of Eliot's memorial service in the Abbey, a frail silver-haired octogenerian, a figure of the past, appeared to pay last respects to his old friend. Ezra Pound, still Odysseus-like, committed to living out the epic poem which had been his life. Several months later, though gripped by illness, Pound paid a final tribute to Eliot when he wrote, "His was the true Dantescan voice—not honoured enough, and deserving more than I ever gave him . . . I can only repeat, but with the urgency of 50 years ago: READ HIM."

It was a vital message, from one still active in the promotion of his "enthusiasms," for those,

> *O HELPLESS FEW IN MY COUNTRY,*
> *O REMNANT ENSLAVED! . . .*
>
> *TAKE THOUGHT:*
> *I HAVE WEATHERED THE STORM,*
> *I HAVE BEATEN OUT MY EXILE.*

> —Ezra Pound.

Badge and insignia of the American Medal of Freedom, awarded to T. S. Eliot. (Mrs. T. S. Eliot)

Selected Bibliography

Adams, Alexander B. *John James Audubon: A Biography.* New York, 1966.

Astor, Michael. *Tribal Feeling.* London, 1963.

Balsan, Consuelo Vanderbilt. *The Glitter and the Gold.* New York, 1952.

Blumenfeld, Ralph David. *All in a Lifetime.* London, 1931.

———— *The Press in My Time.* London, 1933.

Brooks, Van Wyck. *The Pilgrimage of Henry James.* New York, 1925.

———— *The World of Washington Irving.* New York, 1944.

———— *The Dream of Arcadia: American Writers and Artists in Italy 1760–1915.* New York, 1958.

Brown, Sanborn C. *Count Rumford: Physicist Extraordinary.* Boston, 1974.

Buckle, Richard. *Jacob Epstein, Sculptor.* Cleveland, 1963.

Chace, William M. *The Political Identities of Ezra Pound and T. S. Eliot.* Stanford, 1973.

Channon, Henry. *The Diaries of Sir Henry Channon.* Edited by Robert Rhodes James. London, 1967.

Chapple, William Dismore. *George Peabody.* Salem, 1933.

Charteris, Evan. *John Sargent.* New York, 1927.

Coburn, Alvin Langdon. *Alvin Langdon Coburn, Photographer: An Autobiography.* Edited by Helmut and Alison Gernsheim. New York, 1966.

Collis, Maurice. *Nancy Astor: An Informal Biography.* London and New York, 1960.

Corey, Lewis. *The House of Morgan: A Social Biography of the Masters of Money.* New York, 1930.

Cornwallis-West, Jennie. *The Reminiscences of Lady Randolph Churchill.* London and New York.

Curtis, Rosemary. *Jennie, the Young Lady Churchill.* Philadelphia, 1963.

Dickinson, Henry W. *Robert Fulton, Engineer and Artist: His Life and Works.* London, 1913.

Dilks, David. *Curzon in India.* 2 vols. London and New York, 1969–1970.

Edel, Leon. *Henry James, the Untried Years: 1843–1870.* Philadelphia, 1953.

———— *Henry James, the Conquest of London: 1870–1881.* Philadelphia, 1962.

———— *Henry James, the Middle Years: 1882–1895.* Philadelphia, 1962.

———— *Henry James, the Treacherous Years: 1895–1901.* Philadelphia, 1969.

———— *Henry James, the Master: 1901–1916.* Philadelphia, 1972.

Edwardes, Michael. *High Noon of Empire: India under Curzon.* London, 1965.

Einstein, Lewis David. *Divided Loyalties: Americans in England during the War of Independence.* New York, 1933.

Epstein, Jacob. *The Sculptor Speaks: Jacob Epstein to Arnold L. Haskell, a Series of Conversations on Art.* Garden City, 1932.

_____ *Epstein: An Autobiography.* 2nd ed. London, 1963.

Evans, Grose. *Benjamin West and the Taste of His Times.* Carbondale (Ill.), 1959.

Farington, Joseph. *The Farington Diary.* 8 vols. Edited by James Grieg. London and New York, 1923–1928.

Fielding, Daphne. *Those Remarkable Cunards: Emerald and Nancy.* London and New York, 1968.

Flagg, Jared Bradley. *The Life and Letters of Washington Allston.* New York, 1892.

Flexner, James Thomas. *America's Old Masters: First Artists of the New World.* New York, 1939.

_____ *The Light of Distant Skies, 1760–1835.* New York, 1954.

Ford, Alice E. *John James Audubon.* Norman (Okla.), 1964.

_____ *Audubon by Himself.* Garden City, 1969.

Frankenstein, Alfred. *The World of Copley 1738–1815.* New York, 1970.

Gregory, Horace. *The World of James McNeill Whistler.* New York, 1959.

Hanson, Willis Tracy. *The Early Life of John Howard Payne.* Cambridge (Mass.), 1913.

Harrison, Gabriel. *John Howard Payne, Dramatist, Poet, Actor . . . His Life and Writings.* Philadelphia, 1885.

Holder, Alan. *Three Voyagers in Search of Europe, a Study of Henry James, Ezra Pound and T. S. Eliot.* Philadelphia, 1966.

Irving, Pierre. *The Life and Letters of Washington Irving.* 4 vols. New York, 1863–1864.

James, Alice. *The Diary of Alice James.* Edited by Leon Edel. New York, 1964.

Johnston, Johanna. *The Heart that Would Not Hold: A Biography of Washington Irving.* New York, 1971.

Josephson, Matthew. *Portrait of the Artist as American.* New York, 1930.

Kenner, Hugh. *The Pound Era.* Berkeley, 1971.

Knoedler, M., & Co. *Washington Irving and His Circle.* New York, 1946.

Langhorne, Elizabeth. *Nancy Astor and Her Friends.* New York, 1974.

Larkin, Oliver W. *Samuel F. B. Morse and American Democratic Art.* Boston, 1954.

Le Clair, Robert Charles. *Three American Travellers in England: James Russell Lowell, Henry Adams, Henry James.* Philadelphia, 1945.

Leslie, Anita. *Lady Randolph Churchill: The Story of Jennie Jerome.* London and New York, 1969.

Leslie, Charles Robert. *Autobiographical Recollections.* Boston and London, 1860.

Levy, William Turner, and Victor Scherle. *Affectionately T. S. Eliot: The Story of a Friendship 1947–1965.* Philadelphia, 1968.

Mabee, Carleton. *The American Leonardo: A Life of Samuel F. B. Morse.* New York, 1943.

McClary, Ben Harris, ed. *Washington Irving and the House of Murray: Geoffrey Crayon Charms the British 1817–1856.* Knoxville, 1969.

McMullen, Roy. *Victorian Outsider: A Biography of J.A.M. Whistler.* London and New York, 1973.

Martin, Ralph G. *Jennie: The Life of Lady Randolph Churchill.* 2 vols. London and Englewood Cliffs (N.J.), 1969–1971.

Morgan, John Hill. *Gilbert Stuart and His Pupils.* New York, 1939.

Morse, Edward Lind, ed. *Samuel F. B. Morse: His Letters and Journals.* New York, 1914.

de Navarro, Mary Anderson. *A Few Memories.* New York, 1896.

_____ *A Few More Memories.* London, 1936.

Ormond, Richard. *John Singer Sargent: Paintings, Drawings, Watercolors.* London and New York, 1970.

Overmyer, Grace. *America's First Hamlet.* New York, 1957.

Park, Lawrence, ed. *Gilbert Stuart: An Illustrated Descriptive List of His Works.* 4 vols. New York, 1926.

Parker, Franklin. *George Peabody: A Biography.* Nashville, 1971.

Parker, Wyman W. *Henry Stevens of Vermont: American Rare Book Dealer in London, 1845–1886.* Amsterdam, 1963.

Pearson, Hesketh. *The Man Whistler.* London and New York, 1952–1953.

———— *Lives of the Wits.* London and New York, 1962.

Pennell, Elizabeth Robins. *Our House and London Out of Our Windows.* Boston, 1912.

———— *The Life and Letters of Joseph Pennell.* 2 vols. Boston, 1929.

———— *Whistler the Friend.* London and Philadelphia, 1930.

Pennell, Joseph, and Elizabeth Robins. *The Life of James McNeill Whistler.* 2 vols. London and Philadelphia, 1908.

———— *The Whistler Journal.* Philadelphia, 1921.

Prideaux, Tom. *The World of Whistler, 1834–1903.* New York, 1970.

Prown, Jules David. *John Singleton Copley.* 2 vols. Cambridge (Mass.), 1966.

Quinn, Vincent Gerard. *Hilda Doolittle (H. D.).* New York, 1968.

Richardson, Edgar Preston. *Washington Allston: A Study of the Romantic Artist in America.* Chicago, 1948.

Rose, Kenneth. *Superior Person: A Portrait of Curzon and His Circle in Late Victorian England.* London and New York, 1969–1970.

Satterlee, Herbert Livingston. *The Life of J. Pierpont Morgan.* New York (privately printed), 1937.

Sellers, Charles Coleman. *Patience Wright: American Artist and Spy in George III's London.* Middletown (Conn.), 1976.

Sencourt, Robert. *T. S. Eliot: A Memoir.* London and New York, 1971.

Sizer, Theodore, ed. *The Autobiography of Colonel John Trumbull, Patriot-Artist, 1756–1843.* New York, 1953.

———— *The Works of Colonel John Trumbull, Artist of the American Revolution.* New rev. ed. New Haven, 1967.

Smith, Logan Pearsall. *Unforgotten Years.* Boston and London, 1938–1939.

Sparrow, Wilfred J. *Knight of the White Eagle: A Biography of Sir Benjamin Thompson, Count Rumford, 1753–1814.* New York, 1964.

Spender, Stephen. *Love-Hate Relations: English and American Sensibilities.* London and New York, 1974.

Spiller, Robert E. *The American in England during the First Half Century of Independence.* New York, 1926.

Stock, Noel. *The Life of Ezra Pound.* London and New York, 1970.

Sutcliffe, Alice. *Robert Fulton and the "Clermont."* New York, 1909.

———— *Robert Fulton.* New York, 1915.

Sutton, Denys. *James McNeill Whistler: Paintings, Etchings, Pastels and Watercolours.* London, 1966.

Sykes, Christopher. *Nancy: The Life of Lady Astor.* London and New York, 1972.

Wagenknecht, Edward. *Washington Irving: Moderation Displayed.* New York, 1962.

Weintraub, Stanley. *Whistler: A Biography.* New York, 1974.

Whitley, William T. *Artists and Their Friends in England 1700–1790.* 2 vols. London, 1928.

———— *Gilbert Stuart.* Cambridge (England), 1932.

Williams, Alfred Harry. *No Name on the Door: A Memoir of Gordon Selfridge.* London, 1956.

Williams, Stanley T. *The Life of Washington Irving.* 2 vols. London and New York, 1935.

Wilson, Edmund. *The Triple Thinkers: Ten Essays on Literature.* New York, 1938.

Index

(Italicized numerals refer to illustrations)